Understanding White Privilege

Knowingly and unknowingly we all grapple with race every day. *Understanding White Privilege* delves into the complex interplay between race, power, and privilege in both organizations and private life. It offers an unflinching look at how ignorance can perpetuate privilege, and offers practical and thoughtful insights into how people of all races can work to break this cycle. Based on thirty years of work in diversity in colleges, universities, and corporations, Frances Kendall candidly invites readers to think personally about how race—theirs and others'—frames experiences and relationships, focusing squarely on white privilege and its implications for building authentic relationships across race.

This much-anticipated revised edition includes two full new chapters, one on white women and another extending the discussion on race. It continues the important work of the first, deepening our knowledge of the recurring history on which cross-race relationship issues exist. Kendall's book provides readers with a more meaningful understanding of white privilege and equips them with strategies for making personal and organizational changes.

Frances E. Kendall is a nationally known consultant who focuses on organizational change and communication, specializing in issues of diversity, social justice, and white privilege.

The Teaching/Learning Social Justice Series

Edited by Lee Anne Bell, Barnard College, Columbia University

Understanding
White Privilege

Creating Pathways to Authentic
Relationships Across Race

Second Edition

Frances E. Kendall

Routledge
Taylor & Francis Group

NEW YORK AND LONDON

Second edition published 2013
by Routledge
711 Third Avenue, New York, NY 10017

Simultaneously published in the UK
by Routledge
2 Park Square, Milton Park, Abingdon, Oxon OX14 4RN

Routledge is an imprint of the Taylor & Francis Group, an informa business

First edition published by Routledge 2006

Library of Congress Cataloging in Publication Data
Kendall, Frances E.
Understanding white privilege : creating pathways to authentic relationships across race / by Frances Kendall. – 2nd ed.
    p. cm. – (Teaching/learning social justice series)
    Includes bibliographical references and index.
    1. Whites – Race identity. 2. United States – Race relations.
    3. Race discrimination – United States. I. Title.
HT1575.K456 2012
305.809–dc23   2012016288

ISBN: 978-0-415-87426-7 (hbk)
ISBN: 978-0-415-87427-4 (pbk)
ISBN: 978-0-203-96103-2 (ebk)

Typeset in Minion
by HWA Text and Data Management, London

This book is dedicated to the women and men of color who have entered into authentic relationships with me because, as Adrienne Rich says, "we can count on so few people to go that hard way with us."

CONTENTS

SERIES EDITOR'S INTRODUCTION

I have been eagerly waiting for Francie Kendall to write about her life-long work on white privilege. *Understanding White Privilege: Creating Pathways to Authentic Relationships Across Race* has been well worth the wait. Kendall has written a compelling and highly readable account of her own coming to consciousness about racism as a white woman, and what she has learned along the way about our role as white people in supporting and perpetuating it. Through her long years of experience as an activist and educator/trainer she has collected a vivid array of stories and examples delineating how white institutions and individuals consciously and unconsciously, overtly and tacitly, support a system that benefits white people at the expense of people of color. These grounded examples hold up a mirror in which white people can recognize our complicity in the "spirit-murdering" system that is racism.

While direct and clear in her indictment of racism and white privilege, Kendall is also a sympathetic and trustworthy guide for how white people can work against these systems. She models the humility and continuous learning required to resist constant recruitment back into the "institutionalized dominance of whiteness" if we are to find muscular ways to resist and challenge its hegemony. With humor, compassion, and responsibility for "my people," Kendall combines unwavering honesty with encouragement for the hard work required to be effective antiracists. Kendall has clearly earned the trust of friends and colleagues of color whose stories she has learned from and honors in the retelling. For any person who yearns for guidance in how to be a reliable and effective ally in the struggle against racism, Kendall serves as an authentic and experienced role model.

While offering a sophisticated analysis, the book is accessible and engaging. Kendall draws on examples from higher education, non-profit, and corporate settings to delineate how racism and white privilege operate individually, culturally, and institutionally. While unwavering in her challenges to white privilege, she is not rigid or doctrinaire, and because she connects theory to practice in a grounded way through the vivid and engaging stories she tells, this will be an incredibly powerful educational tool. It is perfect for the Teaching/Learning Social Justice Series because it connects hard-hitting critique with concrete and hopeful strategies for creating the kinds of authentic relationships across race that are so sorely needed if we are to realize our social justice goals.

Lee Anne Bell

ACKNOWLEDGMENTS

Writing is, in many ways, a solitary adventure. For me, a serious extrovert, that requires on-going connection to people who keep me sane while holding my feet to the fire. I am deeply grateful for the friends who have played that role. I thank:

Sarah Sheppard Levine (1947–2010), my cousin-like-a-sister, who died in the midst of my writing this edition. More than anyone else, she knew the necessity of hope, steadfast love, grace and humor as we walk through life.

Sally Kendall Bundy, my older sister, who has worked to understand my passion and been a cheerleader for moving forward.

Pat Lowrie, my close friend and mentor, who insists that she "just carries the water" when, in fact, she has walked beside, behind, and often in front of me for years.

Denny Stein, my high school roommate and loyal friend, who listens and considers my thoughts about what might be happening in racial situations and graciously admits I'm right.

Sid Reel, Santalynda Marrero, Pat Lowrie, and Sharon Washington who are my posse of women of color who check my moral compass to be sure I'm not experiencing whiteout and drop everything when I call.

Diane Davenport and Sayre Van Young, librarians and friends *extraordinaire*, who for years have answered all kinds of questions. It is invaluable to have one's own personal reference librarian; I have been graced with two.

Andrea Bryck, Margaret Gee, Ethel Manheimer, and Sherry Miller who offer continuous love and support for my work.

Rani and Eytan Urbas and their daughters, Natalia and Tamsin, who have for years fed me spiritually, emotionally, and literally.

Jane Kelleher Fernandes (a deaf white woman), Provost at the University of North Carolina Asheville, who invited me into her deaf experience so that I might understand one person's deaf life and my own hearing privilege. She pushes herself tirelessly to understand being white, renewing my hope that white people will do this arduous and essential work.

Marquita Chamblee who generously gave time, energy, and support to make this second edition a better book.

Colleagues, friends, and participants at NCORE and the White Privilege Conference who expect great work from me, support me, teach me, and help me meet my own standards.

My clients, from whom I learn more than I teach them. I am incredibly lucky to do what I do.

Susan Rawlins, my editor and friend, who will be forever integral to my writing process.

Lee Anne Bell, the series editor for The Teaching/Learning Social Justice Series of which this book is a part, who is a friend and teacher for me.

Catherine Bernard, my editor at Routledge, who has always been generous in her support and appreciation of my work.

PREFACE TO THE SECOND EDITION

It's 4:30 in the morning at the San Francisco airport. I am on my way to Sioux Falls, South Dakota, to speak. I walk up to the security screeners, a middle-aged African American man and an older white woman.

"What am I doing at the airport at 4:30 in the morning?" I ask myself out loud.

"Where are you going?" asks the white woman.

"Sioux Falls, South Dakota."

"For play?"

"No, work. I'm going to speak at a university tonight and at a conference in the morning."

"What do you do that takes you places to speak?"

"I'm speaking on diversity and inclusion, really on racism and white privilege."

"And I'm going to miss it?" the African American man asks, smiling.

To which the white woman responds, "There's no such thing as white privilege."

"Of course there is," says the African American man. "Look at the Senate."

"There's lots of 'them' in the Senate," the white woman says, seeming irritated.

"How many?" I ask.

"I don't know. Lots."

"I don't believe there are any," I say.

Now clearly agitated, the white woman says, "You all are crazy." She looks directly at me as I have turned to go into Security and says loudly, "You ought to go to college!"

The African American man and I smile at each other as I move on.

It was November, 2011, and this was the second such interaction I had had that week. The first occurred when I agreed with an African American woman that she had been treated in a racist way by her white female "mentor" and a white woman inserted herself into a discussion and disagreed. Then she said to me, "Francie, there's racism in everyone, not just white people." I tried to respond that there was bigotry in everyone, but she went on, insisting almost frantically, "It's everywhere, in every country, not just here [in the United States]," as if she sees racism as normal and part of the human condition. While I've had these experiences before with people I don't know well, the frequency of them has grown exponentially, and their tone and shape have shifted. Recently I've been involved in many conversations with people of color in which white people who overhear jump into the conversation to deny what the people of color are saying.

This is about self-concept, white people who feel their goodness has been challenged. Given the state of the economy, the experience and fear of loss—of jobs, healthcare, pensions, and/or homes—the human and financial costs of seemingly endless wars, and the deepening gulf between the haves and the have-nots, there is little tolerance on any side for ideas other than its own. Many people are so fearful, seeing themselves in desperate competition for shrinking resources, that behavior and interactions have gone to extremes. Here are some examples:

The attempted assassination of the white liberal Arizona Democratic congresswoman, Gabrielle Giffords, by a white man who came to a public open air meeting-and-greeting of her constituents. She was shot in the head and critically injured; six others were killed, and thirteen wounded.

A young white gay man, Tyler Clementi, committed suicide after being secretly videotaped while kissing another man. His suicide was one of a rash of suicides occurring, at least in part, because the gay person was being bullied. The videotape was made by Dharun Ravi, his college freshman roommate, an East Indian heterosexual man.

Rand Paul, a recently-elected [2010] Republican Senator from Kentucky, announced his primary election by saying, "I have a message, a message from the Tea Party. A message that is loud and clear and does not mince words: 'We've come to take our government back.'" Later he said that he wouldn't have voted for the Civil Rights Act of 1964 as it was passed: "I think it's bad business to exclude anybody from your restaurant, but, at the same time, I do believe in private ownership." And, if restaurant owners prohibit Black people from eating at their restaurants, it is their right to do that. "This is the hard part about believing in freedom."[1]

The chair of a diversity and multicultural committee at a university in the Midwest said that the real problem at their school was not the Black students, who make up six percent of the student population: "Our problem is we're being overrun by Asians." [2]

Pastor Steven Anderson of Faith World Baptist Church in Tempe, Arizona, prays for President Obama's death: "I hope that God strikes Barack Obama with brain cancer so that he can die like Ted Kennedy and I hope it happens today," he told MyFOXPhoenix. He classified his sermon as "spiritual warfare." [3] In addition, a group of Southern Baptist ministers around the country encourage their congregations to pray that God will kill President Obama and "leave his children fatherless." [4]

On August 17, 2009, President Obama arrived in Phoenix to speak to the Veterans of Foreign Wars (VFW). He was met by people carrying handguns and at least one assault weapon, "the latest incident in which protesters have openly displayed firearms near the president." [5]

These examples show us a part of the context in which we now live. That part is scared, angry, and tending toward violence in various forms. Our country's descent into greater overt animosity coincided with beginning to write this second edition.

Another part of the current picture is that there is a growing cohort of young people, white and of color, who are stepping up to the challenge of pushing their institutions to a new place of comfort in addressing issues of white privilege and other institutionalized inequities. Given the ease with which we could fall into despair, it is vital that we hold both parts of our current context at the same time.

Understanding White Privilege: Creating Pathways to Authentic Relationships Across Race is written for a range of people: those who are in the beginning stages of learning about whiteness and white privilege and those who are actively working toward racial justice. It is written for individuals and those in organizations—colleges and universities and corporations—who grapple with race every day, as well as for those who believe they don't need to. It is written for those who have tried to build authentic professional relationships across race but have felt unable to do so. It is written for those who believe strongly in the struggle for racial justice and need additional information to share with their friends and colleagues. Inviting readers to think personally about how race—theirs and others'—frames experiences, relationships, and the way we each see the world, *Understanding White Privilege* focuses squarely on white privilege and its implications, offering specific suggestions for what we each can do to bridge the racial chasm.

The book provides a context for understanding the ways in which whiteness and white privilege systemically affect how white people and people of color are treated and interact in and out of the workplace. In addition to drawing a broad picture of how those of us who are white receive unearned benefits purely on the basis of our skin color, I have included many stories that speak to the vastly different experiences of whites and people of color because of this system of privilege. My hope is that, by showing the contrasts and connections between people's stories, the ways that racism is built into systems and structures will be revealed. Readers will feel empowered to work toward more just and equitable systems. I hope the book is a resource for creating organizational cultures to which each of us is able to bring all of our talents.

Understanding White Privilege is the result of almost forty years of interacting with institutions about issues of race and privilege. Two of the valuable by-products of my practice are that I am able to witness what is happening nationally in diversity efforts and that I am able to explore how power, privilege, and issues of diversity play out in academic, corporate, governmental, and not-for-profit systems. Historically, institutions of higher education and corporations have viewed themselves as very different from one another. Corporations didn't want to be compared to colleges and universities because the latter were too removed from the real world. Scholars, on the other hand, were aghast at the suggestion that there were any similarities between the academy and corporations. From their point of view, making money was what motivated corporations while universities were concerned with purer matters. Because of the economic issues facing the nation and the world these days, academic institutions can no longer focus solely on "purer matters," though beliefs about the value of money for money's sake still vary. But over the past fifteen to twenty years differences between the corporate and academic worlds have lessened significantly. It is not unusual now to find a former corporate CEO as the president of a college or university, and corporations use academic research to help them create organizational climates that best retain a broad diversity of employees.

In this millennium the differences are blurring, moving my colleague Dr. Harry Gibbs to coin the term "corporademic." While significant differences remain, colleges, universities, and corporations all ask similar questions:

- How can a person's race be such a powerful determinant of her or his experience in the organization, whether it is corporate or academic?
- Why does race continue to be such a significant barrier to collegial relationships?
- How do we become more comfortable talking about race?
- What can we do to begin to build stronger, more effective and honest relationships across race that increase our ability to work together?

My experience is that, while white people in the academy and in corporations have little conscious understanding of the complexities of white privilege and how it affects their daily lives, people of color in all organizations are very clear that primary access to power and influence lies in white hands. The enormous difference between these perceptions means that there is little common ground on which to build relationships and then organizations that best use the talents of all the members of their respective communities. My goal is to provide an alternate lens through which to examine our behavior as well as the institutions in which we work.

In this second edition I am adding two new chapters focusing on strengthening our ability to build cross-race relationships and deepening our knowledge of the history on which our relationship issues exist. Chapter 5, "How White Women Reinforce the Supremacy of Whiteness," begins to untangle the lack of trust many women of color have for white women as a group. While we, as white people, are almost always clearer about being individuals than we are about being members of a group, particularly a racial group, we are of course both individuals and members of various groups. Just as we are each a member of the "daughters" group or the "sons" group, we are also members of the "white" group. Not good or bad, just fact. For those of us who are white women, uncovering the ways in which we are in a privileged group (being white) as well as in an under-privileged group (being women) makes it more possible to build authentic relationships with those who are in two target groups—people of color and women.

Chapter 9, "Talking about Whiteness and Being White," continues and updates the discussion of talking about race which began in the first edition of *Understanding White Privilege*. Much has changed in the tenor of racial conversation in the country in the past six years. While many white people seem far more willing to publicly express their anger toward African Americans and Latinos, they still have difficulty using the w-word— "white"—to identify themselves or others of us in that racial group. That reluctance crosses the political spectrum even though the reasons probably vary. The willingness of white people to name ourselves and others like us as "white" in everyday conversation, just as we identify people of color, is essential to moving toward equal footing in a conversation.

The first four chapters of *Understanding White Privilege* offer a foundation of information and a blueprint for how we can begin to think about white privilege. This is information I believe all of us—white and of color—need. However, Chapters 1 and 2, focusing on personal work and understanding why those of us who are white would do the difficult self-exploration that is required, have been written particularly with white people in mind. Putting the personal work at the beginning reflects my strong belief that, if we don't look at ourselves, our biases and prejudices, and our "blindnesses" first and continually, anything else we do will be built on a shaky foundation. No matter how much work we have done on our privileged status, any time we become complacent about the amount of internal examination we have done, we move quickly to greater complicity with the systems of oppression.

I believe that every one of us has self-examination to do based on the identity groups to which we belong. Systems of privilege are intertwined, each building on the other. While unearned benefits might be withheld from us in terms of one part of who we are, we may receive them on the basis of other parts of our identities. For those of you who are men, for example, how does the patriarchy serve you, even if you are of color or gay or poor? If you are a woman of color and heterosexual, upper-middle class, and Christian, how do the latter elements of your identity give you access to power, resources, and ability to influence decision-makers even though you are of color?

Chapters 5 through 10 are designed to provide deeper and broader excavation about white privilege and to equip the reader with strategies for making personal and organizational changes. As Margaret Andersen put it:

> ...understanding white privilege only as a repertoire of taken-for-granted advantages is not enough. Without also understanding racism and racial stratification as the foundation of white privilege which is the very structure of society, acknowledging white privilege will only generate a sense of relief for dominant groups and will not dissect the institutional arrangements through which racism continues.[6]

To learn about white privilege and not to use that knowledge to bring about changes in our systems serves those for whom the structures of oppression were created. To help us better understand the relationship between us as individuals and the systems in which we function, I am including a model called the Three Levels, first introduced to me by Price Cobbs, that I find very helpful in diversity and inclusion training.

The basic premise of this model is that each of us functions at the personal, interpersonal, and organizational levels concurrently. Often we are unaware that what we personally believe seeps out, greatly affecting our behavior at all three levels. On the personal level we carry all of our thoughts, biases and prejudices, our various belief systems, values and judgments, our ideas, the conversations we have in our heads. Our complacent fantasy is that our personal thoughts are just that—personal—and that no one else has access to them if we don't want to share them.

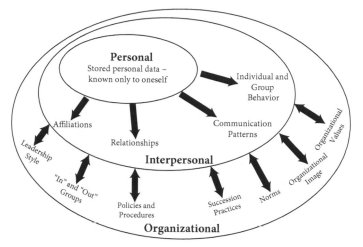

The Three Levels

The second level, the interpersonal, is comprised of our interactions with others based largely on the application of the ideas we carry in our heads. The organizations with which we build affiliations or don't, the groups of people with whom we are most likely to create relationships or not, the ways we talk to different groups of people, and the quality and types of behavior we exhibit with individuals and with various groups all reflect what we hold at the personal level.

At the organizational level are structures and systems that are often believed to have been created by a single leader—"This is the way President Smith runs this university." In reality the ways of doing things are not the work of a president but are most likely embedded in the culture of the organization. Peter Senge, a well-known proponent of systems thinking, says that instead:

> The systems perspective tells us that we must look beyond individual mistakes or bad luck to understand important problems. We must look beyond personalities and events to understand important problems. We must look into the underlying structures which shape individual actions and create the conditions where types of events become likely. [7]

Put another way, my favorite organizational change mantra: "Every system is perfectly designed to get the results it gets."[8]

Let's look at how this process works. As I talk about in Chapter 1, I was born in 1947 and grew up in Waco, Texas, in the midst of segregation. Because my elementary school was segregated, I did not go to school with Black children, but I did go to school with Mexicanos. (A historical note: Mexican children were in white schools based on the treaty of Guadalupe Hildago, 1848, between the United States and Mexico. In that treaty Mexico agreed to cede 55 percent of its land to the United States with the stipulation that the people living on that land would retain ownership of their property. Not surprisingly, the United States reneged. The second important agreement was that those Mexicans would be identified as white. The United States kept that promise, as we can see on census forms, "non-Hispanic white." [9])

As I was growing up, I heard a lot about how stupid Mexicans were, how they were always drunk, and how dirty they were. In third grade when I got an intestinal infection at school, my mother was convinced it was because I used the same bathrooms as Mexican children did. Without thinking about it consciously, all of those comments were stored at my personal level and they played out at the interpersonal level. I never built a relationship with a Mexican student. Even though I spent six years in elementary school with the same group of children, I only remember one boy's name, Domingo. My mother was so afraid that I would date Mexican boys in junior high that she sold our house and moved us to the white suburbs. The spoken and unspoken messages in our culture made it clear to me that Mexicans were not as good as white people. In this instance, it was not about socioeconomic class; the mother of one of the white students was a server at the Piccadilly Cafeteria. Mom never talked about the poor or working class white students in ways that she did about Mexican children: how I had to be careful to wash my hands really well after going to the bathroom, for example.

Many politicians, almost assuredly all white, had evidently grown up with those same messages because, as recently as 1971, legislation was in place that made it illegal to speak Spanish in a public school building in Texas.[10] The point here is not how bigoted Texas is; this kind of legislation is being passed all over the country. It is, rather, an example of how attitudes held at the personal level play out in the interpersonal level and go on to affect one's response to institutional policies, practices, and procedures. The principals and teachers in the Texas schools who had the task of suspending children who spoke Spanish at school usually had no sense of how they were colluding with the underlying racism.

I need to say a few things about the language used in this book. First, I am intentionally using "white supremacy" and "the superiority of whiteness" instead of "institutional racism" because I believe they more accurately depict what exists in the United States. I know that for many whites it is not comfortable language because it brings to mind pictures of the Ku Klux Klan and other white supremacist groups. I hope that it will become clear that I am talking about systems and not individuals. Second, I have struggled over being consistent and capitalizing "white" as I capitalize "Black." I have chosen not to do that chiefly because, for me, it would be too much like the writings of white supremacist groups.

Third, a thought about "blind." I know from working with the deaf community that there is a genuine sensitivity about tossing the word *deafness* around. And I am conscious that I have used *blindness* throughout the book as a metaphor. I have searched for another word, and nothing else works for me at this point. I think it has to do with the hymn, "Amazing Grace," written in the early 1770s by John Newton, a former slave trader who, in the later part of his life, spoke out against slavery: "I once was lost but now am found, / Was blind, but now I see." I feel that it was truly an act of grace that I turned out differently from what I might have become—that I have seen, experienced, felt things that I had no reason to expect to be able to, having grown up in the time and place that I did. So I am stuck, for the present, with *blind*, knowing that in time a better word will replace it. To those whom I offend, please forgive me. To those who have never noticed how casually we use metaphors that pertain to physical and mental disabilities, I hope this note will help you think more carefully.

For much of my life I have looked for white anti-racist role models to provide guidance and spiritual energy. I have found a number of them, some of whom I have known personally and some I have never met. Anne Braden is one I know only by reputation and through her writing: a white Southern woman who bravely defied systems and power-holders when she and her husband bought a house in segregated Louisville, Kentucky, on behalf of a Black couple. She speaks about the challenge that I hope this book addresses:

> The challenge to us as whites is to try to understand what racism is and what it has done, not to just us personally, but to the society we live in, and then to do something about it—about very specific manifestations of it in the here and now.[11]

1
BEGINNING WITH OURSELVES
The Importance of Doing Our Personal Work

"When I walked into the workshop on diversity that you were leading for my organization, I felt sick. Here was another white woman coming to talk about diversity. What could you possibly know? I decided that I would not get involved—that I would sit still, take notes, and say nothing. But you turned out to be different, and by 2:00 p.m. I was totally involved and, in fact, crying because my work situation was so hard. I had never met a white woman before who had looked deeply at what it means to have white privilege and could talk about it so honestly and straightforwardly. Before then, I hadn't heard anyone white who had done so much work on herself about what it means to be white that she was able to have even a glimmer of understanding about what it is like to be a person of color living in a racist society. When I told you that at the end of the workshop, your response was, 'Understanding how race works in the United States doesn't seem like rocket science to me. There are clues everywhere if white people want to see them.' I'll never forget that."

I have been actively involved in addressing race and racism since 1966 when I was a sophomore in college. One of my greatest lessons during that time is that those of us who are white and, by definition, have white privilege must engage in sustained self-examination about how our race affects our lives. If we don't fully understand our individual and collective roles in maintaining a system of white superiority, our relationships with people of color remain superficial, our ability to work in diverse workplaces is greatly diminished, and we fail to create a just world in which everyone has an equitable opportunity to contribute and thrive.

My clarity about the importance of doing our personal work has increased as I have worked and talked with colleagues and friends, both white and of color. The feedback I receive, like that in the story above, regularly reinforces my determination to examine how being white affects what I do and how I do it. Several times a month, as I work with groups on institutionalized racism and white privilege, white participants comment that they wish they knew what it was like to be Asian American or American Indian or Black or Latino/a. The underlying belief is that, if they understood the experience, they could be more sympathetic. "What is it like for you to be white?" I ask. "How is your experience different from others because of your skin color?" Frequently people are taken aback by the question. "I never thought about it," or "I don't really think about myself as white," or "I think of myself as a member of the *human* race, not the white race."

As those of us who are white begin to examine racial privilege, our first and perhaps most important task is to explore what it means for each of us, personally, to be white. I am talking about my own experience here, as the first chapter of *Understanding White Privilege*, for three reasons: to give you a sense of how I came to think so seriously about institutional racism and privilege, to give you an example of one person's self-exploration, and to create a foundation on which the rest of the book will sit. In race-based American society, the white race is the standard against which all others are measured. We can never know what it is to be "other" if we aren't very clear about our experiences as white people. This journey is not simple nor is it quick. It is continuing work. And, while it can be painful, it is essential. In the 1999 edition of her book, *The Wall Between*, lifelong antiracist activist Anne Braden talked about it in this way:

> ...we who grew up white Southerners two and three generations ago learned something else the whole society needs to ponder. We found that when we turned ourselves inside out to face the truth, it was a painful process, but it was not destructive. Rather, it became a moment of rebirth—and opened up new creative vistas in our lives.[1]

When we set out to do intentional personal work, as we must, and to turn ourselves inside out, we have to first know where we want to get to in our understanding and behavior. Then we have to identify honestly where we are now and how we got there, being conscious of how our racial, ethnic, and cultural roots have shaped our perceptions. My experience is that, the older I have gotten, the more purposeful I have become in looking at the many sides of a situation. I ask how my racial experience helps or hinders seeing another's perspective. How has my response to an experience been informed by my Southern culture or by my age or gender?

In many instances, life has happened, and I have then worked to make meaning of what has occurred. I have learned in what Warren Bennis and Robert Thomas call "crucibles"—"transformative experience[s] through which an individual comes to a new or an altered sense of identity."[2] Some of these crucibles were searingly painful, like feeling that I had to choose between my family and what was morally right. Others were unanticipated learning opportunities that presented themselves whether I wanted them or not, like going to the Whitney Museum in New York City to see an exhibit titled "Executive Order 9066" about the Japanese internment and discovering that I had no idea that the Japanese had been interned in the United States. Still others I sought and, while definitely uncomfortable, felt essential to my understanding, like reading *A People's History of the United States 1492–Present* by Howard Zinn.

I can identify six "crucibles" in which my essential understanding of the world and my place in it were changed: experiencing the cognitive dissonance caused by hearing my family's comments about Black people, having my own experiences, and not knowing what to believe; becoming increasingly aware of my family's history and choosing a different path; leaving my family and joining the National Student YWCA; learning what I hadn't been taught about my country's history; returning to live in the South; and looking at my life with Marie. Each of these experiences turned my understanding of the world upside down. There is nothing magical about the process of "turn[ing] ourselves inside out to face the truth." There is only the willingness to be uncomfortable with what we are seeing and hearing and the determination to uncover more that we need to know and then make changes based on what we learn.

I grew up in an upper-middle-class family in Waco, Texas. I was born in 1947, so I experienced the legally segregated South. I remember "white" drinking fountains and "colored" ones, movie theatres where white people sat downstairs and Black people sat in the balcony. The messages I got about race were direct and clear: White people are the regular people, the good people, the valuable people; all others, particularly Black people, are less than human. Some of my learning came subconsciously as I watched and listened to what happened around me: Black people serving white people, taking care of their children, managing their households. Black women were the mother substitutes, working long hours cleaning houses and taking care of white people's children while their own children were at home. Black men were the bartenders, always present at family celebrations and parties. The white men joked with them and acted as though they were just men together. As I look back on it now, that part in particular seems like a bizarre play. Some of the white men could easily have been Ku Klux Klan members, but, during a party, as long as Black men kept their place, white men acted like they were best buddies. The white men—family members and close family friends—regularly told vicious jokes about Black people and "Mexicans." I remember only a few of the white women participating in the slurs and jokes; "ladies" didn't say such things, but none of them ever stopped or contradicted the men. At best, they rolled their eyes and gave a tsk-tsk, "Oh, Bill," and went on with their conversations.

Race was a constant element in conversations. Black people were spoken of in hushed tones at the dinner table, as if the person in the kitchen or waiting on us couldn't hear what was being said. There were frequent discussions of maids among the white women: "It's so hard to get a good one. How did you find her? Does she know anyone?" At the same time there was constant complaining about the maid's work, her "sullenness," her lack of morals about having babies, too many and out of wedlock. There was a basic contradiction about the Black women; my mother enjoined me to "Mind Marie" as she left home, even though she didn't really trust her to do the work she had been hired to do and constantly complained about her. "Black people are nothing like us—their homes are dirty, they live in a terrible and dangerous part of town." Again, a contradiction: Their own homes are dirty, but somehow they are able to keep our homes clean. Frequently I asked if I could go to the home of the African American woman, Marie Jones, who worked for us and raised me, and the answer was always no. By words and implication, Mom let me know that Marie's house was nothing like ours, that nothing was the same, and that it would be neither appropriate nor comfortable for me to be there.

Crucible 1: Experiencing the cognitive dissonance caused by hearing my family's comments about Black people, having my own experiences, and not knowing what to believe. I carried all of those messages that I didn't know I had gotten to boarding school at National Cathedral School for Girls in Washington, D.C., which stands immediately next to the Episcopal Church's Washington Cathedral. I was there from 1961–1965, the height of the civil rights movement. There were two Black girls in my class; they were similar to me in terms of social class and each was a lot smarter than I was. The sophomore class party was held at one of their houses. It was the first time I had ever been in a Black person's home. "The bathrooms were clean, the beds were made, and the small children in the family were neatly and cleanly dressed. I was honestly surprised to find things much as they are in my own home." (From a journal entry, January 9, 1967.) When I walked into her kitchen I stopped dead in my tracks. On the counter, I saw a Mixmaster—it was *exactly the same Mixmaster* that we had at home. I watched as the pieces of what I had believed fall around me, and a voice in my head said, "If Mom lied to me about this, what else has she lied to me about?" I don't think I ever again fully believed what my mother told me. That confusion was only heightened when I repeated a comment I had heard my brother-in-law make about the entertainer Sammy Davis, Jr., calling him a "one-eyed nigger Jew." One of my white classmates slapped me on my face and walked away. I knew I had done something horrible, but I wasn't quite sure what it was, since I was only repeating what one of my elders had said. This last incident was among the many times that I was shocked by the strength of others' responses to my behavior. I think I was testing what I had heard in one environment to see how it flew in another. While I wondered if my brother-in-law's comment was okay, I wasn't clear at that point how vile it was.

How could such a seemingly small thing as seeing a Mixmaster like ours in a Black person's home cause such a powerful response? Child development theorists like Jean Piaget tell us that generally young children want to believe what they are told by the adults in their lives and that they do so without questioning the veracity of what they are hearing. In addition to believing those adults closest to them, they also gather information from the environment in which they live—what they see on TV, what they hear in the grocery store, what they hear from other children. Unless the adults around them consciously and intentionally provide different experiences for them, they are likely to take at face value what they see or hear.

For me as a white Southern child, racial messages were a regular part of my experience. In their dailiness and in their seeming irrefutability, comments about race were not terribly different from those about God or patriotism: There is a Christian God, we love and pledge allegiance to our country, and Black people are inferior to white people. The racial lies that were communicated were delivered with such conviction that I never questioned them. So, when I got concrete information that went directly against what important adults, as well as my Southern culture, had told me, I was thrown into serious cognitive and emotional dissonance. My hunch is that, at some level, I was already beginning to question what I had been taught, but denial is a remarkable force, and it was easier and safer to believe that my mother had told me the truth than it was to listen to relative strangers at boarding school. However, my experience at my classmate's house was concrete proof, and I could no longer block out what I was seeing and learning.

Crucible 2: Becoming increasingly aware of my family's history and choosing a different path. The Mixmaster incident, my first crucible, felt like the story in the New Testament in which Saul was struck by the blind staggers on the road to Damascus. A man committed to the destruction of Christians, Saul was suddenly blinded by God until his eyes were opened to a new reality. He later became the Apostle Paul and worked with and for the very people he had previously persecuted. For me, the view of the world that I had held until that time was totally upended. The second crucible, becoming increasingly aware of my family's history and choosing a different path, took place over the next couple of years, my junior and senior years of high school. While my changing consciousness was more gradual, it was not less emotionally disorienting. Important building blocks that I had always counted on continued to crumble. The school vacations that I spent in Waco became increasingly contentious; I was more argumentative about race and civil rights, and the racial comments and "jokes" from my brothers-in-law and male cousins grew more frequent and vicious. Many dinners ended in shouting and my leaving the table in tears. My mother was horrified by the conflict but had no idea what to do about it; I suspect she was feeling as helpless and hopeless as I was, and I know my provoking such conflict bewildered her.

I felt less and less at home in the Episcopal Church in which I grew up. There I had been overtly taught that we who were white had been made in God's and Jesus' image and covertly taught that there were no contradictions between being a moral, upstanding Christian and actively participating in personal and systemic racism. Because the Washington Cathedral is considered to be the *National* Cathedral, ministers from all over the country and the world preached there; it was a hub of civil rights activity. As I listened to clergy who were involved in civil rights activities and marches, particularly Black and white ministers from the South, I heard graphic descriptions of what was happening to those who were fighting for their freedom at the brutal hands of white people—many of whom identified themselves as Christians—for example, the bombing of the 16th Street Baptist Church in Birmingham in which four little girls were killed, fire-hosing and beating people in the freedom marches, and murdering Blacks and white sympathizers. I began to rethink what it meant to be Christian. One of the most powerful sermons was given by the Very Reverend H.C.N. Williams, a white South African who had for years fought against apartheid. He was then the Provost of Coventry Cathedral in Coventry, England. "Prejudice is the child of a delinquent mind," he said. I was so taken by him and his thoughts that I spent parts of three summers in Coventry, working at the cathedral and living with him and his family. Mr. Williams became a role model and father figure for me. Together we read Christian theologians like Dietrich Bonhoeffer who fought against Hitler's persecution of the Jews and was ultimately killed by the Nazis. I came to feel more at home with him and his family than I ever would again with my family in Waco, Texas.

I thought about the possibility of my family having a "delinquent mind" as I began to question my family's history. My mother's family's business is cotton. Her parents moved from Meridian, Mississippi, where my grandmother's family had owned a plantation and the enslaved people who worked on it, to Cameron, Texas, in the late 1800s. Our history and the individuals in it—my mother, her parents, grandparents, and perhaps great-grandparents—became a burden of personal shame for me, whether that was a helpful way to feel about it or not. I desperately wanted my mother to change, to stand up for what was right and *really* Christian, but, if she didn't, I was increasingly willing to separate myself from her and from other family members. I felt that, if I weren't connected to them, I wouldn't be responsible to change what I saw as their wrongs or their "delinquent" minds. And that was before Mom told me that some of the men in my family, who were mayors, bank presidents, and highly respected businessmen in the community, had also been Klan members. The revelation was mind-numbing.

In the spring of 1965, a classmate asked me if I wanted to participate in the Selma march. By then I must have been talking a different talk, and my guess is that she wanted to see if I was serious about what I was saying. I asked my mother, who, of course, said no, and, while I was probably relieved at that point not to be venturing into such scary territory, I asked my friend to bring me back a button from the march. She returned with a button the size of a dime; it was black with a white equality sign on it. I put it on and wore it throughout my summer in Waco—to church, to the country club, to visit my mother's friends. I even put it on my nightgown. I refused to take it off, even though my mother begged me to. I don't believe that I had really committed myself to do social justice work at that point. I think I was trying it on, literally and figuratively. I had found a way to separate myself from my mother and the rest of my family, to take a stand, and, I'm sure, to pay Mom back for what I saw as her cowardly behavior.

It is important to remember the historical context of my story. I know that my personal experience was similar to that in many other white families: young people fighting to respond differently than their families were to the civil rights struggle in the South. Mine is a particularly Southern experience, like those of Anne Braden, Lillian Smith, author of *Killers of the Dream*, Mab Segrest, author of *Memoir of a Race Traitor,* and many others. Each of us was forced to take a side: either to maintain the system that was in place or to do something different. There was no ignoring the earthquake that was occurring.

Crucible 3: Leaving my family and joining the National Student YWCA. The next four years, 1965–1969, were pivotal. While I became increasingly serious about doing anti-racism work, I still wished desperately that my family would change. A journal entry, dated January 9, 1967, reflects what I was feeling:

> I am still going through a great deal of conflict internally concerning race; I know that I am not able to take a friend home simply because of her color; my family disapproves to a large extent of many of the ideas that are most basic to my being; I am not able to share with my family many of the ideas that excite me most. Intellectually I know I must begin to live a life of my own, but emotionally I feel a responsibility to my family.

In my second week of college at the University of Denver, I went to the Campus YWCA-YMCA (Young Women's Christian Association-Young Men's Christian Association) to hear a talk on tutoring "inner city" children. I spent much of my next four years in the Campus YWCA office. I met people who would become lifelong friends as I threw myself into attending programs on social justice issues, involving myself in the running of the local organization, and then taking leadership in the regional and national offices.

From the beginning, the National Student YWCA offered me a place to work seriously with other women—of color and white—as we looked at whiteness and at racism. Most of the initiatives at the national level were anti-racism based, whether we were participating in workshops on white racism and white privilege, determining the priorities for action on individual college campuses, studying colonialism and racism as they were manifested in South Africa, Central and Latin America, and in the United States, or working with other national student-based organizations. For the first time in my life, I was in the company of many Black women who were teaching me and working with me, pushing me to grow. I was frequently in the presence of Miss Dorothy Height, a giant in the fight for racial justice and president of the National Council of Negro Women for many years, and worked with her as she started the Center for Racial Justice at the National YWCA in 1965. Valerie Russell, an African American woman who was working at the National Student YWCA headquarters when I met her, was one of the most important people for me. She was extremely clear about how racism worked, having watched her mother's life and her vision shortened by it, and she was passionate about tearing down the systemic and personal walls that separated us. Through the power of her anger and love, her freedom songs and prayers, my heart was opened to the possibility of change.

Our student leadership group had real, honest conversations, and frequently we fought about the work we were doing. On several occasions, the women students of color told the white women students that they were not interested in being our educators and to go away and figure out what it meant to be white, to work on *our own* racism, and then to report back. They weren't doing it any more; it was not their job. It shocked many of us well-meaning white women—both students and staff—to have our actions and our motivations questioned. While some of us didn't have any idea what "work[ing] on our own racism" meant, we knew enough to know that, if we didn't invest in that endeavor, the possibility of genuine relationships within and across race would be greatly diminished. The remarkable thing is that many of us made that commitment, in large part because we had advisors and supporters who were as deeply engaged in working on *their* racism and were committed to our understanding the deep implications of being white.

Through the National Student YWCA, I had opportunities that few other white women students had and that were pivotal to my developing understanding of myself as a white person. A central one was the focused work with other white women on systemic white racism and institutional change. In a chapter I wrote for *Journeys that Opened up the World: Women, Student Christian Movements, and Social Justice, 1955–1975*, I described my experience with the Y and talked about the workshops and trainings on white privilege that I had been a part of. Several of the sessions were based on materials that were created by Sally Timmel and compiled to form "White on White: A Handbook for Groups Working Against Racism." The publication was designed to help white people examine our own racism. The following excerpts from the preface give a sense of the tone and the intent of the handbook and of the culture and environment in which I was living and growing. Racism and white privilege were part of my everyday conversation.

> Racism in America is a white problem. It is woven into our institutions and our culture. We must all recognize how we benefit by racism and are caught in its web. Whites can and must change! Change themselves, their institutions, and their culture....
>
> As we begin to use this book, designed to help us come to terms with racism, we must recognize that a book, a set of discussions, does not eliminate racism. It is only when we have transformed the total fabric of our lives that we will have eliminated racism and created a

truly pluralistic society. But we must begin somewhere and beginning with ourselves and the institutions in which we find ourselves is now clearly called for....

We need help to look at ourselves. We need help to understand how we as a people through history have used others for our own ends. We need help to look, without fear, at the meaning of our own lives. We need help to understand that our own worth and power is not lost in a just distribution of power. The emotional weight that racism produces in whites blinds us from a vision of the fundamental changes we must work for and which will, in fact, free us all.[3]

While often uncomfortable with what I was pushed to look at about myself, my motivations for continuing my personal work were clear. In the National Student YWCA I had found a family of students and professionals who loved me and valued me *because of* who I was—my values, my commitment, my passion about race—rather than in spite of those things. When I was with them I felt like I was home, and so I spent more and more time in the company of my chosen family and less and less in Texas.

The decision to separate myself from my family was horribly painful, but it was not difficult. I think that it was an act of survival. I tried to deny many parts of myself: being Southern and my family's being in the cotton business, the blatant racism of some family members and the silence of others, and our upper-middle-class pretensions. I felt strongly that I couldn't become who my inside voice was telling me I should be and stay connected to those things I found reprehensible. It took years of work to become whole and to reconnect with my family, but I was compelled to apply my mind, heart, and hands to creating a better place for *all* of us. My search has always been for wholeness—whether I described it as "being the best me I could possibly be" or re-membering and re-collecting. The belief that change is possible is woven through my life's work.

Crucible 4: Learning what I hadn't been taught about my country's history. In many ways, the fourth crucible was similar to crucible number three. Coming to grips with actual United States history, as opposed to the sanitized version that we are generally taught, pushes many of us into such profound cognitive and emotional discomfort that we resist the information. Moving ahead requires that we again give up what we thought we knew, another fundamental part of our beliefs about the way things are.

Like many, I was a very patriotic child. I said the pledge of allegiance with vigor. I was given no reason to believe that there was anything wrong with slavery, with Texas "capturing" Mexico, with settlers staking claims for Western land and building their homesteads there, or with "our" people killing "savage" Indians. That was the way it was meant to happen. I watched "The Lone Ranger" every Saturday morning, never questioning what *"tonto"* meant—in Spanish it means a fool, half-wit, stupid. I didn't question that someone could "discover" a place where millions of people already lived.

In high school I learned facts about the United States that were less than complimentary, mainly about the South. Because they were so connected to my own personal story, I didn't ask further questions about what had *really* happened as white people took over the nation. I didn't flinch as I learned about the Three-Fifths Compromise, the clause in Article 1 of the Constitution that identified enslaved Black people as each counting as three-fifths of a person in terms of taxation and representation, or about Manifest Destiny, the belief in white people's divine right to expand west, taking control and ownership of all land. It was as though that information wasn't able to penetrate my shell of denial.

It wasn't until I was in college that the veneer cracked. I had trusted, in a childlike way, what I was told about the nation's history. Perhaps I, and we, want to believe that people are simple and decent, that our ancestors, for example, were people of integrity who had the good of all in mind. Nothing had prepared me at gut level for the complexities of our national behavior. I wasn't told, or didn't take in, the information that almost all of the framers of the Constitution were slaveholders. I didn't hear that the army intentionally gave blankets contaminated with smallpox germs to the Native Americans in order to kill them. Or that white people had built the railroads using Chinese laborers who were paid a pittance and asked to do the dangerous jobs that recent Irish immigrant workers would not. I knew Hitler had built concentration camps for the Jews, but I didn't know until I was twenty-six that we had built enclosed spaces in remote locations where we interned Japanese Americans, many of whom were American citizens. For years I had hanging on my wall a print by Sister Mary Corita, then an Immaculate Heart nun, with a quotation from Camus: "I should like to be able to love my country and still love justice." The two felt mutually exclusive then, as they still do in many ways.

These revelations were painful to me for two reasons. First, during that time I became clear that I live in a country that professes to be moral, better than everyone else, and to have created a system of government under which justice is equally meted out. It was horrible to come to the realization that that wasn't the case; I felt like I had been a fool. I had built my sense of the United States on what I thought was reality only to find that I had been lied to, through omission and commission, about much that had really happened. Second, this experience was sadly similar to my learning about my family's history. In each case, I was left feeling that I had no idea what was true and not true, what information and which people I could trust, and that my legs had been knocked out from under me.

Again the Student YWCA caught me as I floundered. My despair was mitigated by the fact that we were taking action at campuses across the country: doing audits of racist activities on college campuses, holding conferences on racism and white privilege, and pushing college boards of trustees to get rid of all stocks in companies that in any way reinforced apartheid in South Africa. I wrote a model that was used around the country for investigating university investments. Being actively involved in making change in institutions reduced my sense of powerlessness and gave me hope that things could change.

Crucible 5: Returning to live in the South. After graduating from the University of Denver in 1969, I moved to New York City, in large part to be closer to the national headquarters of the YWCA. I lived there for five years, and during that time I got my Master's degree from Bank Street College of Education and taught in a demonstration day care center in Brooklyn. All the while, I tried to deny parts of myself, particularly the Southern parts. I did my best to get rid of my Texas accent, and I dodged questions when strangers asked me where I was from or what business my family was in. My mother had died of cancer a couple of months before I graduated from college (my father had died when I was four), so the Texas trips I had made to please her were no longer necessary. I went only at Christmas, and then for a short time. I was too unsettled about who I was to be forced to pretend that everything was fine.

My anti-racism work continued. At Bank Street, my thesis was on racial stereotypes in children's literature; I began to create an anti-racist curriculum for three- and four-year-olds. I remained deeply involved in the Student YWCA, working with other students and adult mentors to push the National Board to adopt the One Imperative: "To thrust our collective power towards the elimination of racism wherever it exists and by any means necessary." I participated in convocations on white racism and white privilege. At one of those conferences, we worked with three facilitators: Robert Terry, a white man and author of *For Whites Only*, Patricia Bidol, a white woman, and Barbara Mays, an African American woman. Barbara said something I have never forgotten. She said that once we began to notice racism we could never not see it again; we had bought a one-way ticket. That certainly seemed to be my reality.

I continued to be haunted by the racism in my Southern culture and by the fear that my family's history reflected on me. While being away from the South was a relief in some ways, I came to understand that, if I was going to be able to do valuable work on racism, I had to figure out what it meant to be white and Southern. At an opening of Sister Corita's new show at a gallery in Greenwich Village, I had my second blind-staggers-on-the-road-to-Damascus experience. One of her serigraphs was a large picture, in black and white, of the outline of a tree and its reflection. In the middle, between the two images, was a quotation in green from Carl Jung: "No noble, well-grown tree ever disowned its dark roots, for it grows not only upwards but downwards as well." I watched the pieces of my life fall around my head again, and I thought, "No, you can't do your doctoral work at Harvard or at the University of Massachusetts; you have to go back to the South." I accepted an offer to study at the University of North Carolina at Chapel Hill in the School of Education.

I lived in North Carolina for six years. During that time I did the work required to receive a doctorate—classes, comps, research, and dissertation. That was the easy part. The real challenge was the personal excavation I did on two fronts. The first and most powerful was accepting myself as a white Southerner. The second was coming out as a lesbian. While the order might seem odd, that was how it felt to me. Coming to grips with being a lesbian was traumatic, given the national culture of revulsion at and fear of things not heterosexual. But I knew that I would not have to give up my "chosen" families—my friends and loved ones, my YWCA connections—over this issue. It would be painful and it would be a struggle fully to integrate that part of my identity, and I knew I would be fine in the end, despite all the internalized heterosexism I carried. My central identity was race, and while my gender, class, and orientation are vital to me, race has remained the center of my life's work.

During those six years in Chapel Hill, I struggled mightily with both guilt and shame: guilt about the ongoing uncountable ways in which I was insensitive and used my race and class privilege; shame about who I was. I wasn't at all sure that I would ever believe myself to be a good person or that I could ever do enough to make up for all the wrongs of my family and other white Southerners. The clearer I became about the horrors of racism in the South and, by extension, my family's plantation mentality, the more excruciating was my pain. I was wrestling with the devil, my own and my country's. Many of my white friends—some gay or lesbian, some straight—thought I was obsessed with race and a pain in the neck. I remember lots of lunches at a restaurant in downtown Chapel Hill. There were pictures of Aunt Jemima on the walls, and every time I ate there I told the manager that they were offensive and asked him to take them down. He never did, of course, but I kept asking. I think I knew that if I caused real trouble, organizing a boycott or picketing, for example, that I would lose my friends. I had already given up my family, and I wasn't at that time strong enough to give up my friends, too. I internalized that sense of weakness and questioned whether I was really who I said I was. I worried secretly if, when push came to shove, I would stand firmly for what I said I believed in. I feared that, at a deep level, I was a fraud.

My dissertation was on teachers' racial attitudes and their use of a guide to multicultural education that I had written.[4] My research was done as I visited rural elementary schools where UNC student teachers were placed. All the student teachers I worked with were white and, with very rare exceptions, so were all the teachers in towns like Mebane and Saxapahaw where the students did their practice teaching. When I began, I had almost no compassion for the teachers; it would probably be more accurate to say that I held them in the same disdain that I did the Southern parts of myself. Gradually, as I began to have some patience for the pace of my own learning, the ways that I evaluated the students and teachers changed as well. Slowly I moved from thinking that they were unteachable to believing that they were worth my time and energy and that they might change, too. Glacial shifts.

Some years later I heard Alice Walker talk about writing one of her books. She said that at one point she heard pounding on the door to her writing room and the voice of her great-, perhaps great-great-grandfather, an Irish plantation owner. He told her that she had to let him into her stories because he was as much a part of her history as her African great-great-grandmother, his slave whom he had raped. The necessity of letting in all parts of myself and my ancestors rang true for me as well. During my years in North Carolina, I came to realize that the South was much more complex than I had originally thought, no less brutal but with many more tangles and tendrils. I had bought the message that the South is the bad racist place and every place else is fine. I also came to understand that the South and the North both benefited, in intentional ways, from slavery. The South had provided the free labor to grow cotton that the North then used in the textile mills, and they shared the profits. In that way the North was able to appear to have clean hands, yet benefit financially. Racism in the North did and does look different, but it is equally pernicious. So the solution was not simply to jettison white Southerners; that would be easy. Eliminating racism in the United States and in our country would be far more difficult. Nothing about any of this part of my journey was simple, but having a greater knowledge of how systems work and greater clarity about my own role in making change gave me a much-needed sense of hope.

Crucible 6: My life with Marie. I have left significant mention of Marie Jones until the last. Writing about the Black woman who raised me is treacherous; I can hear African American friends saying, "Don't go there." From the beginning of this country's history African American women have been forced, either by law or by necessity, to take care of white people's children; they were legally forced by those who enslaved them during slavery and economically after emancipation. While the stereotype is that only wealthy white Southerners were taken care of by these women, working, middle, upper class white people across the country had Black housekeepers—women who tended their children, their houses, and their lives. Most did so at the expense of their own families, giving their energy and time to white children while their own children were left in the homes of relatives or to care for themselves. Not only did they have to keep white people's domestic lives together, they had to act as if they were enjoying it; otherwise the women were called "sullen" and fired. As an African American colleague said, "They acted as if they loved you, but the truth is that they hated you for pulling them away from their own families."

Many of the relationships between the Black women and the families for whom they worked were complex, stretching over generations. Certainly in the South, where for more than two hundred years African American women have been the primary caretakers of white people, often there was and is a sense of almost-family—"family" when it serves the white people to see Black women that way and hired help when it doesn't. Their status in the household is determined by the whim of the white woman who runs the house.

Realizing that I am on very thin ice, I am also clear that writing about Marie is critical, not only because of her continued importance in my life, but also because it might shed light on the tangle of feelings other white people have about the Black women who raised them. The complexities of these relationships are, to me, symbolic of race relations in the United States. There is nothing simple about Black–white entanglements, particularly in the South. We have been and continue to be in each other's lives in many ways, all of which are affected by the institutionalization of the supremacy of whiteness. If we do not hold that truth in our memories, we cannot create a different personal or national reality.

Marie came to work for my family when I was seven and she was twenty-five. By that time my father had died and my mother had gone into deep grief and depression that she didn't emerge from for her remaining eighteen years. My two sisters, who are ten and twelve years older than I, were usually away from home so my mother and I were alone. Because Mom was so inaccessible and no one else was there, Marie was everything to me. She was my nurturer, my disciplinarian, my playmate, my companion, my mother substitute. When she came, I began to pretend to be sick so that I could stay at home with her rather than go to school. I spent my days following her around, learning about life, cooking, ironing, love, and honesty. That practice continued when I was at home until my mother died in 1969. As I got older and began to learn about race, I would rage at her about how little my mother was paying her, about what a racist Mom was as well as a coward for not standing up to the racism in our family and community. One day, she'd had enough. "I am your mother's best friend, and I won't listen to you talk about her like that." Complex entanglements.

Until she died in 1998, Marie was a constant in my life. I have no doubt that she loved me; not long before she died she asked me to adopt her two great-granddaughters and raise them, knowing that I was in a long-term lesbian relationship. In the end it seemed best to all of us that the girls not be moved to California, away from everything that was familiar to them, so they stayed in Texas with their aunts and uncles. Marie knew when she asked, though, that I would have done it happily. In the second edition of *Diversity in the Classroom*, I wrote: "This book is dedicated to Marie Jones who came into my life when I was seven and, by her nature and example, made me question the messages I was receiving about race. She continues to be a powerful force of love in my life." When she died, my cousin sent me flowers. The card with them said, "She was really your last and best parent."

That is the story from my white perspective. But there are many other pieces to it. Her daughter, and probably her sons as well, resented me horribly for what I got from her mother that she didn't, both as a child and as an adult. While Marie was central in my mother's and my life, we were not her center; she had her own life that was, of necessity, shaped around ours. She worked Monday through Saturday from 8:30 a.m. to 3:30 p.m.; she cooked and served Thanksgiving and Christmas dinners at our house before she was able to take care of her own family. She was always reachable by phone if I couldn't find my socks, didn't know how to cook something, or was lonely. While she was working for my mother, she was always our maid first, before anything else. And, while she called me her "white daughter," her sons addressed me as "Ms. Kendall." I was the one who had to be treated deferentially; regardless of our feelings for one another, I could pull rank in ways that she never could.

It was an essential step in my personal work to look honestly at my relationship with Marie and not allow my vision to be clouded by sentimentality. I am not saying that there wasn't a lot of mutual love there, because I believe there was. However, what I know for certain is that, if I were to act as though we had been on equal footing and miss the role that oppression played in our life together, I would misrepresent our relationship. I would also risk losing the respect and trust of people of color, particularly African American women, for whom this is crystal clear—a loss of unimaginable magnitude.

Now, though I have been looking at my whiteness and my racism for 35 years, I hold no illusions that my work is done. I take it as my daily responsibility to explore what it means to be a white, upper-middle class, able-bodied, Christian lesbian whose life work revolves around race. The older I have gotten and the more personal and institutional anti-racism work I have done, the more my life and my social circle are filled with people of color and white anti-racists. I think there are a number of reasons for this: First, it is a result of the willingness of people of color to risk trusting me, knowing that my white imperfections are always on the table for all of us to see. Second, I think it is because of my determination to continue personal excavation as long as I am on the planet. That commitment is evident in most things I do; there is no separation between my work and my life. And, third, I believe it is about grace—forgiveness and acceptance that has been granted to me regardless of whether I deserve it. I can't conceive of a time when I will not be passionate about dismantling the systemic superiority of whiteness.

Doing the personal work required to understand what it means to be white is the foundation for me in striving to build a just world. I believe it is that for all of us who are white. While the process is painful and at times difficult, I don't regret a moment of it. One surprising outcome has been richer and more honest relationships with family members. When I let go of the idea of their behavior reflecting badly on me, the battles I had fought took on a different tone. The conflicts haven't gone away, but my sense of my worth is no longer tied to my family's seeing the light. Because of that shift I am able to show my love to many of them, be clear about where I stand and what I expect of their behavior—respectful treatment and no racist slurs. Interestingly, one of my greatest lessons has come from my relationship with one of my brothers-in-law. Even though we had many screaming matches with each other about race, and still do on occasion, he, among my sisters and brothers-in-law, has been the most supportive of my life as a lesbian. Rather than closing my heart to him because of his racist language, I have chosen to keep myself open to the possibility that he will change. I continue to be forthright about his slips in behavior, and he continues to love me for all of who I am. More than in any other family relationship, with him I have learned to deal with complexities.

As white people, we have to believe that we can change ourselves and our institutions. Without that belief, the system of the supremacy of whiteness continues to work exactly as it was set up to work, and all of our lives are lessened. In its own way, each of the crucible experiences I have identified taught me to look at complexities, and each provided me the opportunity to become more deeply committed to work toward a world in which authentic relationships across race can not only happen but can thrive. My belief is that this is where white people have to begin—by looking at ourselves. Through that personal work, we become clearer about the necessity of changing our institutions, and we work to build a greater repertoire of skills to make needed changes.

2
WHAT'S IN IT FOR US?
Why We Would Explore What It Means to Be White

I sit down on a plane with a copy of Tim Wise's book, White Like Me, *in my lap. This is a working trip for me. My seatmate asks what I do, and, almost begrudgingly, I tell him. Describing my work usually brings questions and arguments, passed off as those of a "devil's advocate." He begins: "Do you really think that there should be race-based scholarships and grants? What happens when, in all of the academic associations, there are racial group-based caucuses—isn't this balkanization?" I know the challenges by heart.*

He's a white academic, a social scientist. He spends his summers on Martha's Vineyard, an island off the coast of Massachusetts that is a summer home for wealthy people. He uses some of the "right" words, says he is "picking my brain," and yet I wonder if he wants to hear my responses or if he is really trying to confirm what he believes. I ask him that.

He ignores the question and goes on: "What one thing would you change? Should you really have Black schools and women's schools or should you work to homogenize?"

I respond. "There's not a silver bullet, a single thing that you could change to make everything all right. What has to be changed is much more complicated than that. This is a system that our white ancestors have built over time, to benefit us, to maintain our power and dominance in this country." His eyes glaze over, and I feel myself sag under the weight of trying to convince him. I speak strongly about my support of HBCUs (Historically Black Colleges and Universities) and women's colleges as a way to prepare those who are the targets of institutionalized racism and sexism to function successfully in the work world.

How do I show him that it is in his interest as a white person to rethink the assumptions in his questions? How do I encourage him to ask different questions, to hold what he sees as true less surely? What facts and statistics or stories would shift his train of thought?

I am regularly asked by people of color, "Why would white people begin to look at themselves and their privilege? What would motivate them to move out of their comfort zone?" My response is a work in progress. For quite a while I shook my head and said I wasn't sure why we would do it. Partly that came from being baffled that systemic racism was apparently so difficult for white people to see. "This is not that hard!" I have said many times in an exasperated tone. And partly I wasn't sure why I had done so much personal exploration about being white—I just knew it was what I was supposed to do.

In "Leading Change: Why Transformation Efforts Fail," John Kotter describes his "eight-stage process of creating major change." The first step is "establishing a sense of urgency."[1] I think about that frequently as I work with organizations and individuals: What can I do or say that will move the leaders in this organization—and they are usually white—to a sense of urgency about this work? I had to become clearer in my answer to "What's in it for us?" I needed to be able to translate what has always been intuitively obvious for me into compelling reasons to share with other white people. My list grew as I worked with corporate clients who needed to be able to see "the bottom line," as I did strategic planning for diversity with senior administrators in colleges and universities, and as I listened to white friends and colleagues like Bob Terry, Gary Howard, and Tim Wise, authors of *For Whites Only*, *We Can't Teach What We Don't Know*, and *White Like Me*, respectively.

Why *would* we explore what it means to be white? Or perhaps: Why *wouldn't* we? If we want to work in open, inclusive, just organizations, if it is important to be congruent in our stated values and our actions, if we want our organizations to thrive, then why wouldn't we do whatever is necessary to understand how to reach those goals? What keeps us from acting in ways that reflect what we identify as our beliefs? Sad to say, we view our efforts in addressing racism as something we do for someone else—not for ourselves. We are not always clear about how creating just and equitable systems and organizations and authentic relationships is in our best interest. Nor are we clear about what maintaining systems of white supremacy costs us personally, organizationally, or globally.

I realize that language like "supremacy of whiteness" or "white supremacy" and "institutional racism" and "white privilege" can be very off-putting, upsetting, and scary. I can hear readers saying, "I'm just living my life here, trying to be a good person, and already in Chapter 2 you're telling me that I'm a white supremacist!" In order to provide some clarity with which to frame this chapter, before going into depth in Chapter 3, it might be helpful to include some definitions of the concepts we're talking about.

My experience with language surrounding the issues of racism, privilege in general, and white privilege in particular is not that we who are white don't understand the definitions of words and phrases, but rather that we resist acknowledging the existence of these forces in our world today. I hope that, by becoming more comfortable with the underlying ideas, we will move to a different understanding of the issues. The following definitions are almost all from the *Random House Unabridged Dictionary, Second Edition.*

Prejudice is "an unfavorable feeling or opinion formed beforehand or without knowledge, thought, or reason" and "unreasonable feelings, opinions, or attitudes, esp. of a hostile nature, regarding a racial, religious, or national group." *Discrimination* has its basis in prejudice, but, because it is behavior and not feeling, the consequences are more serious than those of prejudice. A working definition of *discrimination* is "treatment of a person or thing based on the group, class, or category to which that person or thing belongs rather than on individual merit."

The implications of racism are more far-reaching than those of either prejudice or discrimination. *Racism* is "any attitude, action, or institutional structure which subordinates a person or group because of his or their color."[2] The key to this definition is subordination. Individuals or groups of people are kept in subordinate, less powerful, less important positions on the basis of their color. *Random House* defines *racism* as "a belief or doctrine that inherent differences among the various human races determine cultural or individual achievement, usually involving the idea that one's own race is superior and has the right to rule others" and "a policy, system of government, etc., based upon or fostering such a doctrine." It is important to note that in the United States, while any racial group might view itself as superior, only the white group has the power to institutionalize that belief into laws, policies, practices, and culture and to subordinate other groups based on that institutionally-held power. It is true that everyone is prejudiced and can discriminate. Racism is different. If we bear in mind that racism is systemic, we remain clearer about its connection to privilege. Those of us who are white receive unearned privileges based on our racial group membership that enable us individually and systemically to subordinate individuals and groups of color.

Racist is usually applied to a person, act, or object that embodies the belief of racial superiority inherent in the definition of *racism*. For many white people it is one of the most difficult words to deal with, because when it is applied to you it feels like a personal attack identifying your fundamentally bad behavior. I'll talk more about how to deal with being called a racist in Chapter 8, "Talking About Race: What If They Call Me A Racist?"

Privilege, particularly white or male privilege, is hard to see for those of us who were born with access to power and resources. It is very visible for those to whom privilege was not granted. The subject is extremely difficult to talk about because many white people don't feel powerful or as if they have privileges that others don't. It is sort of like asking fish to notice water or birds to discuss air. For those who have privileges based on race, gender, class, religion, physical ability, sexual orientation, or age, it just *is*—it's normal. The *Random House Dictionary* defines *privilege* as "a right, immunity, or benefit enjoyed only by a person beyond the advantages of most." In her article "White Privilege: Unpacking the Invisible Knapsack," Peggy McIntosh reminds us that those of us who are white usually believe that privileges are "conditions of daily experience which [we take] for granted."[3] Further, she says that what we are really talking about is "unearned power conferred systematically." For those of us who are white, one of our privileges is that we see ourselves as individuals, "just people." Most of us are clear, however, that other people whose skin is not white are members of a race. The surprising thing for us is that, even though we don't see ourselves as part of a racial group, people of color generally do see us that way.

White supremacy is "the belief, theory, or doctrine that the white race is superior to all other races, esp. the black race, and should therefore retain control in all relationships."

> ...we live in a world which has been *foundationally shaped for the past five hundred years by the realities of European domination and the gradual consolidation of global white supremacy*.[4] [Italics in original.]

Although many people think of white supremacy as the beliefs and behavior of groups like the Ku Klux Klan, some contemporary thinkers and writers like bell hooks and Cornel West have begun to use the term "white supremacy" instead of "racism" to broaden and clarify the understanding that the supremacy of the white race is one of the foundation stones of European and United States history.

There are both personal and public costs of maintaining racism and the systemic supremacy of whiteness. As Robert Terry reminds us:

…racism undermines and distorts our personal and organizational authenticity….we become untrue to ourselves and/or untrue to the world in which we find ourselves. As inauthentic persons operating in inauthentic organizations we make decisions that conflict with our real short- and/or long-term self-interest.[5]

The process of looking at what racism and white privilege cost us—those of us who are white and have skin-color privilege—is a difficult one for several reasons. First, many of us don't feel particularly powerful or as if we have privilege. Second, even if we know we have privilege, we are usually only clear about what we gain from being white, not about what it costs us. Third, understanding how we are both beneficiaries and losers because of this system requires that we face the fact that this system didn't just magically appear; it was intentionally constructed and put into place, ostensibly for us, by people who look like us.

So why would we spend this time and effort looking into something we don't want to be connected to? For many people the most immediate answer is that it is the right thing to do. If we do not work to change ourselves and our systems, we continue to be complicit in the oppression of others whether we mean to or not. We do this exploration because our lives depend on it—our physical, psychological, spiritual, and economic lives.

Many of the costs of systemic racism are global. Because we see ourselves and our ways of doing things as superior to everyone else, we have very little knowledge or understanding of other peoples—their religions, their governments, their ways of doing things, or their belief systems. I resist saying "culture" because that's often what we focus on about other people—their food, their dances, their "costumes"—and we are apt to see these as exotic, weird, quaint, foreign. Different from ours.

Many of us isolate ourselves from others in the world; that perspective blinds us to the realities of other people and other countries, particularly those places that are peopled by humans of color. We get so wrapped up in ourselves that others simply aren't in our awareness. I remember, as a child, saving money in a small rectangular cardboard box during Lent to give to people far away. And that's exactly how they seemed—disconnected, starving people in Armenia, Biafra, Bangladesh, Sudan. The Saturday night before I was supposed to present my mite box at church I raided my mother's coin purse, and that was my gift. There was no empathy for or human connection between the recipients of the money and me.

As a country we see ourselves as the center of the world. Even the maps of the world that are used in most public school classrooms have the United States front and center. All other countries are on one side or the other. Not as important. Not central. For me, that is compounded by my geographic illiteracy. I couldn't fill in the countries in Africa or the ones in Asia if my life literally depended on it. The continent I know best is Europe, the one filled predominantly with other white people. What makes this so much worse is that, according to United States Census data for 2000, my doctoral degree puts me in the ninety-ninth percentile of the most educated people in this country. This lack of geographical knowledge is important because if we don't know who lives next to whom we are less able to understand the interrelatedness of their histories, their economies, their conflicts, and their relationships with the United States. We are far less able to consider life from their perspectives. We are isolated in a time of global interaction. We're not prepared to enter into necessary conversations or to work effectively in multinational settings. Many Americans expect everyone in the world to speak English and are offended when they don't. There is little expectation that United States citizens will be multilingual, and, institutionally, there is not a great push for it. The weight of responsibility is on others to be able to communicate with us.

You might be wondering what all of this has to do with white privilege. Well, a lot, actually. Historically, people who looked like me colonized many of those countries that I, and probably millions of other Americans, can't place on a map. White Europeans invaded those who lived there, took their resources, frequently used the people for cheap or free labor, and profited financially. That was true in Africa, much of Asia, South America, Australia, and North America—all the continents that were, and in many cases still are, inhabited by people of color. Our ancestors, white Europeans, believed it was their moral obligation to "civilize" the people who lived on those continents, believed they had the right to take from them what they wanted and leave them with a superior way of doing things—English, French, German, or Belgian language, manners, and values. Much of the decimation of indigenous cultures was done by white Christian missionaries who saw it as their responsibility to bring truth and the light to the heathens, many of whom lived in ancient and highly sophisticated civilizations—Hawaii, for example. The ancestors of most of us who are white came from countries whose rulers conquered the world, setting up systems and structures that kept the supremacy of white people in place. This is what Charles Mills describes in his book, *The Racial Contract*. White involvement on these continents continues in much the same tradition: Many of our electronics and clothes are put together by cheap labor in countries inhabited by people of color, for example, and the American and European owning class makes an unimaginable profit.

Jobs that were once done predominantly by working class white people are now being done by poor people, many of whom are women, "off shore," in countries where the populations are of color. The financial benefits of this system to upper- and upper-middle-class people, most of whom are white, are obvious, and the costs to working class whites in the United States are clear. Further, the United States continues to engage in wars in countries of color; poor whites and Black and Latino men and women are most of our foot soldiers as well as the great majority of our casualties. This was true in Viet Nam, Granada, and Kuwait, and is true today in Afghanistan and Iraq.

This "racial contract" also has costs for wealthier white people. Those who attend even our most selective colleges and universities often don't gain the knowledge and skills they need to work effectively in the global marketplace. The curriculum is decidedly unbalanced, presenting students with a white, male, upper class lens through which to view the world. With very few exceptions, there is not a critical mass of indigenous people of color in any of the most selective schools. If white upper-middle and upper class students were sharing classrooms with a variety of students who were racially diverse, their education and preparation for work life would be enhanced. That was acknowledged in the Supreme Court's rulings in the University of Michigan cases, *Gratz v. Bollinger* and *Grutter v. Bollinger* in 2003. But, for a variety of complex reasons, equitable access to higher education continues to elude most students of color.

In 2012 the global economy is in serious trouble and the divisions between the "haves" and the "have nots" have grown exponentially. Funding has been repeatedly cut from public colleges and universities; classes have been cancelled and departments have been closed. Tuition has soared, and loan programs have been reduced. In economic downturns, people of color and poor white people suffer the greatest impact.

The costs of ignoring or downplaying systemic racism in organizations have been discussed from various points of view—focusing solely on "diversity" without addressing oppression, speaking specifically to the experience of people of color in predominantly white organizations, or talking openly about racism in organizations. The great majority of books and articles use one of the first two points of view to look at organizational issues.

The corporate sector has long been the leader in understanding why a diverse workforce is a business advantage. Authors like Taylor Cox, Jr. (*Creating the Multicultural Organization*), Frederick A. Miller and Judith Katz (*The Inclusion Breakthrough: Unleashing the Real Power of Diversity*), and *The Business Case for Diversity 4th Edition* (DiversityInc; staff publication), have written convincingly about diversity being a "bottom line" issue. While they don't situate their arguments in the issues of privilege and whiteness, many in the business world are very clear that all-white companies are not financially expedient because they are less able to meet the needs of a diverse client base.

There has been some, though a great deal less, written for the lay reader on the efficacy of "diversity" in academic institutions. Without the clear focus on the bottom line that the for-profit world has, academe doesn't have such a driving force for making changes. In the last ten years or so, books have been written about recruiting and retaining faculty, staff, and students of color and about struggles in academia for people of color, for example *What Makes Racial Diversity Work in Higher Education: Academic Leaders Present Successful Policies and Strategies*, edited by Frank W. Hale, Jr., and *Faculty Diversity: Problems and Solutions*, by Joann Moody. Preparation for the University of Michigan cases on admissions spurred significant research on the value of racial diversity in higher education. Those efforts have continued. In the almost ten years since *Grutter*, the research and conversations have focused mainly on numbers—bringing in more students of color—and creating hospitable environments for students of color in predominantly white institutions so that students stay. An article that was particularly useful to me appeared in the *Chronicle of Higher Education* in January 2010. It described research that "provides colleges something of immediate and practical value: Guidance on how to tweak their policies to maximize educational benefits and minimize harm."[6]

A mid-range collection of articles and books identifies race as an issue, but stops shy of talking about racism. An article from *Industry Week*, February 6, 1989, "No, You *Don't* Manage Everyone the Same," is far too relevant almost thirty years later; the author talks about corporations "finding daring, different ways to manage an increasingly diverse workforce" in which senior managers pushed to put issues of race, gender, and ethnicity into the open and to keep them there rather than acting as though they didn't exist.[7] David Thomas and John Gabarro's book, *Breaking Through: The Making of Minority Executives in Corporate America*, and Thomas's terrific article on cross-race mentoring, "The Truth about Mentoring Minorities: Race Matters," in the April 2001 issue of the *Harvard Business Review*, highlight the centrality of race and ethnicity to who we are, in the work- and school-place and in our everyday lives. A great majority of the books that address race straightforwardly have historically been written by people of color. Joe R. Feagin, a white male professor, has for years been an exception to this rule. (See bibliography.)

It is important to distinguish between the first two bodies of literature and those that focus on the disparate organizational experiences that white people and people of color have because of racism. Four books are useful to mention here. All are by African Americans, three are about the corporate world, and one is about academia. For *The Rage of a Privileged Class*, Ellis Cose interviewed many middle-class Black people who believed the myth that, if they followed the rules of the white world, they would be able to escape America's racism. However, the text on the jacket cover refers to:

> ...the depth [of] discrimination that haunts even the most affluent and best-educated African Americans...all with stories of their continuing encounters with prejudice, of its damaging effects on their lives, their careers, their children, and of the painful insensitivity whites continue to display toward blacks, no matter how well-dressed, well-connected, well-paid, and competent they may be.[8]

Three books focus on the experiences of African American women: *Our Separate Ways: Black and White Women and the Struggle for Professional Identity* by Ella Bell and Stella Nkomo, *Double Burden: Black Women and Everyday Racism* by Yanik St. Jean and Joe R. Feagin, and *Shifting: The Double Lives of Black Women in America* by Charisse Jones and Kumea Shorter-Gooden. Each provides a clear picture of the role that racism plays in Black women's daily lives in the business world. Caroline Sotello Viernes Turner and Samuel L. Myers, Jr.'s *Faculty of Color in Academe: Bittersweet Success* is different in two ways from the other books mentioned; first, the authors interviewed a broad range of people of color—Asian and Pacific Island Americans, American Indians and Alaskan Natives, Hispanics, and American Blacks/African Americans—and, second, the interviewees were faculty in academic institutions. The stories about racism are different in context from those about the corporate world, but not particularly dissimilar in content: people not being promoted, shifting back and forth from being invisible to white people to being under constant scrutiny, having to do three times as well to be considered as competent as white people, and having one's skin color receive more attention than the skills and abilities for which one was hired.

The life of people of color in organizations, academic or corporate, is very different from that of white people. Yet racism is frequently left out of the diversity discussion. I think this is due, in large part, to the desire to smooth over the hostile environments of predominantly white schools and companies. It's as if, if we don't talk about it, it doesn't exist. However, if white people don't talk about the dominance of whiteness and the related endemic racism within organizations, we address only the manifestations of the systems and not the root causes. We look at only a part of the task that faces those of us who want to create equitable and hospitable work and school cultures. Many of us who are white still resist remembering that race, ours and others, is always present in the conversation. Little has been written by white people that delineates the white experience as a *racial* experience in the work world or addresses the huge costs of the systemic superiority of whiteness to all of us. An exception to this is *Unlikely Allies in the Academy: Women of Color and White Women in Conversation*, a recent book edited by Karen L. Dace. It includes chapters by white people and women of color and provides models for how we might become allies to women of color in the academy.

In both academic and corporate settings, people of color regularly report that, because of their race, they still don't have access to mentoring, promotions, hospitable work environments, senior role models, committee appointments, and so on that would allow them to contribute all of their talents to the workplace. It is clear that the issue here is race. When white employees at the middle and senior levels talk about not feeling appreciated or that their talents are being fully used, it is rarely their sense that this is because they are white. This lack of perspective and understanding negatively affects all of us every day, bringing about a sense of isolation, alienation, and resignation on the part of people of color and a lack of trust for those of us who are white. Obviously, this is expensive, both financially and in terms of morale, for the organization. Let's look at a few of examples of how this phenomenon plays out.

I had the following conversation with a senior partner of a law firm that had the stated goal of recruiting and retaining lawyers of color, African American lawyers in particular.

Client: Why is it in my best interest for Black men or women to succeed? We have a sink or swim culture for everyone. Some white men fail, too.

FK: How many white men do you have?

Client: Twenty-three.

FK: How many Black people do you have?

Client: Two. And do you know how hard it was to get those?

FK: So why would you let them sink? What does that prove?

Client: It's the same thing we put everyone through. If we did it differently, we would be catering to them. We treat everybody the same here.

I always get nervous when someone says to me, "I treat everybody the same. I don't see differences." First, I don't believe them. If we are able to see, we notice differences among people. Second, treating different people as though they were the same is not a terribly good strategy even if it were possible because people are different from one another and need different things. Just as most of us don't treat our grandmothers and our peers in the same ways or the electrician and our partner in the same ways, we behave differently with different colleagues. I think that what many people believe is that "same" equals "fair." Everyone gets two weeks of vacation, the same pay depending on years of service, and the same holidays. While I could talk about this approach from many perspectives—good management practice, employment law, meeting employees' specific needs—let's look at it through a racial lens. Systemically, those of us who are white and those who are of color are rarely treated "the same." Individually, does treating everyone the same mean treating everyone like they're white until they prove themselves otherwise by acting "too Black," or "too Latina," or "too Native"? Or does it mean that we do not see them for who they are?

In this particular law firm, as in many other workplaces, the African Americans I talked to felt strongly that they weren't seen as individuals or valued for what they brought to the practice. The assignments they were given were not as good and they had no mentors while some of the new white hires were being groomed for success from the beginning. Nor did there seem to be any open conversation or understanding of the experience of being Black in the surrounding community dealing with housing, treatment at stores and restaurants, access to social organizations. Both said that they would not recommend this firm to other Black people.

So what did the firm and its white employees lose by not acknowledging the systemic racism in the community and in the firm or the impact that race and racism have on each of our experiences? It lost time and money involved in recruiting the African American people. Talent that was searched for, hired, and subsequently not developed. Support from other employees as the firm tried to move the organization forward on diversity. It lost image and reputation of the organization among other people of color, credibility that the organization is truly committed to do what it says it will do, and access to Black clients. It lost trust in the sincerity of the recruiting and retention efforts by both people of color and white people and opportunities to gain new skills while mentoring across race.

In another instance, an African American woman was hired to be the director of the Office of Multicultural Affairs at a small liberal arts college. She reported to a white woman who was the Vice President of Academic Affairs and second in command of the institution. She came into the position with a great deal of fanfare regarding the role she would play in creating a diverse institution. She also came in with a great deal of hope that this school would be different from others, that this institution was seriously committed to fulfilling their stated goal of preparing all students to thrive in the 21st century global village.

After a brief honeymoon period, she began to have concerns. At the vice president's request, she drew up a three-to-five-year strategic plan, with a budget to fund the identified initiatives appropriately. The plan was shuffled back and forth between the president's and vice president's offices, with each person telling her "in confidence" that the other was reluctant to move forward with her plan. There were several requests for her to redo sections, though the requests were always couched in terms of doing "minor adjustments."

She was the only person of color on the president's cabinet; she had been invited to attend the meetings because of "the important work she was doing." During these meetings she felt invisible, not addressed or included in the conversation except when she was put in the spotlight and asked to speak for all people of color at the school; other cabinet members regularly talked over her after they had asked for her opinions. Initially, her relationship with her boss, the vice president, seemed warm, though she knew enough to be cautious. In their meetings, she was careful not to identify race as a campus problem very often and to have all of her facts straight before she did. The situations she brought up were always treated as isolated incidents, and the vice president either asked that she just "make them go away" or refuted the racial connection in the problem. In time, the vice president and the president told her that she was "obsessed" with race and saw it everywhere she looked.

After two years, with the strategic plan stalled because of inaction by the president and vice president and she herself seen by her colleagues as ineffective, the woman began to look for another job. She felt good about some of the programs she had sponsored and about her relationships with the few African American students who were there. However, she was exhausted by her day-to-day experience of being: the voice that was expected to speak for all Black people and understand the needs of all other people of color; the one expected to resolve the racial issues on campus and to do so without clearly identifying them as racial; the cheerleader for the Office of Multicultural Affairs because the senior leaders had stopped reiterating their commitment and many of the white liberals had shifted their focus to other things. She felt beaten down and no longer capable of doing her job.

The costs identified in the first example are common to all three stories. There is an important difference, however, between the corporate scenario and this one. The primary motivation for people like this woman in choosing to work on issues of diversity in colleges and universities is the desire to make change, to be part of creating a good environment for all students, particularly those who are otherwise ignored or overlooked. The same might be said for the young African American lawyer, in terms of creating a fair and just judicial system for people of color, but the financial remuneration is much greater and professional focus is not always racial. The decision to do work on race in an academic setting, if you are a person of color, requires bringing your head and your heart to the job and removing the screen between professional and personal. Frequently professionals of color are the sole support for students of their race, so it is difficult to separate oneself from them. Often I have heard staff and administrators of color say, "We can't leave. We have to take care of the children." Given that, one's vulnerability is much greater.

In this case, the African American woman lost belief in herself and her competence: "My sense of self is so low that I don't think I can do this job any longer." The organization, by constantly overvaluing white people and undervaluing people of color, has made its employee(s) incompetent. The organization lost her energy, her creativity, and her loyalty. It also lost the willingness of people of color to speak up because of having continually not been heard or having seen others like them not be noticed; new insights and different ways of doing things because it takes so much energy just to show up and constantly reeducate white people about racism; forward momentum of white people who are just beginning to understand the racial issues and address them; and collective energy when one person leaves or is recruited away by another institution—"All of us are diminished by the loss of one."[9] Furthermore, the institution will lose more employees as the support network dwindles.

In a third situation, I had been working with the senior administrators— the president and her cabinet—of a large and extremely diverse community college for some months. Forty-four languages were spoken on campus; many of the students were recent immigrants themselves while another large component were first-generation Americans and first-generation college students. There was a lot of racial diversity in this group as well.

It had been a frustrating experience for me. The conversations had remained superficial and "nice," with no one willing to move below the surface to talk about what was really going on racially in the college, with the students and in the team of administrators. I knew that at least one of the vice presidents, the African American man who was Vice President of Student Affairs, did not feel that he could say what was on his mind for fear that he would be seen as "an angry Black man." So I kept asking questions: "How do race and ethnicity have an impact on the experience of students?" "What is happening in classrooms that is giving students skills to work successfully in a diverse workplace?" "How are you using the ethnic and racial experiences of your students to enhance the quality of learning?" "How does your race affect you as you do your job?" And I waited for them to answer. Finally, a breakthrough…

The Chief Financial Officer—the Vice President of Financial Affairs—began. "Because of the stereotype that Latinos only care about their families and want to have a good time, I am always very serious at work. I rarely mention my family or what I do when I am not at work. I don't talk about those things that I care about most."

And then the Student Affairs Vice President spoke up. "I leave my Black self at home and I try to be race-less here. I deny a big part of who I am so that I can fit in. The problem is that it doesn't really work. The white people still see me as Black, of course, and other African Americans resent me for not being who I am."

I mentioned the statistic from *How to Calculate Diversity Return on Investment* by Edward E. Hubbard which estimates the cost to an organization in which people feel they can't bring all of themselves. Hubbard has found that approximately 40 percent of such an employee's time is spent managing the issues around which she or he feels unwelcome—race, gender, sexual orientation, religion, physical disability. [10] "So," I went on, "you're paying these folks for 100 percent of their time, and they're using about 60 percent for work. That seems like a lot of money to be wasting."

The president, a white woman, seemed to be thinking and sorting her words. "Well, actually," she said, "I don't feel like I can bring my Jewish self here, either."

The costs in this situation are similar to the ones in the other stories. However, there are some important additional ones: loss of the variety of perspectives that come from diverse racial and ethnic experiences; loss of the possible synergy in the group because so many of the members' thoughts and ideas go unspoken; loss of authentic role models for students, staff, administrators, and faculty because people aren't able to be who they are; and disaffection with the job and the institution as a result of the basic sense of being alien and unwelcome. In the end, if they can afford to, if they have the class privilege, people leave. Often they fear that the next place won't be any better, that there is no greener grass, just different weeds. "Sometimes it's easier to stay with the weeds you know," as the old saying goes.

There is a lot to be gained by acknowledging that race is a central part of each person's experience. Just as organizations must be clear about the costs of not keeping the topics of race and white privilege as a regular part of conversation and a lens through which they assess situations and make decisions, they must also understand what they would gain by doing so. For example, greater ability to interpret situations. Race is not always the answer, but it is always a possible factor in what is going on. Additionally, the organization would gain a higher degree of honesty in conversations, meetings, and feedback as well as more respect for speaking the truth, even if it means making others uncomfortable. Greater tolerance of discomfort usually means richer conversations that lead to stronger teams and more creative ideas and decisions. The result is greater mental flexibility and the willingness to imagine a different experience as well as happier, more productive employees who can server a broader range of people.

By far the most compelling and gut-wrenching costs for me of keeping the supremacy of whiteness in place are psychological, emotional, and spiritual. I also think they are the diciest to write about. Every time I come up with an example of those costs, a voice inside my head discounts what I'm thinking and repeats comments that I've heard from one client or another: "That's too soft a reason. Give me cold hard facts," or "What kind of psychobabble is that?" or "Not everyone grew up in a racist family like yours," or "We took care of racism a long time ago."

And yet, even though we can make a strong case for diversity and awareness in business and we are able to calculate the costs of a system that inflates the worth of one group while deflating the value of others, those aren't the examples that move me, or apparently us, to continue to look at our whiteness and to work with other whites as they do the same. What grips me is coming face to face with the damage we have done, are witness to, and perpetuate while remaining emotionally removed.

In her book titled *Born to Belonging*, Mab Segrest quotes from the Civil War diaries of Mary Boykin Chesnut, a white Southern woman, a slave's mistress, who "vehemently supported the Confederate cause"[11] and was a slavery apologist. Chesnut describes a "tragedy" she saw occur at a slave auction:

> A mad woman taken from her husband and children. Of course she was mad, or she would not have given her grief words in that public place. Her keepers were along. What she said was rational enough, pathetic, at times heart-rending. It excited me so I quietly took opium. It enables me to retain every particle of mind or sense or brains I have, and so quiets my nerves that I can calmly reason and take rational views of things otherwise maddening. [12]

Segrest goes on to say, "Necessary to the slave system was the masters' blocked sensation of its pain, an aesthetic that left him insensible not only to the fellow human beings he enslaved, but to the testimony of his senses that might have contradicted ideologies of slavery."[13] Suddenly my inability to understand our actions has a possible explanation: We anesthetize ourselves.

It would be easier if I were able to say, "We only did that once." But, of course, that's not the case. We have continued our senseless use of "the soul-destroying anesthesia necessary to the maintenance of power"[14] for hundreds of years. What happened to the hearts of white politicians, including Andrew Jackson, who carried out the Indian Removal Act, the march now known as "The Trail of Tears"? Or who created boarding schools with the explicit purpose of removing American Indian children from their families and forcing them to assimilate to white, Christian ways? What did the doctors and national public health professionals feel as they planned the 1932 to 1972 Tuskegee Syphilis Study in which 400 poor, Black, mainly illiterate men were convinced they had "bad blood" instead of syphilis and were deprived of care and of effective drugs? With the governor's approval, white men created vigilante groups in 2005 to watch the California-Mexico border, ready to shoot Mexicans attempting to come into the United States illegally. The Department of Homeland Security encourages racial profiling of Arabs, Arab Americans, and "Arab-looking" people.

According to 2011–2012 statistics from the Southern Poverty Law Center, hate crimes have doubled over the last decade. Two-thirds of the hate groups are organized white supremacist groups who in their charters deem everyone except white Christian heterosexual people to be lesser beings. The Department of Justice has recently identified 200,000 hate crimes, of which three percent are murders. By far the most targeted are LGBT—lesbian, gay, bisexual, transgender—people. The second most targeted are Muslims.[15]

I am unable to reconcile planned horrifying behavior with seemingly decent people. I have talked publicly for some time about the pathology of white people, but listening to Mab Segrest read about taking opium while watching a slave auction provided the first explanation that helps me make sense of our behavior of anesthetization. Surely the blacksmith must have dissociated while creating tiny shackles for African children captured to become slaves, as many of us did when the president of Mexico referred to the jobs Mexicans were doing as ones *even* Blacks would not do? Certainly the German architects must have anesthetized themselves and dissociated from designing the concentration camp showers as some of us do when we hear language like "He gypped me," or "I really jewed him down," or "I'm free, white, and twenty-one." I imagine that neighbors who watched their Japanese friends taken away to "internment" camps shut down their hearts, as most of us do today when read about toxic waste dumps built in predominantly African American or Latino neighborhoods.

We can't talk about white privilege without talking about pathology—ours—that keeps us from seeing the connections between this behavior and each of us as an individual. In her book, Segrest speaks of it as the "metaphysics of genocide: people don't need to respond to what they can pretend they do not know, and they don't know what they can't feel."[16] What do we pay for this daily anesthetizing, this process of dissociating? What does it cost us?

While reading the chapter titled "Losses" in *White Like Me*, I began to make notes about my personal losses generated by the system of the supremacy of whiteness in which all of us, white and of color, live. The list was surprisingly easy to create. Loss of respect for family members and loss of relationships with them, some that have been re-established and some that never will be. The huge amount of energy spent in creating distance to remain outside the toxic environment in which I grew up. The loss of personal trust in and safety with those who were closest to me, adults who were supposed to be protectors but were, in fact, the perpetrators. The verbal and psychological abuse during which the "n-word" was used as a bludgeon because I was fighting against their racial attitudes. Comments like "Sorry we're late, but a nigger waited on us at McDonalds and it took too long," and "He was killed in a car accident by a stupid drunk Mexican." Would the death have been less painful if the driver had been a drunken white? I have lost heart connection with some of my family.

We have created and sustain a pathological system in which our positive sense of self is based on the negative sense of someone else. Our whiteness and superiority are dependent on others being non-white and inferior. I remember reading *All Souls: A Family Story from Southie,* by Michael Patrick MacDonald, about a poor Irish family in Boston. They lived in the projects, died from overdoses of drugs and alcohol or were murdered, and even so the mother of the family was grateful that they weren't Black. "Ma was thrilled, as if she had died and gone to heaven [,] by getting a place in the all-white South Boston housing projects."[17]

For years, I thought that growing up in Waco, Texas, in my cotton-business family, was the cross I would have to bear. I remember a friend giving me a copy of Wayne Muller's *Legacy of the Heart: The Spiritual Advantages of a Painful Childhood.* As I read, I mentally threw it against the wall, thinking, "What fool would call all that pain a 'spiritual advantage'?" And now I laugh at myself as I realize that a "spiritual advantage" is exactly what I have used it as. It is because of those experiences that I am able to sit with other white people in their pain and grief about race and know that I didn't die from the pain and that there's a good possibility that they won't, either.

A few years ago I facilitated a two-day session on developing dialogue skills for difficult conversations. During the workshop I showed a video, "In Whose Honor," about a Native American woman protesting the use of an Indian as mascot at the University of Illinois. I knew that using the film with this group was risky because of a nearby university that has an "Indian" as its mascot. There had been recent fights between white and Native students at the local high school over the issue. In the process of planning for the workshop, I spent several hours on the phone talking to the people who had invited me to come—one who knew my work and had read some of the things I've written and another who was head of the host organization and was trying to see if I was going to be "neutral" enough. Both were white women. We began to build a relationship, and that process continued over the three difficult days that I was with them. Soon after I got home, the second woman called to talk. What follows are my notes from our conversations, one in November and another in May. In the first, I mainly listened, providing reassuring comments about the importance of her sticking with this process. In the second conversation, which I initiated, I took a different kind of notes. I called her for two reasons. First, I wanted to see how she was and what had happened since we had last talked. Second, I had been so moved by her depth of thinking and honesty that I thought her internal struggle would be a good role model for other white people. (I use these notes with her permission.)

November

Client: I do not mean to take advantage of your time, having an inkling of how busy you are. So, if you are not comfortable with continuing communication, just let me know. However, on the off chance this is okay...I am really struggling with my thoughts since the seminar last weekend. I am struggling with the difference in my feelings between the movie, "In Whose Honor," which made me cry, and the talk from the tribal leader, which made me angry. [The community's tribal leader had talked about the difference between the history we're taught about the interactions between American Indians and white people and what really happened.] I am observing the thoughts going through my head, and some of them are rather disturbing. There does not seem to be anywhere to go or any resolution to the issues. Do you live your life not at peace? Sometimes it wakes me up at night. Over my life, I have developed tremendous ability to block out things I can't deal with emotionally. I think I am on that verge, to a certain extent. I'm not sure what to do, and I have to go on. Do you ever just block it out? If not, what do you do?

May

Client: I was so upset about the mascots that I called a radio call-in show to tell them how hard this is for Native people. This is painful, not like a burn, but that really deep-down ache that makes me not want to look. I'm still really angry at the tribal leader and the visual image he left us with—the heads of Indians on sticks and the Pilgrims dancing around them. I'm *sure* he said it for effect. It's not fair.

FK: What if it's true?

Client: I don't know. Maybe it's the same kind of anger of the woman in "In Whose Honor." Helpless. Like "What if it *is* true?" I feel guilty about feeling angry at the tribal leader because of everything that's gone on since. There has been lots of violence between Native and white teens about using Natives as mascots.

FK: You can't go back to being innocent. It only goes one way.

Client: I wish it would go away! It's so hard to carry around all the time....Just a little part of me feels that way. White teens in town are saying, "Why can't they just leave us and our mascots alone?" I feel like a fraud. Sometimes I agree with the other white people. I look back longingly at the times I didn't know. Just a little. The same thing keeps coming up again and again and again: racial tensions between Native Americans and white boys at basketball games. The decision was not to play the Indian schools. They [the Native Americans] get angry. Why? It's so painful. And it's easier to go with the anger than the pain.

I remember learning about Manifest Destiny in the fifth grade. I remember saying, "Of course. That's how it was supposed to be. Why would you even have to name it?"

And I don't have any place to go with these thoughts. Sometimes I feel like a stranger in a strange land. Everyone in my life is going one direction, and I'm going another. If this is how I feel with just a thimbleful of understanding, what must it be to live with this all the time? It's just so much my struggle. Sometimes it just feels silly. I discount these feelings because there is nobody to talk to about them.

I'm not longing for the lack of knowledge. I'm longing for the lack of pain. Part of it is if just this dawning understanding is this

> hard for me....I think, "This can never have been that bad and if it was...." I don't want to not live here any more! I'm proud to be an American! And yet, now when I go to pin on a flag or sing the national anthem...I don't know, it's different.

In the end, those of us who are white can't choose not to get the privileges we are granted, but we can choose how to use them to make personal and systemic changes. If we choose to live as whole persons, maintaining our head and heart connection and refusing to anesthetize ourselves, our fears fade about being seen as betraying our race, and our determination is strengthened.

My life has long been a process of ridding myself of the effects of anesthesia. A piece on "self-recovery" in bell hooks' book, *Talking Back*, provided a useful way of thinking about my process of connecting my heart and my head, that of re-membering and re-collecting—bringing back together those pieces of myself that I had cut off so that I could stand the pain of watching racism and inhumane treatment in me, in my family, and in the world. hooks led me to *The Raft Is Not the Shore*, a book of conversations between Thich Nhat Hanh, a Vietnamese monk and Zen master, and Daniel Berrigan, a Jesuit priest and poet. In it, they each talk about re-membering. Berrigan sees it one way: "As a surgeon would, we 're-member' an amputee or a broken body or a skeleton. It means that we put broken lives together, into one body."[18] Once we acknowledge that we who are white have cut off parts of ourselves so that we can continue to take pride in ourselves as good, well-meaning people, rather than understanding the complexities forced on us by systemic superiority of whiteness, what can we do?

Thich Nhat Hanh sees re-membering in another way: "In French they have the word *recueillement* to describe the attitude of someone trying to be himself, not to be dispersed, one member of the body here, another there. One tries to recover, to be once more in good shape, to become whole again."[19] I think that most of us who are white don't even know that we're not whole. We feel like something is missing, but we're not sure what. Some sense of ourselves as whole human beings is not there, because for us to be whole and present every day means that we have to re-member ourselves, and that is painful. We pass it off as "I'm a mutt—a Heinz 57" or "I don't even think of myself as white." Or we stay in our heads, like my airplane seatmate in the story at the beginning of this chapter, looking for one magic bullet to fix the problems that hundreds of years of systemic oppression have wrought.

How do we white folks make race our issue? This is a question that will run throughout this book. How do I present the best invitation I can to others who are racially like me but in a different place emotionally and intellectually? I sit staring at my computer, chin resting on my left thumb with my forefinger over my mouth as if that will keep the sadness, despair, bewilderment inside. A voice in my head says, "It is not that hard to see why race matters. This is not rocket science. This is not brain surgery. Maybe it's heart surgery." To reconnect with our hearts, we have to deal with the feelings, un-anesthetize ourselves. Look squarely in the eye a reality that is different from the ones that we have acknowledged before. And understand that it is for *us* that we do it, not for someone else. I work with a primary assumption: Until we as white people are clear about what it means to be white, the issue of race in this nation and in the colonized world can never fully be addressed. We must know about ourselves before we can learn fully about others.

So why would we do this? Whether I like it or not, I know that many of us will not begin to grapple with being white until it is clear that it is in our personal best interest—the old "what's-in-it-for-me"? So I began to list ways we would benefit from understanding what it means to be white in the context of the systemic supremacy of whiteness. For example, we could make genuine connections with people, each of us bringing all of our identities with us. Our view of the world, of history, of reality would more closely match what is known and understood by many people of color. Because we would have something of a shared reality, we would be better able to develop more authentic working relationships. If we were clear about being white, people of color would be more likely to trust our racial perspectives in our interactions. Further, the more we recognized race as an important variable, the more intentional we would be in assuring that there are diverse voices at the table that could enhance problem-solving and reach more creative outcomes. The clearer we were about the ways in which the supremacy of whiteness is built into policies and procedures in our institutions, the more likely we would be to work toward creating equitable hiring, recruiting, and retention mechanisms. If we were aware of the impact of our race on ourselves and on others, chances would be good that we would be able to make and be committed to making different decisions and making decisions differently. Moreover, we would be able more truly to meet the needs of all students, asking "What do students of color need?" and "What do white students need?" if whiteness were explicit. We would be clear that white employees in the organization need skills in understanding their racial perspective and would provide for that development. By focusing on our race, we would become better able to see many sides of a situation and thus better able to act in advance of problems rather than always reacting. Finally, we would do our personal work because our good intentions are not changing our institutions in the ways we would like to change them. We would have to try different strategies based on a clearer reality: How does my race play a role in what is going on?

If we go back to the understanding that we live in a system that uses whiteness as the standard and holds white people as normal, then we see that others are being assessed as not normal, as less than the standard. If we sit quietly for a moment with that level of clarity, without throwing up roadblocks of resistance, we might get to a deeper understanding of the costs of maintaining the system as it is, the costs to others and the costs to ourselves.

So, as we move to Chapter 3 and to a lengthier discussion of whiteness and white privilege, we hold these questions: What is the psychological and physical damage to us as white people of always having to be the standard? What is leached from our humanness to remain, systemically, the oppressor, who must not see the wider results of our behavior? What do we pay for anesthesia—alcohol, anti-depressants, food—to continue to be able to believe that being "well-meaning" is enough?

Of course, the other sides of these questions are also essential. What would we gain by being able to be simply ourselves? Not having to be better, not having constantly to prove that we are superior and right? Not having to establish dominance? What would it be like to feel that all others are as valuable as ourselves? What if we believed in the humanness of each person? What if we understood that each of us is connected to all others—that, if others aren't able to thrive, we aren't either? How would our mental and physical health improve if we didn't go to such lengths as Mary Chesnut described—"so [quiet] my nerves that I can calmly reason and take rational views of things otherwise maddening"?

3
WHAT DOES IT MEAN TO BE WHITE?

Some years ago I was a guest speaker in a predominantly white class at a community college in California. When I introduced myself, I talked about being white and the impact that has had on my life. Most of the students were either listening or pretending to, but one young woman appeared agitated. Suddenly she burst out, "I don't want you to see me as white!" I was a bit taken aback; she had very white skin and red hair. I wasn't sure I could see her as anything else. "How would you like me to see you?" I asked. "I want you to see me as Jane!"

Separating whiteness and white privilege is a bit like trying to unscramble an egg—pulling apart the yolk and the albumen. Although different from one another, they are mixed together, inseparable. Jane's sentiments are not unusual; they reflect the combination of being white and privileged. Many of us who are white have little sense of what that means for our lives, and we are not particularly interested in finding out. It doesn't seem relevant. We see ourselves as individuals rather than as members of groups, and we often feel little connection to others in our racial category. Because we are in the dominant power group racially, we are able to define how we are seen by other white people. Generally we choose to be viewed as individuals, and we take offense at those who point out our group membership. Our life task, as I see it, is to examine at increasingly deeper levels what it means for us to be white and then to alter our behavior so that we are better able to change our systems to be just and equitable and ourselves to enter into authentic cross-race relationships.

As I said in the first chapter, I began to think in earnest about what it means to be white when I was about twenty. Before that, my focus was more on what it meant to be me: a white, Southern, upper-middle class young woman whose family was in the cotton business. As I became more involved with the National Student YWCA, my perspective broadened. I started to understand the concept of whiteness and to realize that I had an identity that was greater than being an individual or a member of my family or of my Southern culture: I was part of a group of people who, while very different from one another, shared a skin color, a history, and a set of everyday experiences that people with other skin colors didn't have. I started to examine what I would come to call "my people"—white people as a group—and our common reality, past and present.

What does it mean to be called "white?" Is race real? Or is Jane right, that if I don't "see [her] as white" then her skin color won't have any meaning? There is a lot of theorizing about when race arose as a concept and as a tool to quantify the relative value of human beings, though many date it to the late 1600s or early 1700s and tie its origins to the European Enlightenment. Is race a biological reality? The response to that question has changed significantly during American history, but two elements have remained constant. First, the "official" conversations have been among white people. Very rarely has anyone of color been allowed to be part of the debate, even though people of color have been speaking and writing about whiteness for more than three centuries. Second, the purpose (and result) of the "scientific" study of race has been to prove that white people are biologically superior to people of color, in particular to Black people.

Throughout the eighteenth and nineteenth centuries, the belief was that race was a biological phenomenon. Not only was it assumed that people inherited intellectual skills and abilities from their forebears, but also that all people could be ranked based on their race: Black people were of lower quality and intelligence than anyone; American Indians were closer to white people, it was thought, and so of higher intelligence than Blacks; and whites were superior to everyone else. There was consensus among the white men in power that people were genetically programmed to lead or to follow, to be the decision-makers or those about whom decisions were made. While there was a range of thinking about the impact of genetic inferiority—some white people believed that Black people could be brought up to white standards through education and training while others argued that their situation was hopeless—there was fairly solid agreement that Black people were genetically inferior to whites.

Even our heroes concurred. Benjamin Franklin wanted the population of America to be white. "Why increase the Sons of Africa, by planting them in America, where we have so fair an opportunity, by excluding all Blacks and tawneys, of increasing the lovely white and red?"[1] Thomas Jefferson was a man of serious contradictions. He was an architectural genius and a statesman of note. He was also a slaveholder and the owner of a Black woman, Sally Hemmings, with whom it appears he had as many as four children. In *Notes on the State of Virginia*, Jefferson wrote, "I advance it, therefore, as a suspicion only, that the blacks, whether originally a distinct race, or made distinct by time and circumstance, are inferior to the whites in the endowment of both body and mind."[2] Abraham Lincoln, known widely as the Great Emancipator, freed the slaves, but he did not believe that the Black race was equal to the white race and was in favor of "having the superior position assigned to the white race."[3]

It wasn't until relatively recently that we had hard scientific evidence that race is not a biological phenomenon but a *man*made concept, a social construct. Episode 1 of "Race: The Power of an Illusion" outlines in detail that "race has no genetic basis. Not one characteristic, trait, or even one gene distinguishes all the members of one so-called race from all the members of another so-called race."[4] Why, then, do we so easily categorize people by race and place those races in hierarchical order? Episode 2, "The Story We Tell," explains that there was great scientific effort in North America during the 1800s and early 1900s to create the illusion of biological racial differences in order to justify the treatment of those who were not white.

"Social construct" is academic language for an idea or concept designed to serve a social purpose. Here the social construct is that some people have greater inherent worth than others—white people being superior to people of color—and laws, customs, and culture were built up to reinforce that thesis. Also, there was intentional inventing of scientific "facts" to underscore the construct. A hierarchical system identifying the value of each race was created, with white people on the top and Black people on the bottom; because it was "scientific," the hierarchy gave the superiority of whiteness substance through which to rationalize behavior. In order to keep power and privilege in the hands of white people, particularly white men, information was fabricated, disseminated, and used as a basis for action to reassure white citizens that, for example, the genocide of American Indians and the enslavement and brutal treatment of Africans were necessary to keep them in their respective positions.

Part of the culture that was built to hold the construct in place came from connecting the name "Caucasian" and white people. In "Why Are White People Called Caucasian?" Nell Irvin Painter identifies Johann Friedrich Blumenbach as the person who popularized the application of "Caucasian" to white people. An eighteenth-century social scientist who paradoxically believed in the "unity of mankind,"[5] Blumenbach studied the skulls of people from around the world and created a system of racial classification. The name "Caucasian" refers to the Caucasus Mountains, two ranges in what was then Russia and is now Chechnya, which he believed were extraordinary and produced "the most beautiful race of men."[6] Blumenbach identified Caucasians as the "primeval" race because Noah's Ark had rested on Mount Ararat after the Biblical flood; that mountain is part of the Caucasus range. More than two hundred years later, "Caucasian" continues to refer to those people who are held up as most beautiful and racially superior.

Another part of the supporting culture that ensured the maintenance of the supremacy of whiteness occurred in what historian David Roediger in his book *Working Toward Whiteness* calls "the long early twentieth century"—the 1890s until after World War II. During that time immigration, combined with race, became the central action of America's history. The great majority of the thirteen million new immigrants—people from eastern, central, and southern Europe—came into the country through Ellis Island between 1901 and 1915, a time when, essentially, only white people could immigrate. Although they came in as Italians, Greeks, Latvians, and so on, two things happened: First, over time they assimilated and "became" white, and, second, they learned and began to reinforce the bigotry that was already firmly ensconced in America's culture, customs and laws. At various times, Italians, Greeks, Jews, and Poles weren't considered white. But, by the end of World War II, they had access to jobs and financial assistance (the GI Bill, for instance) that African Americans, Japanese Americans and many Chinese Americans, American Indians, and dark-skinned Mexican Americans did not. While they had all been GIs, banks, real estate developers, and communities did various things to keep people of color, particularly African Americans, out. Banks red-lined neighborhoods, not giving loans for houses in those areas; neighborhood covenants were drawn up saying that houses couldn't be sold to Black people; realtors wouldn't show houses in particular neighborhoods to Black or Latino people.

Inclusion in the "white" group was costly for the arriving immigrants. New Americans were expected to act like Americans, White Anglo-Saxon Protestants (WASPs). The rule was that they stop speaking their own languages and begin speaking English only, that they give up their own cultures' ways of cooking, celebrating holidays, and dressing. The fewer external reminders of their backgrounds present in public the better. They had to assimilate, become American, even while they were often told that they were not as good as those who had arrived earlier.

The anti-immigrant prejudice was enormous; if that's a surprise, list the slurs and jokes you've heard about Italians, Poles, Russians, Slavs, Irish, and Jews. The more of themselves, their beliefs and customs, and their languages they were willing to give up permanently, the more quickly they were admitted into the white club and were given some of the benefits that were reserved for whites, like access to suburban neighborhoods, acceptance at neighborhood bars and restaurants, and being welcomed at grocery stores, gas stations, public swimming pools, and schools. These examples show that ethnic segregation did not just happen in the upper class but in the middle class as well.

"Since the concept of race was invented, and race doesn't really exist, what is all the hubbub about? Why can't I simply identify myself as a person and move on?" These are questions I hear frequently from white people. For some, the questions come from genuine confusion. "I don't understand. I'm a good person. Why does it matter what color my skin is?" For others of us, there is a sort of passive resistance. "I never even think about being white." But we must have thought about it and then dismissed it as not worthy of consideration. For still others of us, there is resistance with attitude.

Recently, I was speaking to a group of administrators in a medical organization about what is required to be an ally to people of color if you are white. I talked about getting up in the morning, looking in the mirror, and asking myself how being a white woman was going to affect me today. In a frustrated and angry tone, one of the participants asked, "Why can't I just be color blind and see myself in the mirror as a member of the *human race*? Isn't that our goal?"

"Well," I said, "I don't think that is our goal. I, for one, don't want to be seen as 'just a human being.' I want to be seen as who I am—a woman, a white person, a fifty-seven-year-old. I don't want to be colorless or androgynous. What I *do* want is to live in a time when our worth is not based on our skin color or our gender, when all of who I am is important and valuable. That's very different from lopping off pieces of myself—my race, my age, my sexual orientation, my Southern-ness—to make others comfortable."

I have thought long and hard about why there is such resistance to identifying as white. There are some obvious answers. First, being white is often equated with being bigoted, even a member of the Ku Klux Klan. That makes sense to me. Why would we want to identify ourselves with what we see as a reactionary fringe group? Second, those of us who are white have rarely been singled out personally based on our skin color. Though we regularly identify others as being members of racial groups, it's not something we want done to us. It feels accusatory and not about us individually. That is part of how systemic white privilege works: Whiteness is assumed unless a person is identified otherwise. Frequently, when I ask about the racial composition of a group, I'm told that there are seven percent Asian Americans, nine percent African Americans, and eight percent Latinos/Hispanics. That is presented as a complete answer, even when the combined percentages only add up to twenty-four percent. While that kind of answer is most typical from white people, I also hear it from people of color. The race of the rest of the group is left unmentioned.

This phenomenon takes another form. When talking about a total population of students or faculty or employees, the question usually is, "What do our African American students need to be successful here [in this predominantly white institution]? What can we do for our Asian students?" Almost never do I hear, "What do our white students need as members of a racial group?" This is troubling for a couple of reasons. The first is obvious—white students are thought about as "students," not white students. The second is that there is little or no attention paid to the need to help white people understand what it means to be white.

It is partially to this lack of clarity about the importance of whiteness that whiteness studies literature attempts to speak. People of color have been writing about white people and whiteness for at least a hundred and fifty years; Harriet Jacobs wrote about the white people who enslaved her in *Life of a Slave Girl* in 1861. In "The Souls of White Folks," an essay in his book *Darkwater,* W.E.B. DuBois spoke about the clear eyes through which the "Darker Peoples" see white people:

> In the awful cataclysm of World War, where from beating, slandering, and murdering us the white world turned temporarily aside to kill each other, we of the Darker Peoples looked on with mild amaze.... Here is a civilization that has boasted much. Neither Roman nor Arab, Greek nor Egyptian, Persian nor Mongol ever took himself and his own perfectness with such disconcerting seriousness as the modern white man. We whose shame, humiliation, and deep insult his aggrandizement so often involved were never deceived. We looked at him clearly, with world-old eyes, and saw simply a human thing, weak and pitiable and cruel, even as we are and were.[7]

Many of us who are white have never thought about our skin color; it doesn't occur to us that others would write about us as a racial group. And, because our schools' curricula are so heavily white-oriented, many of us haven't read works by Black, Latino, Asian American, or American Indian writers. There is a far graver consequence to that than just not having a balanced perspective. If we only hear what we are saying, if we only have our perception, we begin to believe that what we're saying is true and that everyone shares our views. That experience is reminiscent of many Americans' response to the September 11, 2001 attack, a genuine question of "Why do they hate us?" Had we been hearing from sources other than ourselves for the twenty-five or thirty years before that, we would have had a better understanding about how negatively many see the actions and attitudes of the United States. But, because we surround ourselves with our own words, we are unprepared. Words like those of DuBois about white people come as a surprise. For decades, whiteness wasn't talked about by white people. It didn't need to be; it was just the way things were.

Within the last fifteen years, some white people have come to the conversation about whiteness. From my perspective, some of the talk is useful, but much of it serves to keep us in the center of the race conversation. In short, I am of two minds. In April of 1997 I attended a conference at the University of California at Berkeley called "The Making and Unmaking of Whiteness." I had very mixed responses: I was struck by the apolitical, academic tone of many of the papers read. I found the lack of feeling and connection to human beings extremely disconcerting. It was as if the presenters, predominantly white men, were talking about a group of which they were not a part: "White people we studied did this" or "This is how white students responded to this test."

There were two presenters who redeemed the conference for me. The first was Mab Segrest. After what seemed like a long string of white men, she read a paper titled "The Souls of White Folks." In it she talked about herself *as a white person* and the impact of that on her experience. It was there that I heard her read the piece from Mary Chesnut's diary that I quote in Chapter 2. As she left the podium, one of the men on the panel of presenters made a comment dismissing her presentation, saying something like, "Well, we can all do autobiographical work. We certainly don't need any more of that." His comment and most of the other papers I heard that day confirmed my fear that the whiteness "scholarship" was to be as removed from life as a great deal of other academic work and that it would not be about the active dismantling of white supremacy that I was hoping for.

There was, however, one other splendid paper. Cheryl Harris, an African American law professor, read "Whiteness as Property" which had been published in the *Harvard Law Review* in 1993. As she spoke, I made a clear historical connection between race and class, between the Southern cotton business and the owners of northern mills, and the intentional exploitation of the free labor of African slaves and the cheap labor of the working class mill workers. It was a light bulb experience for me.

For those of us who work on systemic racial oppression, whiteness literature is useful because it pushes us to become clear about what we think and where we stand. We also hear different perspectives than our own. Of course, there is a range of thought about what the focus of conversations about whiteness should be, its purpose and direction. White identity development, white culture, and dismantling white supremacy are three areas of study.

Any time those of us in the oppressor group shift focus, those who are in the oppressed group should be wary. I have often said that white people will do *anything* not to talk about their race and to avoid our responsibilities to take apart these systems that keep us primary. One has to look at whiteness studies to see if that is what is happening. For me, those who identify as "race traitors"—Ignatiev, sometimes Roediger, Garvey, and others—display the privilege of highly educated white men when they say that "The key to solving the social problems of our age is to abolish the white race, which means no more and no less than abolishing the privileges of the white skin," as though individuals not "acting white" will have any impact at all if we don't dismantle structures that hold supremacy in place. When I heard Ignatiev's paper given in 1997, I was reminded of a bumper sticker I had seen around Berkeley: "Visualize the End of World Hunger." It feels like a slogan that only highly-privileged, well-fed people would think up. Without serious and sustained action, visualization doesn't change anything; similarly, "abolish[ing] the white race" feels like an easy, "radical" idea that requires nothing of us and comes from a privileged white male perspective.

Part of me says that, while important, general whiteness studies is not where my patience or passion lie. As with the general diversity literature briefly discussed in Chapter 2, one might venture to say that it is designed, consciously or not, to tinker with some things, change a few others, and keep the rest as they are. Most of it does not go far enough for me. It starts with what is, which is always essential, but it keeps things generally the same. There is little strategic discussion about how to bring about the root changes necessary. Sometimes I believe we get in our own way: "My board is not ready for such a deep and complex conversation as changing the systemic ways we do things. We have to begin with a little piece like hiring. And we have to call what we're doing 'multicultural competence' instead of 'white privilege.' The board just won't go there." I am clear that, to change the ways things work, you have to divide the task into do-able parts. However, I think we sometimes underestimate those with whom we work, feeding them, for example, bite-sized pieces of an apple rather than showing them the whole apple and then cutting it into slices to make it easier to digest. The potential costs are similar to the diversity conversation in the corporate sector: If there is no clear assessment of systems of superiority and how they are kept in place to advantage some and disadvantage others, then it is just so much talk that makes us (the power holders) feel good about ourselves but results in no real change.

Another part of me knows that there are works that are vital that might be considered part of the whiteness literature. Though I would be more likely to put them in the race literature, they are peripherally connected to whiteness. In the legal field, critical race theorists like Cheryl Harris, Kimberlé Crenshaw, Stephanie Wildman, and others look at race, gender and law from an "outsider" perspective—standing back and looking in at the legal system. By writing from that perspective, they raise issues in a way that is profoundly helpful in understanding how white supremacy is embedded in law.

There is another area that is more clearly part of the whiteness literature and seems essential to me: the perspectives of white college students about what it means to be white. Three books, each sobering and enlightening, are particularly important: *Breaking the Code of Good Intentions: Everyday Forms of Racism* by Melanie Bush, *Two-Faced Racism: Whites in the Backstage and Frontstage* by Leslie Houts Picca and Joe R. Feagin, and *Being White: Stories of Race and Racism* by Karyn D. McKinney. As we listen to students' voices, one of the recurring themes throughout is whiteness-as-everyday-ness: "...I could tell my life story without mentioning my race"[8] That is precisely because the students are white. Because of the self-identified lack of racial awareness among white students and because of the potential roles they will play in the future, young white students deserve our focus; regardless of whether it is fair or right, many of the nation's future leaders are in that group.

Joe Feagin and Debra Van Ausdale looked at young children who will grow up to be the students studied by McKinney and Bush: They found a picture that is even more disturbing. In *The First R: How Children Learn Race and Racism*, Van Ausdale describes an understanding of systemic racial oppression and the creation of those patterns in children as young as three. White children told children of color that they couldn't be the leaders because they were Asian or Black, that only white children could, and they excluded them from play specifically because of their skin color. While white children used racial epithets against children of color, no children of color spoke to white children that way. Feagin and Van Ausdale make it clear that children learn race roles as they learn sex roles, from all that they observe around them. They recreate racial power roles, as they do gender roles, either as oppressor or oppressed, and understand what they are doing.

When I first read this, it went so against the grain of what we who are white think is common knowledge that I had trouble believing it. Further, it contradicted all that I was taught in my master's and doctoral courses about children's development. Yet I know how easily children learn gender roles: Girls watch, boys do. That inactive/active power distinction is regularly represented in ads and on toy boxes. I see it so often that, while I am infuriated and disturbed by it, I am not surprised. When I thought about gender conditioning, what I was reading about race roles wasn't hard to believe. The basis for rejection of children of color is race. Rarely are white children excluded *because they are white*. Even if they are, this is not the experience that they or their parents face on a daily basis, as it is for children of color and their parents. Further, the white children knew they might get in trouble for their behavior, so they hid it from the teachers. In doing so they internalized the behavior which then became part of normal action.

> ...the need to conceal racist behavior results in racial identity becoming a central part of young children's social repertoires....for white children, racist thought and practice are "normal" and conventional, and they make use of learned distinctions to structure their behavior toward others....for most white children, as for most white adults, there is little in the way of a broad moral dilemma posed by racist thinking and action. What has often been framed as a basic moral issue is really an issue of everyday routine....[9]

So, if structural and personal racism is understood and part of "everyday routine" at age three, without that posing much of a moral dilemma, of course a white college student is able to "...tell [her/his] life story without mentioning [her/his] race" and white adults are enabled, in fact empowered, to be resistant to the mention of our race. When you put those pieces together, you arrive where you would expect. Jeff Hitchcock's book is called *Unraveling the White Cocoon*. That's what being white usually means—living wrapped up and removed from racial reality. We don't have to think about it, and we know that. We learn not to, and yet no other group in our country has that option. Race is one of the central criteria by which our society is organized, and our privilege allows us to ignore its existence as it relates to us.

Two other keys to understanding what it means to be white are important: the attempt to move toward being "color-blind" and the ways in which the supremacy of whiteness has been built into law. The first—the fantasy of being "color-blind"—brings us to the current political rhetoric of "post-racialism" suggesting that race is no longer an issue in the United States, while racial politics and oppression run rampant. The second—white by law—makes clear how determined we have been to maintain the superiority of whiteness and positions us to begin to understand white privilege and how it was put and remains in place.

In 1966 when I was a freshman in college, I gave my mother a copy of *What Color is Love* by Joan Walsh Anglund. It is a small book with sweet little drawings, and the last line was something like "Isn't love more important than color?" That was certainly the gist of the book. A central theme of that time, the civil rights era, was that color should not determine someone's worth or alleged intelligence, nor should it affect someone's right to vote, see a movie, drink from a fountain, or get a fair trial. Many of us fought to remove color from a list of indicators of anything important— who you should date or marry, who should be president, who you go to school with. Color shouldn't matter, period. It was just something you "happened" to be. Integration in the United States was about assimilating Black people into white society; the goal was to make them more like us.

Today the objective of being "color-blind" is much the same. I put it in quotation marks because I don't believe being color-blind is possible in terms of race. I think it is used to obscure what is really going on. If we aren't forced to deal with color—ours or others'—we can pretend that we don't live in a society totally stratified by race. We can act as though there are no racial disparities in healthcare, ability to purchase a home or rent an apartment (given the same financial history), or get a job, get police protection, and on and on. If we don't "see" color then we don't have to question why Black and Latino/a children aren't doing as well as white and Asian children on standardized tests; we can see this as individual children having individual difficulties. Race isn't relevant. There are white people who want to believe that race doesn't matter and that if you obey the Golden Rule everything will be fine. Because we are all alike under the skin, we all basically want the same things, or so the thinking of some well-meaning white people goes.

In organizations, "color-blindness" often shows up in this way. Some years ago the Director of Human Resources at a large pharmaceutical company contacted me with a concern. Three African Americans had recently left the company, citing a hostile environment and their inability to get promoted. Prior to their leaving, they had complained to HR that the manager of the engineering division was oblivious to these issues. The director was calling to ask if I would come in and do diversity training.

During an organizational assessment that included a series of interviews and focus groups, several red flags were raised. Two related to "color-blindness" and came up in interviews with members of the senior team. One person said: "There is no reason to look at our differences here; all of us are on equal footing. Don't talk about disparities or past inequities; people know all of that and are tired of hearing about it. If you come in to the managers talking about how some of us have privileges and others don't, you'll be met by hostility." Another told me: "What we want to do is attract qualified minorities, not second-class ones. All we have to do is be sure that people have an equal opportunity to get in the door. After that, it's all competition, and the employees who have the most to offer will be successful." (This is exactly what the person told me at the law firm I described.) A third said: "You're making too much of this race thing. People don't see employees as black or brown or green or purple. They just see them as people. What we are looking for is a 'color-blind' institution; give people a chance to apply and qualifications will do the rest."

Following my presentation of the assessment, a group of senior managers and the director of HR worked with me to create an organizational diversity plan. The three-year program focused on answers to this question: In terms of diversity, what organizational values do we want to see reflected in policies and procedures, employee behavior, and our employee composition? There were a couple of things that I knew from the beginning would have to be addressed.

One of the senior managers quoted above gave me a clue to a reason that the company was having difficulty recruiting and retaining Latino and Black managers: "...We want to attract *qualified* minorities here, *not second-class ones.*" While I have seen many job applications stating that "Qualified minorities and women are encouraged to apply," I have never seen one that says, "Qualified white candidates are encouraged to apply." One aspect of white privilege is to assume that whites who apply for a job are qualified. This is not the assumption about candidates of color. As my friend David Tulin says, "White men are assumed qualified until they prove themselves unqualified while people of color and white women are assumed unqualified until they prove themselves qualified." The senior team spoke for many other white managers who were comfortable with the way things were.

I also realized that we would have to begin the conversation soon about the costs of acting as if race doesn't matter. A flag was raised by the comment that "People don't see employees as black or brown or green or purple. They just see them as people." If white people in an organization don't understand the role race plays in their lives and in others', they will not be able to attract the greatest and most varied talent; they will not have the skills to mentor and coach those who are different from them; nor will they have the greatest likelihood of achieving their organization's vision and goals. The call for color-blindness was revealing. My experience is that "color-blind" is code for "You are welcome here as long as you don't remind me that you are different from me or make your race an issue. If you make me aware of your race, your career here will be limited." That undermines all seemingly positive messages the organization sends. This has impact on productivity, effectiveness, and loyalty to the organization.

The drive for "color-blindness" also affects our collective psyche. In order to believe that it is possible, we have to sit in delusion. We have to act as though we really can't see the difference between brown and white skin. Its absurdity becomes clear if we shift the "blindness" to sex and/ or gender. Consider saying, "I just don't see sex" meaning the physical differences between men and women. [As I write this a transgender friend taps me on my mind's shoulder and says, "So why is that so important?" I don't know enough yet to write that book.] And while I guess it's possible for someone to believe they don't "see gender," I've never heard anyone say it. We are as gender-ized as we are racial-ized; we are as controlled by patriarchy as much as we are by the supremacy of whiteness; they are inextricably entwined. As with all socially constructed paradigms, meaning has been attached to skin color. Thus the old saying: "If you're Black, get back; if you're brown, stick around; if you're white, you're right." In her book, *Seeing a Color-Blind Future: The Paradox of Race*, Patricia Williams says, "We must be careful not to allow our intentions to verge into outright projection by substituting a fantasy of global seamlessness that is blinding rather than just color-blind."[10]

The current push for a "color-blind" society on the part of some white politicians and many other Americans is ironic at best. That desire belies the fact that color and race have always been deeply embedded in America's legal systems. In fact, one can trace the history of racism in this country by looking at laws regarding citizenship and immigration—initially who was considered a citizen and, then, who could become one by immigrating to the United States at any given time. This was important because with citizenship came the privileges of voting and the ability to own land. The supremacy of whiteness and immigration law are intertwined. The laws were designed to keep power and control in the hands of white people, so who was white was the linchpin on which the legal cases were determined.

The longer I work on white privilege, the more convinced I am of the need to know and understand the history of the United States and the ways in which race and color have played out here and in other countries that were colonized by western Europeans. Periodically, preparation of something I'm writing requires me to do research so that I am better able to build an historical context for what I'm thinking and saying. I had already begun to look into how whiteness is and always has been codified in the American legal system when a client called. He had invited me to make a presentation on white privilege at his highly selective liberal arts college. One of the vice presidents got nervous about my topic because he thought it was "too political" and asked if I could do "something more scholarly." My academic arrogance and my training—and a dose of "Don't dare me!"—set me on a fifteen- or twenty-hour journey through history books, legal texts, and descriptions of Supreme Court decisions. At the end, I had learned a tiny bit about history and a lot about how much I don't know. What follows is a very brief sketch of how whiteness has been embedded in American history since the signing of the Constitution in 1787. I have divided the cases by which race they pertain to—African American, American Indian, Asian, and Latino/a—because how each race was dealt with historically instructs us about the unstated but real pecking order of racial groups today. As always, the past informs the present.

In 1787, the Constitution of the United States was written. Article 1, Section 2, states that, for the purposes of representation and taxation, "the whole Number of free Persons, including those bound to Service for a Term of Years [white indentured servants], and excluding Indians not taxed, three-fifths of all other Persons [African slaves]"[11] will be considered. What this means is that an African slave was identified as three-fifths of a person and white people were considered whole people. The assumption of whiteness as a "neutral baseline"[12] was put in place. In Congress's first words on citizenship, in the Act of March 26, 1790, naturalization—the ability to become a citizen—was limited to "any alien, being a free white person who shall have resided within the limits and under the jurisdiction of the United States for a term of two years."[13] Being white remained a prerequisite to naturalization until 1952.

While there are many cases regarding enslaved Africans, two are obvious and important markers in history. The first is the 1856 *Dred Scott v. Sandford* decision in which Dred Scott, a slave, sued his owner, John Sandford, for freedom for his wife, his daughters, and himself. As this was before the Civil War, there were still slave states and free states. Scott argued that he was no longer a slave because he had been moved out of the South by his former owner, sold to a new owner (Sandford), and was now a citizen of a free state. Chief Justice Taney delivered the opinion of the court: "The question before us is, whether the class of persons [the descendants of African slaves] compose a portion of this people [citizens]?…We think they are not, and that they are not included, and were not intended to be included, under the word 'citizens' in the Constitution, and can therefore claim none of the rights and privileges which that instrument provides for and secures to citizens of the United States." He went on: "On the contrary, they were at that time considered as a subordinate and inferior class of beings, who had been subjugated by the dominant race, and, whether emancipated or not, yet remained subject to their authority, and had no rights or privileges but such as those who held the power and the Government might choose to grant them."[14] I include these words from Taney because the tone is so clear and important. For him, it was simply not a question.

The second is the 1896 *Plessy v. Ferguson* decision in which Plessy sued to be able to ride in the "white" car of the train. Plessy, who was biracial but phenotypically white, charged that "the refusal to seat him on the white passenger car deprived him of property—'this reputation [of being white] has an actually pecuniary value'."[15] Plessy raised two central questions of constitutionality: first, whether or not it was constitutional to segregate by race, and, second, whether the separate but equal clause in the Fourteenth Amendment to the Constitution was constitutional. Justice Brown, in speaking on behalf of the court, found the separate but equal statute to be "reasonable" based on "established usages, customs, and traditions of the people, and with a view to the promotion of their comfort, and the preservation of the public peace and good order."[16] He went on to say: "We consider the underlying fallacy of plaintiff's argument to consist in the assumption that the enforced separation of the two races stamps the colored race with a badge of inferiority. If this be so, it is not by reason of anything found in the act, but solely because the colored race chooses to put that construction upon it."[17] It was not until the *Brown v. Board of Education* decision in 1954 that the separate but equal decision was overturned.

The Fourteenth Amendment, added to the Constitution in 1870 following the Civil War, made all people "born or naturalized in the United States" citizens, regardless of individual states' laws. Thus, people of "African nativity, or African descent"[18] could became citizens, but the law continued to withhold that right from Asians and American Indians.

Obviously, there was no question about American Indians immigrating to this country—it was their country everyone else came to. In the Supreme Court's decision of *Dred Scott v. Sandford* is the following comment about American Indians: "The situation of this population [African Americans] was altogether unlike that of the Indian race. The latter, it is true, formed no part of the colonial communities, and never amalgamated with them in social connections or in government. But although they were uncivilized, they were yet a free and independent people, associated together in nations or tribes, and governed by their own laws. Many of these political communities were situated in territories to which the white race claimed the ultimate right of dominion....It is true that the course of events has brought the Indian tribes within the limits of the United States under subjection to the white race; and it has been found necessary, for their sake as well as our own, to regard them as in a state of pupilage, and to legislate to a certain extent over them and the territory they occupy."[19] Then, like now, American Indians were taken out of the picture. "In a state of pupilage" to be turned into white people, contained on reservations, or wiped out. In many ways their existence is missing from history, as they are absent from our present awareness.

While many legal cases revolved around race, it is the cases that specifically dealt with the issue of citizenship and naturalization that most clearly defined who was white and who was not. Though not explicitly stated, the historical determination was that there were two groups of people—Black (clumping all non-whites together) and white. People who wanted to become citizens, then, based their cases on their ability to prove they were white. Courts determined on a case by case basis who was white and who was not. They also had to decide *why* someone was white or not. These decisions were based on "common knowledge" rationales and "scientific evidence" rationales.[20] The former was sort of an "Anyone can tell that this person is not white" perspective; the latter was connected to studies being done on brain size, facial features, and shape of head.

Chinese immigrants originally came to the United States during the Gold Rush that began in 1848—in fact, their name for the United States was "Gold Mountain"—and by 1860 41,000 Chinese had come to California to seek their fortunes. First they were welcomed, but, as the gold proved harder to get, the Chinese were driven out of the goldfields by brutal treatment—forcing them to pay taxes that no white person had to pay, stealing their property or burning it down, and murder.[21] By 1867, many had fled California and gone to work building the transcontinental railroad, where they were paid much less than their white counterparts and were often given the most dangerous jobs. Blaming economic problems on the Chinese in California, an Anti-Chinese Union was formed in 1876. Dennis Kearney, of the California Workingmen's Party, stated: "We declare that white men, and women, and boys and girls, cannot live as the people of a great republic should and compete with a single Chinese coolie in the labor market."[22] And, by 1879, California had built powerfully racist language into its state constitution. Article XIX of the California Constitution of 1879 protected the State "from the burdens and evils arising from the presence of aliens" and also stated that "No corporation now existing or hereafter formed under the laws of this State, shall employ, directly or indirectly, in any capacity, any Chinese or Mongolian."[23] In 1882, the United States Congress passed the Chinese Exclusion Act, prohibiting Chinese laborers from coming into the country. In 1884, amendments were added to strengthen the Exclusion Act.[24]

In 1905, a Japanese and Korean Exclusion League was formed, and in 1907–1908 a "Gentlemen's Agreement" was signed between the United States and Japan stating that Japan would limit emigration by denying passports to most laborers. The California Alien Land Law was enacted in 1913 stating that only aliens "eligible to citizenship" could own or inherit land. Japanese were not eligible to become citizens because they were neither white nor of African descent. Eleven other states passed alien land laws between 1917 and 1943. And, in 1942, President Franklin Roosevelt signed Executive Order 9066, interning all persons of Japanese ancestry.[25] No groups of German Americans or Italian Americans were interned.

As you read this history of anti-Asian hatred and discrimination, which is only a fraction of what the Chinese, Japanese, and East Asian Indians had to endure, think about how much of this information you knew already. Having spent most of my educational life east of the Rockies, I had no idea of the breadth of Asian oppression in our history. It wasn't until I moved to California and took a class at the University of California at Berkeley on California immigrant history that I added this piece of institutionalized white supremacy to the puzzle. I believe that one of the elements of the racial contract is that we are never supposed to get the whole picture at once. Getting a more complete picture makes it harder to dispute or to minimize.

The last puzzle piece—the experience of Mexicans in the United States. I have chosen to look only at Mexican history relative to immigration for a couple of reasons: first, because of its geographic connection to several states and, second, because the number of Mexicanos is swelling rapidly in the United States. A few cases to remember: In 1921, when national origins quotas were created to end immigration of people from other than "western and northern European stock," Mexicans were exempted because agriculturists lobbied to maintain the flow of cheap immigrant labor.[26] In 1930, a Texas appellate court determined that Mexican American children couldn't be separated from children of "other white races, merely or solely because they are Mexicans."[27] The court identified them as white. But in 1942, in *Inland Steel Co. v. Barcelona*, an Indiana court looked at the issue of whether Mexican Americans were white. Based on information from the *Encyclopedia Britannica* about the racial composition of Mexico, the court decided that "Mexicans" shouldn't necessarily be identified as white.[28] At the beginning of the Depression, jobs that Mexicans had been doing either disappeared or were taken over by destitute whites, and Mexican laborers were no longer wanted in the US. Federal immigration officials began a "repatriation campaign," and 400,000 people were forcibly returned to Mexico. More than half were United States citizens.[29] After the Depression, Mexican workers were brought back into this country because cheap labor was needed, only to be rounded up again in 1954 when the federal government deported over 3.7 million people of Mexican descent—Mexican American citizens and non-citizens—in a program called "Operation Wetback."[30]

As I compiled this list of cases and information, I was stunned. First, while I had read the United States Constitution in junior high and high school, it had not sunk in that racism and the supremacy of whiteness were in the very first article of the Constitution—Article 1, Section 2. The Three-Fifths Compromise: You don't have to pay taxes on all of your slaves as though they were whole people, but you also can't count them as whole people when you are calculating the population to determine representation in Congress. A Black person was rendered three-fifths of a person while a white indentured servant was counted as whole. Carved in the foundation of the nation, the devaluing of Black people haunts us still.

One of my goals in preparing this speech had been to overwhelm the audience with the number and content of cases dedicated to retaining the superiority of white people. Of course, as I read Ian Haney López's *White by Law*, it was I who was undone by the careful construction of race that was intended to keep "my" people in charge. I had known this before, but studying the laws gave me a much clearer picture of how the brutality to human beings of color could be viewed as almost incidental to maintaining power and property. It was all about power—the use and abuse of others whom they deemed less valuable to maintain their wealth and property. That we degraded black-, brown-, red-, and yellow-skinned people for hundreds of years to hold onto what white people thought was rightfully ours, and used the power to build that greed and resulting hatred into laws and systems is abhorrent.

Throughout this book, I talk about the brutal treatment of brown people with roots in Mexico. While historically they have chosen to identify themselves by various names—Mexican, Mexican American, Chicana/o, Latina/o—or we have chosen for them—Hispanic—our nation's treatment of them has remained the same. We have brought them in or returned them to their historic homeland (even if they were United States citizens) as we pleased, and, in doing so, we have torn families apart. We forced those who were migrant workers to work in horrible conditions—few or no toilets in the fields, substandard housing, the fumes of pesticides all around them—promising to pay them a pittance, but withholding money to "cover" their rent and the food they had to buy from the landowner's store. We have lied to them about themselves, excluding them from white history, the most recent example of which is a decision in March of 2010 by the Texas Board of Education to exclude Cesar Chavez from textbooks. Following that vote, Mavis B. Knight, a Democrat on the Board, said, "The social conservatives have perverted accurate history to fulfill their own agenda." [31]

The inhumane treatment of Latina/o immigrants boggles my mind. It's one of those times when my race- and class-privileged self shouts, "Don't tell me! I can't hear any more." And the voice of my colleague Leslie Setlock, whom I quote later, comes to me: "Pull up your big-girl panties and deal." This article from *The Nation* describes intentional trafficking of human beings based on greed.

> ICE's [Immigration and Customs Enforcement] reliance on facilities like the Irwin County [Georgia] Detention Center has put small rural towns at the center of one of today's most contentious policy arguments—how to enforce immigration law. A yearlong investigation by *The Nation* shows how much politics has come to rule detention policy. Even as Georgia and Alabama passed harsh new immigration laws last year designed to keep out undocumented immigrants, documents obtained through the Freedom of Information Act reveal that *politicians from both states were lobbying hard to bring immigrant detainees in. ICE succumbed to the pressure, sending hundreds of detainees to the financially unstable facility in Georgia that promised to detain immigrants cheaply. That promise came at the expense of the health, welfare and rights to due process of some 350 immigrants detained daily in Ocilla.*[32] [Emphasis added.]

This reminds us all too clearly of slavery. It's a heavy recognition.

In the ability to create those laws and take actions such as the Alabama and Georgia politicians were able to do is the definition of *privilege*: the institutional power of individuals to construct systems based on their needs and values. As we begin to examine privilege more deeply, my hope is that the meaning of whiteness is clearer from a variety of perspectives, and that that serves as a foundation for understanding how systemic oppression and white privilege work.

4
UNDERSTANDING WHITE PRIVILEGE

Some years ago I was facilitating a two-day corporate diversity training session in Dallas. During the first day and a half I had talked a lot about institutionalized racism in terms of the differences in daily life experiences. The people of color in the room described situations in which they felt they had been treated differently than they would have been had they been white, for example, being followed around in stores by security guards and sales people, being routinely stopped by police officers when they hadn't broken any laws, and so on. Most of the white participants were not buying it; some were more adamant than others that the stories were mere coincidence.

During the lunch break on the second day, two people—a white woman, Debbie, and a Latina, Josephina—both went shopping. By chance, they turned up in the kitchen department at the same store and bought similar rugs. The Latina got into the checkout line first; the white woman was two people behind her in line. The Latina took out her American Express card to pay. The salesperson took the card and asked for two additional pieces of identification. After the sale was rung up, she handed the woman the sales slip and said, "Be sure to keep this accessible because the guard will want to see it as you leave." The Latina said, "Thank you," and left to come back to the training. When we resumed after lunch, the white woman raised her hand. "Okay," she said. "I got it. Josephina and I both happened to go to the store…," and she described the events. "After Josephina left, it was my turn. I handed the saleswoman my American Express card, she rang up the sale, rolled the sales slip up in the rug, put it in a bag, handed it to me, and wished me a good day. She didn't ask me for any more identification, didn't warn me about the security guard, who didn't even notice as I left. I would never have believed it if I hadn't seen it with my own eyes."

There are several things about this story that make it a good beginning for our discussion of white privilege. First, even though Debbie had been listening to employees of color talk about their painful experiences for a day and a half, she had essentially chosen not to believe what they said; she had continued to say that she thought the different experiences were individual, not race-based. She used her privilege of expecting to be educated about race by the people who were most affected—those of color—and then chose not to believe them. Often, unless the stories are undeniably horrendous, white people don't seem to be moved. We anesthetize ourselves so we won't have to feel the pain that people of color experience because of our behavior. Also, throughout the first part of the session Debbie and other whites had told the people of color that they were "too sensitive" and were "always looking for race." No matter how much the participants of color had tried to educate the white people, the white people had the privilege to belittle and dismiss their concerns. These are examples of how white privilege plays out, and, while they may look subtle to white people, they certainly are not to people of color.

My belief is that we want a better world in which each of us can live. If that's the case, what can we do? The first step is to become clear about the basics of white privilege, what it is, and how it works. Given that there will be a lot of information in the rest of the chapter, I thought it might be useful to include a list of assumptions about white privilege right up front.

This information falls into the category of "it (almost) goes without saying," things I so take for granted that too often, rather than state them, I talk as though everyone already understood them. My friend Pat Lowrie calls it the mortar between the bricks.

I have alluded to some of them already, and others are new. There is nothing magical about this list. It is simply a place to start. First, that the superiority of whiteness is a social construct, created by some white men but in all our names. That this construct informs both the past and the present and affects each of our lives daily. That all of us who are white receive white privileges. They are systemically bestowed on us impersonally, but they affect us personally. We can't not get them, and we can't give them back. Our choice is to use them in such a way as to dismantle the systems that keep the superiority of whiteness in place. One of the primary privileges is having greater influence, power, and resources. White people make decisions that affect everyone without consulting anyone else. As white people we keep ourselves central, thereby silencing others. We can include or exclude others at our whim. If we look at race in North America as only a Black–white construct, we miss the true purpose of the system. We must be aware of how the power-holders oppressed all people of color to achieve their objective to shape the country as they wanted it. Racism is one of several systems of oppression. Others are class prejudice, sexism, heterosexism, the institutionalized primacy of Christianity, able-bodied-ism, and weight policing. These systems work together toward a common goal: to maintain power and control in the hands of wealthy, white, heterosexual, Christian, able-bodied men. Examining the intersections is essential to understanding the intentional and finely crafted nature of the system. Finally, that this system is brilliant, but not impermeable to change. We can dismantle it if we know it well and work together toward that goal.

White privilege is an institutional, rather than personal, set of benefits granted to those of us who, by race, resemble the people who hold the power positions in our institutions. One of the primary privileges is having greater access to power and resources than people of color do; in other words, purely on the basis of our skin color doors are open to us that are not open to other people.

In 2010 the racial composition of the United States was: white, 64.7 percent; Hispanic or Latino, 16.3 percent; Black or African American, 12.2 percent; Asian, Native Hawaiian or other Pacific Islander, 4.6 percent; and American Indian or Alaskan Native, 0.9 percent.[1] Let's compare those figures to see how white privilege plays out in a variety of areas. First, the gaps in wealth by race. In July of 2011, the Pew Research Center released a study on the wealth gaps between whites, Blacks, and Hispanics—the wealth ratios of households by racial groups. For example, "the median wealth of white households is 20 times that of Black households and 18 times that of Hispanic households.... [T]hese lopsided wealth ratios are the largest since the government began publishing such data a quarter century ago."[2] Remember that wealth is a household's assets minus the household's debts. In 2009, the mid-point of wealth of white households was $113,149. (Half of white households had more than that amount and half had less.) The midpoint for Hispanics and Blacks was staggeringly less: for Hispanics it was $6,325 and for Blacks it was $5,677. Let's put that in perspective. The average annual tuition at a private four-year college is roughly $35,000. The additional expenses—housing, dining, books, clothes, transportation, and sundries—bring the yearly cost to about $70,000. The cost for a public four-year institution might be $25,000 to $30,000 yearly, including expenses, for in-state students, and roughly twice that for people who pay out-of-state tuition. (Two-year public colleges are much less expensive.) If your household wealth is $5,500 or $6,500, chances are extremely good that a four-year college is not in your future. White people have 20 times that possibility.

The nation's senior elected leaders provide another lens through which we can look at the facts of white people as a group having far greater access to resources and power than Black or Latina/o people do. There are 100 United States senators, two per state. All things being equal, based on racial make-up of the country, there would be 64 or 65 white senators; there are 96. There would be 16 Hispanic/Latino senators; there are two. There would be 12 Black senators; there are none. There would be four to six Asian Americans; and there are two. There would be one American Indian or Alaskan native; there are none. The House of Representatives has slightly more equitable numbers, but not by much. There are 438 members of the United States House of Representatives. Of those, 361 (82 percent) are white; 44 (10 percent) are Black; 25 (5.7 percent are Hispanic/Latino; seven (1.6 percent) are Asian American; and one (0 percent) is Native American.[3]

All of us who are white have white privileges, although the extent to which we have them varies depending on our gender, sexual orientation, socioeconomic status, age, physical ability, size and weight, and the like. For example, in 2010, women were 47 percent of the labor force and held 51.5 percent of managerial and related positions. Of that 51.5 percent, roughly 88 percent were white, 6 percent were African Americans, 3.8 percent were Latinas, and 2.8 percent were Asian Americans.[4] These statistics help make clear my statement later in the book about white women being seen as barriers by people of color, particularly women. Literally, the career path of African Americans, Latinas/os, and Asian Americans must go through white people to get to the top echelon. Unless we believe that white women or African American men and women are inherently less capable, we have to acknowledge that our systems are treating us unequally.

White privilege has nothing to do with whether or not we are "good" people. We who are white can be jerks and still have white privileges; people of color can be wonderful individuals and not have them. Privileges are bestowed on us *solely because of our race* by the institutions with which we interact, not because we deserve them as individuals. We are sometimes granted opportunities because we, as individuals, deserve them; often we are granted them because we belong to one or more of the favored groups in our society. At some colleges and universities, for example, sons and daughters of white alumnae and alumni may have lower grades and test scores than other applicants; they are accepted, however, because they are "legacies"—their parents graduated from the institution. That is a privilege that the sons and daughters did nothing to earn; because of where their parents had gone to school, they were put ahead of other applicants who had higher test scores and grades.

Throughout history and into the present, bestowing privileges on white people was and is intentional, like its counterbalance, withholding privileges from people of color. In many instances it is also malicious. I have already mentioned several examples of control by inhuman treatment. There are lots of others: breaking apart Black families during slavery, sending mothers one place, fathers another, and babies and children yet another; removing American Indian children from their homes, taking them far from anything they knew, and punishing them if they tried to speak in their own languages; slaughtering tribal people rather than abiding by the treaties that we had entered into with them; using Chinese laborers to build the transcontinental railroad, paying them sixty cents on the dollar that white men were paid, and cutting off their food supply when they went on strike for better wages.[5] While painful to hold in our consciousness, it is important to remember this side of American history, so we are dealing with an accurate picture.

Further, it is essential to be conscious that the patterns set in history are continued today, not only in the systematic discrimination against people of color in housing, health care, education, and the judicial systems, but in the less obvious ways in which people of color are excluded from many white people's day-to-day consciousness. Think, for example, of how rarely you see a positive story about a Native American or a Latina/o on the front page of the newspaper. Could you name ten women of color, other than people in sports, film, and music, who have made major contributions to our society? The freedom not to notice our lack of knowledge about people of color is another privilege that is afforded only to us. All of us, including students of color, study the history of white Western Europeans every day in our public schools.

White people can't not get white privileges, and we can't give them away, no matter how much we do not want them. For example, going back to the story at the beginning of the chapter, imagine if Debbie had said to the salesperson, "Moments ago I saw you treat my friend, who is Latina, very differently from how you treated me," and then explained what she had witnessed. Even if the salesperson acknowledged and changed her behavior, which is unlikely, the policies on which her actions were based would most probably not be changed. Debbie's white privilege remains intact.

I used to say, rather glibly, that we white people receive our skin color privileges prenatally, meaning that we get them from the beginning. Then, as I became more familiar with health care disparity, I realized that, in actuality, race is a significant variable in pre- and post-natal morbidity. In the United States, the infant mortality rate per 1,000 live births for African American babies is 14 and is only 6 for white babies.[6] Even before birth and immediately after, there are disparities in health care solely based on the color of their skin that cause one child to live and another to die. We are more likely to attribute the differences to socioeconomic class, regardless of what the data show. I think that is because we don't want to take the issues of racism seriously; many white people have difficulty accepting that our nation has a racial problem.

In a racial attitude survey published in the *Washington Post*,[7] 13 percent of white people thought that African Americans had more economic opportunities than white people did, while only one percent of African Americans thought they had more opportunities. Seventy-four percent of Blacks believed they had fewer economic opportunities, while only 27 percent of whites believed that. This survey reflects many others identifying the divided perceptions of racial inequality. While people of color understand the necessity of being able to read the white system and to know what life for white people is like, those of us who are white are able to live our lives knowing very little of the experiences of people of color. Remember in Chapter 3 the comment of a white college student who said she could tell someone all about her life and never talk about race? If we don't know about our race, if our race is not consciously important to us, then it is difficult to understand why someone else's race is so important to her or him. Understanding racism or whiteness is often an intellectual exercise for us, something we can work at for a while and then move on, rather than its being central to our survival.

Further, we have the privilege of not knowing how to deal with racial situations without looking incompetent. Almost always, when I ask a white senior administrator how she or he responded to a racial comment or situation, I get a shrug of the shoulders and the response, "I didn't do anything. I didn't know what to do." Chapter 8, "Talking about Race," focuses on what one might do. The shrug response shows that there is no consequence for the white administrator who didn't know what to do; there is no expectation that she or he should know. However, had that administrator been of color, there would be the assumption of incompetence and at least a look expressing disbelief and disappointment. "What do you mean you didn't do anything? You're the one who is supposed to know what to do. This is your area." And probably some of that would have been spoken.

Another white privilege is the ability to make decisions that affect everyone without taking others into account. This occurs at every level, from international to individual. The following story could look like an oversight: "Oops, I forgot to ask other people what they thought." However, in my experience it is typical behavior for white women who want women of color to join them in their endeavors.

During a visit with an out-of-town friend—another white woman, a librarian—we began to plan a conference for librarians on racism that we named "Librarians as Colleagues: Working Together Across Racial Lines." We talked and talked, making notes of good exercises to include, videos to use, materials that might prove helpful. It was clear that we needed a diverse committee to work with me, the facilitator, and we created one that would include all voices: two white women (one Jewish), a Latina, a Chinese American woman, straight women and lesbians, and several African Americans. By the end of our conversation, I was extremely excited and couldn't wait to contact the women on the "planning committee." At the first meeting with these women, I talked about my history of working on issues of racism and particularly my own work on what it means to be white and Southern. Then I presented what my friend and I had thought up as the plan for the conference, and all of us talked about the particulars. In other words, I presented my credentials as a "good white person" and then proceeded to create a conference that was what my friend and I had planned without any input from people of color. At our second meeting, the women of color pointed out that I had fallen into the classic trap of white women: the come-be-part-of-what-we're-doing syndrome. "If you truly want us to work with you to create a conference, we will. But it means starting over and building a plan together. If you want us to enter the planning process in the middle and add our ideas to yours, we're not interested."

For those of us who are white women, too often we see ourselves only as women, believing that we are "sisters under the skin," all suffering under the same oppressor: the white man. That is part of our racial privilege, to be able to ignore our whiteness. Women of color generally don't feel that way at all because, due to the supremacy of whiteness, race is viewed as their primary identity. This is one of the complexities in relationships between women of color and white women. In the next chapter, "How White Women Reinforce the Supremacy of Whiteness," these relationships and interactions will be examined in depth.

Being white enables me to decide whether I am going to listen to others, to hear them, or neither. I also silence people of color without intending to or even being aware of it, by talking over them, talking around them, not asking their opinions, or not considering the omnipresence of race as I view a situation. For example, a colleague of mine, an African American woman, attended a conference on dialogue. Of the forty-five people there, she was one of four who were not white. The whites were highly educated, bright, and, for the most part, liberal. As the meeting unfolded, it became increasingly clear that, if the women of color didn't mention race, no one would. The white people were not conscious at all that race—their race—

was an integral aspect of every conversation they were having. When the women of color did insert the issue into the dialogue, the white people felt accused of being "racist," became defensive and hurt, and wanted reassurance from the Black, Latina, and Asian women that they were "good" people. In this instance, it was the culture of the organizing group itself that preordained how the interactions would be framed, the whiteness of the tone of the conversation that was to take place, what would be discussed, and who was welcomed to be a participant. The planners didn't believe that race was an element in the conference, regardless of whether or not people of color attended. The white participants didn't include the reality of others in their dialogue, and, when my colleague raised the issue, she was made to feel that she was "causing trouble."

White privilege allows us not to see race in ourselves and to be angry at those who do. I was asked to address a meeting of white women and women of color called together to create strategies for addressing issues of social justice in women's health care. Each of the women had been working for years in her own community on a range of problems from health care to school reform. As I spoke about the work that is required for white women and women of color to collaborate authentically, the white women became nervous and then resistant. Why was race always such an issue for women of color? What did I mean when I said it was essential for white women to be conscious of how their race affects every hour of their lives, just as women of color are? They were all professionals, some said; why did it matter what color they were? The silencing of dialogue here occurred because the white women didn't want to face being white or see the race of the women in the room as an issue. It did not occur to them that their daily experience was different from that of the African Americans, Latinas, and Asian Americans in the room. Had I not been asked to raise the question, the responsibility of doing so would have been left to the women of color.

One of the most difficult groups of people I work with is white people who see themselves as "liberal" or "progressive." The white people in the meeting I just described were definitely in that group. Often it is they who are most offended when I suggest that all of us who are white have personal work to do. They begin to talk defensively about their credentials: "I marched with Martin Luther King," "I was in the Peace Corps in Africa," and then the absurd cliché, "Some of my best friends are Black." I believe there is an honest sense of "I get this. Why aren't you talking to those people who are really the problem?" What they don't realize is that they are the best hope, if they can only be moved beyond defensiveness and arrogance. I have long appreciated this passage from bell hooks' book *Talking Back*:

> When liberal whites fail to understand how they can and/or do embody white-supremacist values and beliefs even though they may not embrace racism as prejudice or domination (especially domination that involves coercive control), they cannot recognize the ways their actions support and affirm the very structure of racist domination and oppression that they profess to wish to see eradicated.[8]

So, while they are my greatest challenge, I see them as an essential place to put my energy. They are often the ones who are already convinced in an organization—those who have to be pushed to act but want to be seen as good people.

One of my biggest "hot buttons" is white people who are willing openly, often proudly and with attitude, to state that race is not "their issue." During a break in a corporate diversity training I was leading, I was talking with one of the participants. He was twenty-something, white, Jewish, and openly gay. He told me that he had recently bought a house in an African American section of the city and that some of the families were not happy that he was there. They had let him know that in their comments about buying a house "out from under" an African American family. "But you know," he said to me dismissively, "they are going to have to worry about that. Race is NMI." "*NMI*?" I asked. "Yeah, you know, race is Not My Issue." I was so taken aback by what he had said and so distressed by his cavalier attitude that I knew it was best to walk away, take a deep breath, and drink some water. I wondered why the anti-Semitism and the anti-gay bigotry he had probably experienced even in gay-friendly San Francisco hadn't shaped an understanding that all issues of institutionalized hatred are connected. But, I reasoned with myself, being discriminated against as a lesbian has not necessarily forced me to be aware of or sensitive to other people's pain, so why should he be different? Nothing I could say at that moment would help him understand the messages his comments were sending to other white people and to people of color, and so I waited to plant small seeds of change in his and other people's minds. Luckily this was a five-day training and the incident occurred on day one, and, also fortunately, I was working with a good team of trainers. Together we could provide lots of learning opportunities. By the end of the session, I think he had begun to see things a little differently.

Believing that race is "Not My Issue" and being members of one or more groups that also experience systemic discrimination, we use the privilege of emotionally and psychologically removing ourselves from the "white" group, which we see as composed either of demonically racist people who spout epithets and wear Klan robes or of white, straight, healthy males. For those of us who are white and women and/or lesbian or gay, our experience of being excluded from the mainstream hides us from the fact that we still benefit from our skin color. By seeing ourselves as removed from the privileged group, we are all the more oblivious to our silencing of people of color.

As white people, we have the privilege and ability to discount an individual of color, her or his comments and behavior, and to alter her or his future based on our assessments. One of the most frightening aspects of this privilege is that we are able to do enormous damage with a glib or off-hand comment such as "I just don't think she's a good fit for our organization" or "I don't think his research is up to our standards." Promotions and tenure have been denied on the basis of such comments. Because they come from someone with privilege, they are given more weight. Potentially damaging remarks include speaking of those most affected by racism as "wounded" or "victims" and thus as defective. Identifying a member of an oppressed group as wounded is patronizing: "She is really a member of the walking wounded because of racism and sexism." Although it is absolutely true that racism and all the other -isms are damaging, by speaking of it in such a removed way, the responsibility is potentially shifted from "the supremacy of whiteness" to "she/he who can't cope." Another example is rephrasing or translating for others, as if they cannot speak for themselves, without appearing rude to others like us. "So what Mai is saying is…." Or "Juan, do I understand what you're saying? You are saying…." Or being allowed, by others like us, to take up most of the airtime, even without saying much of substance.

Often we suggest that people of color need to "lighten up" and not take things so seriously. It is all right for us to joke and criticize others for not seeing humor, but we're offended when we're told that our humor is not appropriate. I was at a staff meeting of a new client, and we were introducing ourselves when an African American man with dreadlocks came in. One of the white women said, "Here's Dread Head," and another said, "Oh, hi, Dread." I was so startled by what seemed to be incredible racial insensitivity that I wasn't sure what to do. I knew how I felt about what they had done, but I didn't know how he felt. I waited until I had eye contact with the man. "Hi," I said, "I'm Francie Kendall. I bet you have a real name." "Yes, I do. Hi, my name is Jonathan." I didn't want to belabor the point with Jonathan there, but I knew I had to say something. When I was alone with the white woman who had hired me I told her how taken aback I had been. I tried all kinds of ways to get her to see my point, but she continued to say that they meant nothing by it and that "Dread" didn't mind, not wanting to explore how problematic behavior permeated their organization. I had been hired to facilitate a daylong retreat called by the staff; they wanted the president to hear their concerns that they felt were not taken seriously. I couldn't move him to pay attention, either. Race was only one of their problems; genuinely paying attention to those with less power, whether that was based on race, class, gender, or sexual orientation, all of which were involved, was what they faced. I don't know that they had the motivation to do it.

Another way that we dismiss people is by saying or implying that, as a woman (or a gay person or a working class person), you know what the person of color is going through. "I know just how you feel. When the children in the playground made fun of me because I was fat...." I am not suggesting that race is the only cause of pain and discrimination. I am pointing out one of the ways white people suggest that someone else's experience can't be any worse than that we ourselves have experienced or can understand. Or we ask why people of color always focus on the negative, as if life can't be that bad. A similar way of discounting someone's experience is to say, "You always focus on race. I remember at two meetings last year...." And then commenting, "I know we have a way to go, but things have gotten better." (The subtext of that is: "Stop whining. What do you want from me, anyway? Didn't we fix everything in the '60s?" Or "I know what your reality is better than you do.")

Another mechanism by which we dismiss others is seeing and keeping ourselves central. For some years, writers of color have been discussing the experience of living in the margins while white people live in the center. In one of her early books, *Feminist Theory: From Margin to Center*, bell hooks explains it:

> To be in the margin is to be part of the whole but outside the main body....Living as we did—on the edge—we developed a particular way of seeing reality. We looked both from the outside in and from the inside out. We focused our attention on the center as well as on the margin.[9]

We have and regularly use the privilege of seeing white people as normal and all others as different-from-normal. In describing heterosexuals' privilege, Allan G. Johnson also identifies a white privilege.

> They have the privilege of being able to assume acceptance as "normal" members of society...liv[ing] in a world full of cultural images that confer a sense of legitimacy and social desirability....[10]

We express this privilege in many ways. We use ourselves and our experiences as the reference point for everyone. "I'm not followed around in the store by a guard. What makes you think you are?" We change the subject if we feel it has drifted to focus on race. "I don't really think the issue is race as much as it is class." We bring a critical mass with us wherever we go. Even if I am the only white person in a room of senior administrators and managers of color, I know that most of the other power holders and decision makers share my skin color. We believe that we have an automatic right to be heard when we speak because most leaders in most organizations look like us. (Obviously, this privilege in particular is significantly altered, though not eliminated, by the intersections of socioeconomic class, gender, and sexual orientation.)

We use the experience of being deprived in our lives to lessen our responsibility for the privileges we receive as white people. The pain and sense of being less-than, often based in reality, may emanate both from our personal life experiences—my father died when I was four—and from our membership in groups from which privileges are systemically withheld— being poor or Jewish or gay or deaf. In our minds, this somehow lessens our responsibility for receiving or colluding in systemic white privilege. For example, I often hear, "I don't have white privilege because I'm working class." White working class people do not have the same socioeconomic privileges as white upper-middle-class people. While class privileges are being withheld, they are given the same race privileges as other white people get on the basis of skin color.[11] We shift the focus back to us, even when the conversation is not about us. A classic example of this is white women crying during conversations about racism because they feel guilty about being white and women of color having to put their pain aside to help the white women who are crying. African Americans and gays and lesbians, in particular, are expected to take responsibility for other people's responses to and discomfort with them.

One of the areas in which we have the greatest power and privilege is in shaping "appropriate" language for everyone. Since the early '90s on college campuses, I have watched politeness and "civility" become cardinal rules in predominantly white institutions. More times than I can count, I have observed the stated need for "civility" used to silence faculty, staff and students of color, and white activists. We use our white privilege to define the parameters of conversation and communication, keeping our culture, manners, and language central. We do this by requesting a "safe" place to talk about race and racism. This often means "safe" from hearing the anger and pain of people of color while being able to say racist things without being held accountable for them. We set up informal rules for communicating in the organization, failing to share those rules with people who are different from us, and penalizing them publicly and heavily when they make mistakes. We create institutions that run by our culture's rules but act as if the rules are universally held, such as what time meetings start, how people talk to one another, the "appropriate" language to use.

There are substantial costs to all concerned for holding the control of communication and potential conflict so tightly. I heard this story while presenting at the National Conference on Race and Ethnicity in Higher Education. Actually, I heard it many times there; while there were different nuances, the stories were essentially the same, and the people sharing their experiences were all Black women. Lately the number of these experiences seems to have grown exponentially. The common threads are: an organizational culture in which politeness to white people is mandated at all costs; an inability to deal with conflict, particularly if African Americans are the ones raising issues; a lack of understanding of cultural differences in communication styles; a lack of commitment to having different racial and cultural voices at the decision-making table; an undervaluing of the perspectives of people of color; and double standards for addressing "bad" behavior. Each story began with a meeting of upper-level administrators and special assistants, and in each case the African American woman was the only person of color in the group. The woman grew increasingly frustrated with the assumptions being made about the surrounding community, the ability of the African American students to be successful and whether they "fit" with the school in the first place, and the glib and disingenuous "politically correct" verbiage of one of the most senior people. The people at the meeting were, as each of the storytellers told me, working their "last nerves." In each case, one assumption too many was made, and the Black woman "went off," telling the group exactly how she felt. One woman said that her "Shanana side"—her evil alter ego—had shown up, and she had spoken more plainly than she usually did about the racism in the institution and in the people at the meeting.

What each woman did was regrettable and probably inappropriate. However, the penalties levied on each for the mistake were way out of proportion to the incident and far exceeded that given to the senior men in the group who acted out. Some women were forced to apologize while others were severely chastised and spoken to as though they were children. One of the repercussions was that white people moved the women to the margins, not engaging them in conversation or allowing their insights to influence decision making. The responsibility for the situations and their outcomes was placed solely at the feet of the African American women. That caused them to question themselves, their self-control, and their ability to do their jobs. It was another step in the experience that Patricia Williams calls "spirit-murder":

...racism is as devastating, as costly, and as psychically obliterating as robbery and assault; indeed they are often the same. Racism resembles other offenses against humanity whose structures are so deeply embedded in culture as to prove extremely resistant to being recognized as forms of oppression....As in rape cases, victims of racism must prove that they did not distort the circumstances, misunderstand the intent, or even enjoy it.[12]

I can imagine many of the white people in these meetings reading this story and believing that the spirit-murdering has nothing to do with them. A white woman familiar with one of these situations said that, after having to apologize, the African American woman looked just as Patricia Williams described: "She is here in body, but her spirit is not."

The situation is obviously complex. Each woman made a mistake and acted "unprofessionally" by white communication standards. However, several things disturb me about the story. First, the white people at the meeting had little understanding of their roles in creating difficult environments for honest, hard conversations. My hunch is that the white people didn't think they were having conversations about race. Second, because they were in their own cultural reality, they were oblivious to the growing impact of their continued conversation on the lone African American. Third, they were also unconscious that, in a conversation filled with their assumptions, they were continuing to create a hostile environment for people of color. Fourth, going back to bell hook's comment about liberal whites, while the assumptions being made about the campus and community climate and the "fit" of the Black students were not ill-intentioned, the perspectives of the white people at the meeting "embod[ied] white-supremacist values and beliefs."[13] Fifth and finally, in this organizational context, each woman was pushed to make an expensive mistake by speaking out. She gave the senior leaders the opportunity to discredit the ongoing institutional change initiatives for diversity and to blame the slowdown or shutdown on the "ineffectiveness" of the African American women. The cost to the school is huge; it loses the woman's valuable insight, a loss that could seriously hamper its ability to recruit and retain racially diverse students, faculty, and staff.

Like the privilege of determining what is "appropriate" language for everyone, the privilege of writing and teaching history only from the perspective of the colonizer has such profound implications that they are difficult to fathom. As white people we believe the stories we were taught are true, often failing to question and discrediting those who do. There are many privileges here. First, we are able to live in the absence of historical context.

It is as if we are not forgetting our history, but acting as if it never happened. Or, if it did, it has nothing to do with us. For most of us who are white, our picture of the United States, both past and present, is sanitized to leave out or downplay any atrocities we might have committed. Our Disneyland version of history is that our white ancestors came here, had a hard time traveling west, finally conquered those terrible savages, and settled our country just as we were supposed to do—Manifest Destiny. Next, we are taught that we are the only ones in the picture. If there were others, they obviously weren't worth mentioning. An example of this is the white crosses at the Little Bighorn Battlefield indicating where white men died, as if no Native Americans had been killed there. (I've been told that markers have recently been added for American Indians.) Third, we are able to grow up without our racial supremacy's being questioned. It is so taken for granted, such a foundation of all that we know, that we are able to be unconscious of it even though it permeates every aspect of our lives. Charles W. Mills describes this phenomenon in his book, *The Racial Contract.*

> ...*white misunderstanding, misrepresentation, evasion, and self-deception on matters related to race* are...psychically required for conquest, colonization, and enslavement. And these phenomena are in no way *accidental*, but *prescribed* by the terms of the Racial Contract, which requires a certain schedule of structured blindnesses and opacities in order to establish and maintain the white polity.[14] [italics mine]

While we are deprived of critical thinking by being given such a rudimentary view of our heritage, our ignorance is not held against us. We are taught little complicated history to have to think about and question, and so we have few opportunities to learn to grapple with complexities. We end up with simplistic sentiments like "America—love it or leave it" because we have only been taught fragments of information. We're told that George Washington couldn't tell a lie about cutting down a cherry tree, but we aren't told that he owned African people who were enslaved or that he most likely has descendents by those slaves. We don't often have to wrestle with the fact that one of the biggest fights in framing the Constitution was over maintaining slavery.

We have the privilege of determining how and if historical characters and events will be remembered. From Viet Nam to the Japanese internment to the Alamo to the Filipino-American War, we retain an extremely tight hold on what is and is not admitted. We do this as a culture, and we do it as individuals. We control what others know about their own histories by presenting only parts of a story. Because similar textbooks are used across the country, everyone, regardless of color, is told the "white" story. Japanese Americans are told that their families' internment was purely a safety precaution, just as white children are. Native American students see Walt Disney's *Davy Crockett* alongside their white schoolmates, learning that their great grandmothers were "squaws" and their ancestors were "savages." We all learn the "tomahawk chop" during baseball season. None of us sees a whole picture of our nation that includes the vast contributions of those who are not white.

We are able, almost always, to forget that everything that happens in our lives occurs *in the context of the supremacy of whiteness*. We are admitted to college, hired for jobs, given or denied loans, cared for by the medical profession, and we walk down the street as white people, always in the context of white dominance. Part of the reason that doors open for us is our unearned racial privilege. But we act as if and often believe that we have earned everything we get. We then generalize from our notion of our deserving the opportunities we get to thinking that, if a person of color doesn't get a job or a loan, it's because she or he didn't earn it. We are able to delude ourselves into thinking that people of all colors come to the table having been dealt the same hand of cards. We act as if there are no remnants of slavery that affect African Americans today, that the Japanese Americans didn't have to give up their land, their homes and businesses, or that Latinos weren't brought back into what had been their country to do stoop labor. We can disconnect ourselves from any reality of people of color that makes us uncomfortable because our privilege allows us to believe that people basically get what they deserve or because we feel helpless to do anything about another group's pain. So we can be kind, good people who, because of race and class privilege, are so removed that we don't have to see or experience others. Without that personal experience, we have no understanding of or motivation to address others' lives.

In March, 2002, Franklin D. Raines, then the Chairman and CEO of Fannie Mae, gave the Charter Day address at Howard University. The title of his speech was "40 Acres and a Mortgage," referring to the promise made in 1865 to newly freed slaves that each family could have 40 acres of tillable land on the coast of Georgia and the islands off that coast which are now Hilton Head and Kiawah. Obviously, we reneged on that promise, as on many others. In response to the studies that report that the great majority of Americans believe we have achieved racial equality, Raines decided to look at how it would be different if there were no racial gaps.

If America had racial equality in education and jobs, African Americans would have two million more high school degrees...two million more college degrees…nearly two million more professional and managerial jobs…and nearly $200 billion more income.

If America had racial equality in housing, three million more African Americans would own their homes.

And if America had racial equality in wealth, African Americans would have $760 billion more in home equity value. Two hundred billion dollars more in the stock market. One hundred twenty billion dollars more in their retirement funds. And $80 billion more in the bank. And that alone would total more than $1 trillion more in wealth.[15]

The data in Raines' speech is an example of the phenomenon that Cheryl Harris talks about in "Whiteness as Property."[16] We have the privilege of having our race serve as a financial asset for us. We are the beneficiaries of a system that was set up by people like us for people like us so that we can control the financial aspects of our lives more than people of color are able to. There is much research that shows that race, when isolated as a variable, overrides the variables of class and gender in influencing institutions' financial decisions. I am able to count on my race as a financial asset, even if I have nothing else to offer as collateral. I can take my whiteness to the bank.

We have the privilege of being able to determine inclusion or exclusion (of ourselves and others) in a group. We can include or exclude at our whim. "She would be great here, but her research doesn't focus enough on Latin America." And, moments later, "She would add a lot to our department, but she is just so…Chicana!" Patricia Williams speaks to this pattern in *The Alchemy of Race and Rights*.[17] She tells a story of a man first telling her she makes too much of race and that he doesn't even think of her as Black. Then he tells her that he wished they could find more Africans like her. "I felt myself slip in and out of shadow, as I became nonblack for purposes of inclusion and black for purposes of exclusion; I felt the boundaries of my very body manipulated, casually inscribed by definitional demarcations that did not refer to me."[18]

We have the ability as white women to focus on gender and commiserate with other *women* about men if we don't want to be aligned with other whites. We are able to slip in and out of conversations about race without being questioned about our loyalty or called an Oreo or a Banana or a Coconut. We can speak up about racism without being seen as self-serving. We can even see ourselves as good at standing up for others and mentally pat ourselves on the back. We expect and often receive appreciation for showing up at "their" functions—the Multicultural Fair, the NAACP annual fundraising event, the Asian Women Warriors awards celebration—as if they don't really pertain to us. If we aren't thanked profusely by people of color, we can give up because we feel unappreciated.

For those of us who are committed to the continued "hard work of excavating honesty,"[19] the intentional crafting of the systemic supremacy of whiteness is one of the most difficult and painful realities to hold. It would be more comfortable to believe that racism somehow sprang full-blown without our having had anything to do with it. We would rather remain unconscious of decisions that reinforce white privilege that are made by a few on behalf of all white people.

However, if we are to understand the racial context of the twenty-first century, we have to grapple with Charles Mills' statement that the Racial Contract "requires a certain schedule of structured blindnesses and opacities in order to establish and maintain the white polity."[20] We must ask how we participate in not seeing the experiences of people of color that are so very different from those of white people. We should question our resoluteness to identify class rather than race as the primary determinant of opportunity and experience, particularly when there is so much evidence to the contrary. In short, white people can continue to use unearned privilege to remain ignorant, or we can determine to see clearly and live differently.

5

HOW WHITE WOMEN REINFORCE THE SUPREMACY OF WHITENESS

At a book reading of The Diversity Calling: Building a Community One Story at a Time,[1] *I saw a long-time colleague, an Asian American woman who is a Buddhist, a warrior, a writer and poet. She told me two stories.*

"I sent a book manuscript about being an Asian American Buddhist mother living in California to an editor at a large, well-known publisher. This person was a white Buddhist practitioner to whom I had been referred by a mutual friend. She rejected the manuscript as not being marketable and suggested I try to write something more like the bestselling books of Buddhist teacher and nun Pema Chodron, who is a white American woman. The reason she cited for rejecting the book was that my lifestyle wasn't mainstream enough for the majority of American parents to identify with—for instance, I buy organic food for my family and I don't go to shopping malls."

My friend also told me about meeting a white woman at a Buddhist event where she was teaching. The white woman was surprised to meet an Asian Buddhist and remarked, "There are so few Asian Buddhists."

During my forty years of consulting with predominantly white colleges and universities attempting to create hospitable climates for the faculty and students of color, some schools have made changes in obvious ways: creating racially-based student clubs, beginning to serve ethnic foods in the dining halls, and so on. Yet those of us who are attempting to bring about institutional and interpersonal change continue to run up against unyielding resistance in every area of the institution and across all groups of stakeholders.

The stories above exemplify issues that exist between women of color and white women and the resistance of white women to seeing what is going on, either at the personal or the organizational level. Embedded in the culture in which all of us live and work is a message that white women are more central to everyday experience in the United States than women of color—Asian American, African American, Latina, or Native. That belief is reinforced over and over: in management and senior positions in virtually every organization, in Congress, in movies and on television, in magazines, in fiction and non-fiction, in advertisements, in lists of women who are held up as heroines—the signs are everywhere. If that is not immediately clear to you, make a list of ten heroic white women in American history; now make a list of ten heroic women of color. How much harder was it to think of women of color than white women? We aren't told those stories.

The first anecdote shows how the message of who is valuable underlies the reactions of an individual or a group of individuals. It then becomes institutionalized as the publishing corporation supports the decision of its employee. In case you're thinking that this incident might be just a fluke, the story is amplified by other publishing stories. [See http://www.angryasianbuddhist.com/2010/12/on-white-women-and-buddhism.html.] The editor's suggestion that my colleague might try to write like Pema Chodron was telling; evidently she believes that women are women, and that the race of the woman has little to do with her experience or perspective. Many white women assume that. However, my friend sees the world through her Asian woman's eyes, just as Pema Chodron can only see the world through her white woman's eyes. Chodron talks about this in her work.

The second story is particularly mind-boggling since Buddhism is an *Asian* religion. It is important to note that the white woman's cluelessness was probably reinforced by seeing Buddhist magazines and books presenting white women as the representatives of American Buddhism. In other words, the woman's perceptions were underscored by the messages sent by the media, intentionally or not. She accepted that view, not having done much thinking about Buddhism, past and present. Both stories bring us to the problem of intent versus impact. Somehow we fool ourselves into believing that, if we don't intend to do something, we are not responsible for the impact of our behavior, particularly if we are following the informal policies of the organization for which we work. But our intent has nothing to do with whether or not people suffer from our actions.

What causes white women to close our eyes to the experiences of women of color and refuse to take our own race into account? Do we not want to lose our image of ourselves as good people? Is it that consciously seeing the treatment that many women of color face would require us to act? Are we comfortable with our lives and know that speaking up to the white men in charge would jeopardize not only our jobs but also our relationships with those men? We are in frightening financial times; many people and institutions are dealing with fewer resources than they had ever imagined they would. In fear of scarcity, we contract our hearts and hunker down. "Work is hard enough without being involved in more staff development on diversity." "My personal and emotional resources are stretched to the limit." "I don't want to feel anything more and particularly not guilt!" "Why should I invest myself in other people? I can barely take care of myself."

Expecting that only some of us will survive and so pitting ourselves against and undercutting one another means that work becomes more stressful for everyone. People with privilege draw hard circles around themselves to try to protect themselves and people who are like them. At this point in our nation's history, racism and bigotry are rampant. The lead-up to the 2012 presidential election is more overtly hate- and race-based than we have seen in a long time: a bumper sticker says "Don't Re-Nig in 2012," and the person who makes and sells it says there's nothing racist about it; a candidate telling voters in Puerto Rico that if they want statehood they all have to learn to speak English (which is not true). There are new or pending laws in several states aimed at the Latinas/Latinos who have been dubbed "illegal aliens," removing from them from due process. The sentiment underlying those laws appeared in a recent basketball game as the opposing team's band chanted "Where's your green card?" at a Puerto Rican Kansas State player. One of the main outcomes of the racism aimed at Latinos—their lowered access to post-secondary education—is played out on college and university campuses daily, seriously injuring the climate of those institutions for all students, of color and white. White students get to see themselves as better, the truly human, based on another group's less-than-human status.

I believe that most of us want to do the right thing, but we don't know what that is. Without crucibles—"transformative experience[s] through which an individual comes to a new or altered sense of identity"[2]—we maintain our distance. We white women often feel that race doesn't pertain to us; "We're all part of the same race, the human race," is the frequent retort. We don't see ourselves as part of the problem, and therefore we don't feel responsible for being part of the solution. How do we put ourselves in situations that become crucibles, places where we emerge from our defenses?

First, we must recognize that women of color and white women experience largely different realities. For example, an August 2003 Bureau of Justice Statistics study predicted that 32 percent of African American boys born in 2001 can expect to spend some time in prison during their lifetimes as opposed to 5.9 percent of white boys born in the same year. To attempt to deal with this, most mothers of African American boys train their sons about how to behave when they are in public—in stores, on the street, driving a car, on the subway—to always to keep their hands visible, not to run in public (particularly if they are carrying anything in their hands), to pull up their pants, not to wear their hats sideways, to be cautiously polite to white people who approach them. That's a lot to have to remember when a kid is just going to the store. White parents don't have to teach that.

Trayvon Martin, a 17-year-old African American boy, was walking back from a 7-11 to the house of a friend of his father's in a gated community in Sanford, Florida. A man who considers himself a captain in the neighborhood watch saw him, called 911, and told the police he looked "suspicious" and "up to no good," as if "he was on drugs or something. It's raining and he's just walking around looking about....[S]omething's wrong with him, yep...he's got something in his hands [a can of ice tea and a bag of Skittles]." While many of the facts are still undetermined, we do know that a white/Hispanic man with a gun shot dead a Black boy who was carrying a bag of Skittles. It is not unusual. A woman I know, an African American mother, responded this way on Facebook:

> This is the type of situation that is the parents of a Black son's worst nightmare. We live with the constant awareness that they will likely never be treated with anything other than suspicion and fear simply because of who they are and how they've been portrayed in this country throughout history. And the truth is, no matter how old and responsible and law-abiding they grow up to be, the reality of what happened to Trayvon and thousands of other Black men is still present.

So how might this be a transformative moment for those of us who are white, whose reality is so different? Imagine what it would be like to know that your son is never really safe *because of his race and gender.* Imagine living with the fact that you are not able to protect your boy-child, no matter what you do, because of his skin color. Imagine getting a call from your child's father giving you the news that your son is "gone."

We all exist in institutionalized systems of the supremacy of whiteness. These systems were built and are maintained to benefit those of us who are white. Thus it is essential that we know ourselves and how being white affects our lives; know our histories and how they affect our present-day behavior; identify ways in which we collude with the systems of the supremacy of whiteness; and change our behavior, remembering that we do it *for ourselves*, not to look good to others.

What does it mean to know ourselves? In the context of creating alliances with women of color and with other white people regarding issues of race, knowing ourselves requires us first to identify ourselves as white. Second, we have to remember white people's history. We resist acknowledging the concepts of privilege in general and white privilege in particular as they relate to our lives, our behavior. As Pema Chodron says in her book, *When Things Fall Apart*,[3] "The trick is to keep exploring and not bail out, even when we find out that something is not what we thought. That's what we're going to discover again and again. Nothing is what we thought." The difficult part is that we think we do know. Finding out how little we have been taught about the experiences of others and how vital it is to know more is often another kind of overwhelming, crucible-like experience.

Frequently we say, "But I didn't have anything to do with history. I'm just here, living my life, minding my own business." The problem with such a mindset is that in the contemporary world, even though we may not recognize it, we are so interconnected that in systemic ways it *is* all our business. We can no longer afford to fail to see those ties. In her essay "Resisting Amnesia," the late Adrienne Rich quoted Lerone Bennet, a noted Black historian: "There is nothing you can do in history that will free you of the historical responsibility of being born at a certain time, in a certain place, with a certain skin color."[4] Rich went on to say:

> But you do have a choice to become *consciously* historical—that is, a person who tries for memory and connectedness against amnesia and nostalgia....But we all need to begin with the individual consciousness: How did we come to be where we are and not elsewhere?[5]

Over the years many women of color, particularly African Americans and Latinas, have told me that white women are their greatest barrier to success. That's because in most schools and universities white women have a high percentage of middle management jobs—assistant professors, assistant vice presidents, vice chancellors, assistant deans, and so on. While white men hold the ultimate power, women of color have to move through the white women to get to the senior positions, and, most often, white women hire other white women or white men to fill mid-level positions, rather than promoting the women of color: "...the power positioning of many Whites [sic] make the pathway for other individuals of color to 'make it' on a larger scale next to impossible."[6] In many instances, women of color are the ones who trained the white woman or man who eventually gets the job. Here's an example I heard from one of my colleagues:

> A Black woman with a master's degree has served as an organizational development consultant and management coach at my university and has been overlooked for promotions and awards. This has gone on for years, despite the recognition her group received as a result of her work and the praise her management clients have given her. Meanwhile, the Black woman's white female boss gave a promotion, a raise, and recognition for outstanding work to a white woman with less education who has played a role with no visibility or interaction with client groups.

Because we are white we are able to do thoughtless or foolish things that affect women of color negatively, and we are not held accountable for these acts. If the woman complains, she is seen as a whiner or "too sensitive." The women of color describe invasive and infantilizing behavior like asking an African American woman if it's okay to touch her hair. The white woman probably thinks she is being friendly, getting to know the other woman. "That's how you learn about differences, right?" This may seem like a small thing to a white woman, but let's examine it more closely—another opportunity to think about how we can better see the Black woman's reality. Imagine having a woman of color with whom you do not have an intimate friendship touch your hair or your face so that she can "learn" about "differences." Actually, I can't imagine it. And there is no way the woman of color can object that wouldn't come back to haunt her. Similarly, we might ask an Asian woman where she is from and comment on her good English. Her response might well be, "I grew up in Los Angeles. I'm third-generation Chinese American." I'm reminded of the title of Mia Tuan's book: *Forever Foreigners or Honorary Whites?—The Asian Ethnic Experience Today.*

Generally white women in academic settings think of themselves as collegial and welcoming; some tell stories about how standoffish women of color have been to them and how they are obsessed with issues of race. "They seem so angry. I really don't know what to do." Others work to make women of color feel comfortable, but they make thoughtless comments like "The manager works us like slaves here" or "I don't know what to call you because you're always changing it. Are you a Hispanic or a Latino or a Mexican?"

Women from all groups of color describe unrelenting micro-aggressions by white women, such as questioning whether a given incident was *really* about race rather than simply accepting the perceptions of women of color; introducing a woman of color only by her name and the white woman standing next to her by her name and title; dismissing the comments or even the presence of women of color—"Oh, Juana, I forgot you're here." Repeatedly I hear about patterns of behavior like planning a meeting, changing the time, and "forgetting" to inform the woman of color so that she either arrives late for the meeting or misses it altogether. This reinforces the stereotype of Latino, Black, and Native people as always being late. If the stereotypes were not so widely known, I might not be so sure that this "forgetting" is actually passive-aggressive. As more staff and faculty of color join an institution, the frequency and mean-spiritedness of these comments and actions seems to increase; perhaps some white people are threatened by having to accept growing numbers of people of color as their equals.

Most white women are shocked when I tell them that many women of color see us as the "enemy." (I put the word in quotation marks because it's the word that is used regularly—not always, but often.) This reaction is particularly true of women who pride themselves on being liberal and well meaning. They become defensive, even resentful. "I've done my best. I've bent over backwards. There's nothing else I can do." Clearly built into that response is the feeling that the white woman is being welcoming out of the goodness of her heart to "help" this person of color.

In her powerful essay "Is the Benign Really Harmless? Deconstructing Some 'Benign' Manifestations of Operationalized White Privilege," Frances V. Rains describes the use of dialogue on racism as giving the appearance of commitment to make change. Most often, however, there is little forward movement following the conversations. "Dialogue becomes a means of vaccinating oneself against having to take action based on this concern."[7] We further protect ourselves by defining racism as one person's act: calling a Latina/o a "wetback" [for having swum across the Rio Grande River to enter the United States illegally], using the "N-word," or denying a person of color service in a restaurant. "[A] construction of racism as overt, individualistic behavior provides a cloak of immunity from scrutiny. Immunity carries with it a certain power, for being immune means not having to be mindful of that from which one is exempt."[8] Rains identifies five "seemingly benign" reactions that white people, women and men, use to keep from looking at institutionalized racism and our collusion with it. Often, rather than holding a person with privilege accountable for his or her behavior, we make light of it, characterizing it as harmless. "Oh, she didn't mean it," or "She was having a bad day. Just let it blow over," or "Boys will be boys. Don't make a big deal of it."

The first "benign" response is the "sense-of-entitlement reaction," in which white people believe that everything they get is deserved, naturally owed to them. The conversation about affirmative action is a clear example. This decades-long wrangle has had legal elements and emotional elements, both centered on privilege—white privilege and wealth privilege. While white wealthy people have had, throughout history, unearned access to higher education through legacy admission—being accepted *whether you are qualified or not* based on a parent's having gone to that school— or through knowing someone who knows a member of the generally all-white and all-wealthy board of trustees, we see that as normal, the way the world works, "an assumed set of invisible guarantees,"[9] Rains says. As white women, we might not have been trustees, but our white husbands or brothers or fathers or properly-positioned male friends might well have been. So it is startling to us privileged white people if those things don't work as they "should," the supremacy of whiteness in action. "What do you mean I wasn't accepted at Berkeley? I thought Proposition 209 [passed in 1996, it ended affirmative action in California] got rid of all those Latinos and African Americans who weren't qualified anyway, assuring me a place. And then you let in all those Asians. That's why we call UCLA the University for Caucasians Lost among Asians."

The second not-so "benign" reaction is the "citation-of-exceptions response." This is often used to point out that there can't really be racism because there are these examples of "exceptional" people of color who have been successful. The status quo is fine; racism is over. A much-used example of this phenomenon is Condoleezza Rice. "Look at all she's done. If these other people would try as hard as she did, they would be able to accomplish something, too." We name Colin Powell, Sonia Sotomayor, Barack Obama, and feel much better about the state of the nation. By identifying the exceptions, we get to shade our eyes from the systemic reality that, in truth, there are few people of color outside of sports and other forms of entertainment who become nationally-known figures. That's the way the system works.

The "well-I-can't-speak-for [fill in the blank with a color] response," the third "benign" reaction, fascinates me since I rarely hear people with privilege say they can't speak about anything and anyone they want to. This "benign" reaction pertains to white academics in particular who say, "Well, all of the readings in my class are by white people, because I can't speak for Black people or Asians or Latinos or Native people" or "I wouldn't presume to know about the tribal customs of the Lakota so

I don't teach about them." Initially, the response sounded convincing. "That's right," I thought. "I don't know about Lakota experiences. So I'm not the one to teach a course in Native American literature." However, if there isn't someone with that experience to be the teacher, by my not stepping up to the task I miss an opportunity to study and learn and the students miss a richness of experience that they can't get any other way. I realized that often drawing this line around who we can and can't speak for is an excuse for not taking responsibility for including the views of people of color in the curriculum, in discussions, in perspective-taking, and in decision-making. White male academics are left to teach only about white men. How handy. The implication is that we neither have to learn about people who are different from us nor do we have to listen to them talk about their experiences. We can cast "them"—anyone different from us—aside as either not relevant, not worthy of mention, or not interesting enough to learn about. That doesn't sound "benign" to me. It sounds like using alleged politically-correct sensitivity to preserve things as they are. The hegemony of whiteness remains unspoken and unexamined.

Guilt is the focus of the fourth "benign" response. This particular expression of guilt is fairly straightforward—not easy for any of the people involved, but predictable. Here's an example of how it unfolds: I was co-facilitating a day-and-a-half institute at the NCORE. We were talking about whether focusing on whiteness and white privilege serves to keep white people at the center of all conversation or is a part of dismantling white supremacy. An African American woman talked about the pain of the racism she was experiencing at her university. What was happening to her was awful and it was painful to listen to. A white woman sitting at a table in the corner of the room began to cry. I did what I usually do—kept right on with the conversation, looked for a box of Kleenex, and put it on the table in front of her, saying, "Nobody ever died from crying." In other words, you don't have to stop the conversation to take care of her. She'll be fine. I looked up, and many of the African American women and men were rolling their eyes. They have seen this happen far too often. Usually a white women's tears derail the conversation, putting the focus on her and shifting it from what the person of color is saying. We went on with the conversation, paying the white woman little attention. After the woman of color stopped speaking, I turned to the white woman and asked her what had made her cry. She began to talk about how guilty she felt as she was listening to the African American woman.

Rains talks about how the sense-of-guilt response maintains the white person's privilege of not taking responsibility for her or his response to hearing about a racialized experience from a person of color. By crying, she moves the focus of the conversation away from racism and the person of color who was speaking and puts it on herself. "By viewing the 'guilty feelings' as a consequence of hearing the painful experience with racism in her life, the responsibility for the guilty feelings then shifts"[10] to the African American woman. (The implication is "I wouldn't feel so guilty if you weren't telling this story.") The African American's "personal feelings and risk of disempowerment become secondary in deference to the feelings and needs of the already empowered."[11]

In her book *The Alchemy of Race and Rights*, Patricia Williams extends the analysis of what happens in this interaction between the white woman and the African American woman:

> Though there is certainly an obligation to be careful in addressing others, the obligation to protect the feelings of the other [white people who are listening] gets put above the need to protect one's own; the self [the person of color] becomes subservient to the other, with no reciprocity; and the other [the white person] becomes a whimsical master.[12]

The fifth and final not really-"benign" reaction is the "color-blind and racial neutrality response." Because I talked about the phenomenon of "color-blindness" in Chapter 3 "What Does It Mean to Be White?" I'll be brief here. In her essay, Rains introduces Joyce E. King's theory of "dysconsciousness—an *impaired* consciousness or distorted way of thinking about race as compared to, for example, critical consciousness."[13] It is this impaired consciousness that allows us, white people, to pretend that we don't see color. It is absurd even to entertain the notion that those of us who have the visual ability to see can miss that aspect of an individual. That, of course, is not really what it's about. I'm coming to believe that it's really about white people making a decision, using their privilege of not seeing a person of color as a whole being but rather as lesser and partial, a different "species" as a white woman identified Black and Latino people to me recently. On the surface, for some people it's about conflict avoidance: "I just don't want to get into it." For some it's superficially about the embarrassment of having the negative beliefs and not wanting to be caught. But, at root, it's about feelings that suffuse the white person's head and our culture, internalized superiority that relies on the Other's being inferior and thus less powerful.

Here are stories I've been told in the last year about women of color dealing with "the enemy."

From an African American woman diversity officer: "Our provost, a white woman, wants to 'move past' race and gender. She wants us to be 'inclusive' of everyone and not focus on specific identity issues. 'What we need to know,' the provost said, 'is how to recruit and hire in an *unbiased* way.' Yet our faculty remains 94 percent white while our undergraduate student body is 30 percent of color. The people of color we do hire leave or don't make it through the tenure process."

From a Latina faculty member: "I was told by my department chair [a white woman] that my students complained that they can't understand my English. My first language is English! My chair told me that if my student evaluations don't improve my tenure will be in jeopardy."

From an African American woman faculty member: "Our department chair [a white woman] does not see race as relevant. She explained to me that she and her colleagues see diversity in a 'more nuanced way.' "

From a white staff person: "There are two problematic groups of faculty and staff on campus, the Hispanic faculty and staff group and the Diversity Council. The Diversity Council is just an angry group of people who meet with each other to complain."

What messages do women of color hear from the white women? First, you're putting too much emphasis on race; second, my white race is "not relevant" and your race shouldn't be, either; third, people of color are "problematic" and not qualified to teach at this school; furthermore, you're whining, making a big deal out of nothing, and you don't fit in. At each of these schools, the faculty is overwhelmingly white and there are a significant number of students of color.

I've been hearing the comment about discussing diversity in a "more nuanced way" more and more frequently. In every instance, the white professors see themselves as too sophisticated to have "mundane" conversations about such things as race. They say that now, given that we have an African American president and thus have "moved beyond color," we should be talking about diversity in perspective, in approaches to teaching, in pedagogical theory and so on. This is another way in which white women are refusing to see how race has shaped their lives and that they are colluding with others to keep things as they are, to keep systemic white supremacy in place.

Still other white women are determined to act differently, to build real alliances, because they know it benefits them to see and deeply understand a breadth of experiences and realities. While it is hard to hear that your actions have had a seriously negative impact on another, it is those very discussions that provide hope that we can move forward together. Speaking about experiences of hearing truth from women of color, my colleague

Leslie Setlock said recently, "[I] have had many similar bubble-popping conversations. In my opinion, while they certainly aren't pleasant, they are necessary."

Before we move on to talk about the role our histories play in separating us, here are some questions to ask yourself. Do you perceive yourself simply as a human being or as a human being who is also a member of larger groups based on gender, sexual orientation, religion, socioeconomic class, physical ability, race, and so on? How do these various identities change the ways that you and others see you? What people do you surround yourself with, at work and socially, to affirm the stories you have told yourself about who you are and to protect you from having to be uncomfortable?

What keeps us from seeing how inextricably our pasts, and therefore our presents and futures, are woven together? We were all presented with white history as though it were the complete story. People of color are relatively non-existent in schoolbooks, and there is rarely a hint that there are other perspectives about what we are told occurred. This distortion of our nation's history over-privileges some and under-privileges others.

As I discuss in Chapters 1 and 2, to know my history and work to be a genuine and reliable ally on issues of race meant that I was forced to face the reality of what it means to be a white person from the South. I spent a long time looking at my family's history in Mississippi and Texas as cotton growers, a history which continues to play out in our lives today. My journey forced me to look at my family's values and beliefs and decide if those were ones I wanted for myself. I had to choose what sorts of conversations I was willing to enter into with my relatives and what kinds of relationships I wanted to have. This has been a long, profound, and intentional road, filled with ups and downs, finding out things I didn't really want to know, grieving family history, and building life-long relationships with racial justice activists, both of color and white. I wouldn't give it up for anything.

More publicly, a complex example of the fabricated history we have been taught is that of slavery because, as James Loewen says in his book *Lies My Teacher Told Me*, "Textbooks have trouble acknowledging anything that might be wrong with white Americans, or with the United States as a whole."[14] We learned in junior high about the Three-Fifths Compromise in Article One, Section 2, of the U.S. Constitution—counting each slave as three-fifths of a person—indicating clearly that the people being counted were not seen as human at all. "More Americans have learned the story of the South during the years of the Civil War and Reconstruction from Margaret Mitchell's *Gone with the Wind* than from all of the learned volumes on this period."[15] Many of us are oblivious to how the "peculiar institution," a Southern euphemism for slavery, continues to be reflected every day in twenty-first century America. As Loewen says, "Although textbook authors no longer sugarcoat how slavery affected African Americans, they minimize white complicity in it. They present slavery virtually as uncaused, a tragedy, rather than a wrong perpetrated by some people on others."[16] Further, "[t]he very essence of what we have inherited from slavery is the idea that it is appropriate, even 'natural,' for whites to be on top, Blacks on the bottom."[17] As Leslie Setlock says, "A future built on a lie just won't work."

Maintaining the system of the supremacy of whiteness demands that white people be largely oblivious to others' realities, perspectives, and stories. Examples of this are shown in Kathryn Stockett's novel, *The Help*, and the movie that was based on it. Set in Jackson, Mississippi, in 1963, the story is about a white woman named Skeeter who writes a book based on interviews with Black maids about how they feel about the white women for whom they work. One of Skeeter's childhood friends, Hilly, is a white woman so enmeshed in the prejudices of her culture that she won't let her Black maid use the family toilet; instead she has a separate one installed in the garage. Regardless of the many responses about how demeaning *The Help* is and how ahistorical, many people loved the book and the film. Feelings in both Black and white audiences ran the gamut. How do we understand one another's perspectives and how do we discover why we each feel the way we do?

The Help can encourage insight into how we white women see ourselves as racial and gendered beings. A few questions for white women who have read *The Help* or seen the movie: How did you feel about the characters? Who did you care about and who didn't you care about? What emotions came up as you read? Was the history of Civil Rights-era Mississippi something you were familiar with or were you learning about it for the first time? Did you see the story as about the daily struggles of the African American women or about a white woman's facing the facts of her culture? With whom did you identify?

My hunch is that most of us who are white identified with Skeeter, the white woman writing the book who was unconscious about both her class and race privilege. I doubt that most of us saw ourselves in Hilly, the villain of the novel. White women, particularly those who see ourselves as "liberal" or "progressive," would find that difficult to accept; we see our own good traits and intentions. Yet I am fairly sure that many of the women of color with whom we come in contact would talk about how much like Hilly we are. One African American woman said to me, "We have twelve Hillys in our department." Like Hilly, we all receive messages from our culture about a person of color's lack of worth. We then frequently collude with what we've been taught, unconsciously acting to make that person unsuccessful, undercutting her and spreading doubt about her competence. It is easy to deny that part of ourselves, but women of color see through our self-delusion. They have to. Their survival—promotion, tenure, continued employment—depends on it.

Rather than getting defensive or downplaying the connections between our histories and our current experience, it is important to untangle the roots of some of our behavior. In my Southern family, for example, lots of racial jokes and stories were told. Most of them had to do with how dangerous Black men are, a stereotype deeply rooted in our nation's history of slavery, and how stupid, lazy, and drunken Latino men are, another nationally-held stereotype. Black women were always in white people's kitchens, like Aunt Jemima. In the Southwest, Latinas played a similar role.

So, when I read about a crime committed by an African American man, I'm not surprised. Often I don't realize I have registered the reinforcement of the stereotype, but of course I have. When I hear about the laws currently being passed in many states that legalize the profiling, arrest, imprisonment, and deportation of Latinos without any proof that they are here without papers or have committed a crime, I often don't stop to think about what I'm hearing. If I don't know the long history of the United States' abusive treatment of people who have roots in Mexico, I respond with the prejudices based in the many jokes and stories I took in long ago, without necessarily being conscious of what I'm doing. Black men and Latinos become more stereotyped and less human to me.

Then I go to work, taking with me in the recesses of my mind all of the unprocessed and unexamined information I've been exposed to. I sit on a hiring or tenure or promotion committee, and a person of color is a candidate. Unless I am extremely self-aware, chances are good that I will unconsciously judge the candidate based on the stereotypes I hold rather than on that individual's personal strengths and academic achievements. On the other hand, I judge white women and men of my class as individuals, rather than as members of a group that has been defined negatively.

Part of maintaining and colluding with any system is going along with the status quo, not putting our necks out to call attention to what is taking place. We help maintain the supremacy of whiteness or maleness by our silence. To act as allies across lines of privilege requires the privileged people—the white people—to make our thoughts known, to "have the backs" of the people who don't have the unearned privilege we do. Here are examples of colluding with white supremacy: regularly aligning with the white men and women in discussions; working to build relationships with white colleagues, particularly those with formal or informal power; sitting quietly when a white person in a group makes a stereotypic comment, tells a belittling joke, or silences a person of color; continuing to teach a basically white curriculum; not advocating for candidates of color because you're worried about how other white people will see you or what that support might cost you; letting stereotypes shape your perceptions and direct your actions. Remember, the power and privilege imbalance between white women and women of color is similar to that between men and women. Because white men frequently have professional, familial, or intimate power over white women, white women often collude with white men in oppressing people of color. Sometimes this is a conscious choice made by the white woman out of self-interest; sometimes it arises from what Tom Bartlett calls "the dark side of loyalty."[18]

You could instead choose behavior that makes it clear you believe it is important to have a richly diverse organization. Build honest and open relationships with white men so that you are able to tell them when their attitudes and behavior are off-base and support them as they risk going against a member of their group. Take an active role in creating new opportunities for women of color. Co-teach a class with a woman of color, being sure that you don't take over and squeeze her out. Change your curriculum so that it reflects the racial composition you would like to see in your school. Intentionally build mentoring relationships with people who are racially different from you, paying real attention to how *they* want to be mentored rather than how you were mentored or would like to be mentored.

In all this, it is vital to remember that you are changing your behavior because it is in your own interest. You are making choices based on what you think is right, rather than what seems politically correct. This is not about saving someone or showing that you are a good person. It is about creating real conversations with women of color, and, in so doing, taking steps to change the organization.

I have said for many years that people of color are crazy to trust white people, generally, because everything we do in this country is in the context of the supremacy of whiteness—all laws, all systems, all institutions. Remember all of the treaties we signed and then reneged on with Native Americans. Many people of color have extended trust and love to me. While I hope there are times when I deserve that trust, I am also extremely clear that having privilege—any kind of privilege related to the identity groups to which we belong—is not only blinding, as I have discussed, but also extremely seductive. It is easier not to speak up, not to "cause a scene." And it is difficult to turn your back on someone who looks like you, to stand with someone who doesn't have the privilege we do, because, of course, when we step away from the power we have access to, we lose some of the privilege we have. Speaking truth to power is risky and potentially costly. By not speaking up or standing up, however, we break trust with ourselves and who we believe we want to be.

In *The Speed of Trust,* Stephen M. R. Covey talks about ways of building trust, difficult to establish though I think many of us yearn for it. Building trust across differences in privilege is a long process with many tests for the person with more privilege. As people with privilege, we must be diligent about our behavior, not expecting to be let off the hook because our intentions are good. Being clueless is no longer an excuse. In the epigraph for the chapter on trust-building behavior, the author's father, Stephen R. Covey, is quoted as saying, "You can't talk yourself out of a problem you've behaved yourself into." The author adds, "No, but you can *behave* yourself out of a problem you've behaved yourself into…and often faster than you think." The younger Covey believes thirteen forms of behavior are pivotal in building trust. He underscores their importance: "[E]very interaction with every person is a moment of trust."[19]

Behavior 1. "Talk Straight," tell the truth, maintain humility, and don't withhold information so that what you're saying will sound prettier.

Behavior 2. "Demonstrate Respect" while being caring and concerned about the person with whom you are talking. Humility is necessary here as well. Remember that you are no better a person than the one to whom you are speaking, regardless of your position or the unearned privileges you hold based on your identities.

Behavior 3. "Create Transparency" by telling all of the truth in a way that people are able to verify and by speaking openly.

Behavior 4. "Right Wrongs" by making mistakes whole and doing what you can to correct them and going farther. "It's based on the *principles* of humility, integrity, and restitution."[20] In order to act in this way, one has to let go of ego and respond to people in ways that signal to them that they are being treated respectfully and taken seriously.

Behavior 5. "Show Loyalty" has two elements. First, give credit to others for things they have done rather than taking all the credit yourself. Second, be consistent in what you say about others. Little breaks trust more quickly than saying one thing in public and another in private, such as acting respectfully to a woman in front of her and then telling sexist jokes in the locker room. It would take a long time to repair that betrayal.

Behavior 6. "Deliver Results" by doing what you say you are going to do when you say you will do it. Period. That, of course, means that you don't promise what you can't deliver.

Behavior 7. "Get Better" by continuing to learn, working toward understanding white supremacy and your part in it. Lifelong work on ally behaviors is essential, particularly across lines of privilege. If you make a mistake, acknowledge it, and keep learning. Covey suggests developing feedback systems and taking action on any feedback you get.

Behavior 8. "Confront Reality—the good, the bad, and the ugly; especially the bad and the ugly." When white people say there is no racism, that we are in a "post-racial" society, that our goal is to be "color-blind," that other people might be racist but "I don't have a racist bone in my body," and on and on, people of color know that this white person is either lying (consciously or unconsciously) or living on another planet. If you don't know how to talk about racism, go to Chapter 9 "Talking About Whiteness and Being White." There are suggestions for how to begin.

Behavior 9. "Clarify Expectations" before you begin conversations across differences. You can't assume you're saying the same things about expectations even if you're using the same words, so ask clarifying questions. Often what you say is not what I hear and so on. Because we have such different realities, due to the privileges we have or don't have, it's very important to listen, remembering how much we have to learn. See Chapter 8, "Talking about Race: What If They Call Me a Racist?" for specific suggestions about engaging in conversations across differences and about difficult issues.

Behavior 10. "Practice Accountability" by, most importantly, doing what you said you would do *in the ways you said you value*. If you said you would get everyone's input for the report you're writing, get it and put it in.

Behavior 11. "Listen First" before expecting to be listened to. Listen in a way that communicates your integrity and humility.

Behavior 12. "Keep Commitments"—that is the most important thing to do to build trust, and breaking them is the quickest way to wipe out any trust that has been built. Don't promise something of yourself that you don't expect to or can't do or be. Keep a firm view of reality as you make a commitment, particularly in relationship building.

Behavior 13. "Extend Trust" initially to all of the people with whom you work, not just to your friends or those who are like you. The hope is that others will take your cue and behave respectfully and generously as well.

Mainly what is missing in us is the *willingness* to step out and step up. The will to speak and act in ways that promote racial equity and justice requires courage and the desire and ability to build trust. The results are, admittedly, mixed. Loss of friendships and ease of connection with family members are possible with any major change we make in ourselves. However, for me, those losses have been greatly outweighed by being able to live in integrity with what I believe is racially just and to develop relationships with others, of color and white, who are working toward the same end. My hope is that you will each open your mind and heart and increase your will to listen to the words of people of color, believe them, and take action based on what you have learned.

Our fear is that if we open ourselves and our institutions up, we will lose some or all of what we have. We can continue to guard our resources, both material and emotional, or we can choose to do something different. Imagine going to work in a cooperative environment in which everyone is welcome and valued, in which you can breathe with others instead of holding your breath all day. Think about what it would be like to create racially diverse communities in which power is shared, in which you can learn with and from each other, not giving in to the feeling of fear, even if conversations get passionate and hard.

It wouldn't be easy at first; hearing people speak their truths that they've finally been invited to express isn't always comfortable. In fact, it is often messy. But it could change your perspective and understanding, yours and others', if you're willing to believe that change is possible. In their new book *Walk Out Walk On,* Margaret Wheatley and Deborah Frieze talk about people who "courageously step forward to discover new capacities," who, rather than "wait[ing] passively for help to come from the outside," have "the good sense not to buy into the paralyzing beliefs about themselves and how change happens."[21] It would change the experience of being in your organization if there were connected groups of people who had decided together "how to create healthy and resilient communities where all people matter, all people can contribute," where people are willing to have authentic conversations and take action together.

It's not our fault we were born white or at any particular time in history. Our responsibility arises when we make the choice of how to deal with the race and the time we were born into, the choice of moving toward a just world, a world good for everyone. "Historical responsibility has to do with action," said Adrienne Rich, "where we place the weight of our existences on the line, cast our lot with others, move from an individual consciousness to a collective one."[22] We can make those choices.

6

BARRIERS TO CLARITY
What Keeps White People from Being Able to See Our Whiteness and, Therefore, Our Privilege?

At a workshop I was conducting, a white man said he was glad he was white and male and that he wouldn't choose to be anything else. In the next moment, he asked why we were even talking about race; it was not important—he was simply a human being. He grasped what it meant to be white and privileged, and that insight was stored in one file. In a completely different file was the insistence that race isn't important to anyone and that there is no reason to discuss it.

One of the psychological tools that we white people use to protect ourselves from seeing the pain and injustice we regularly inflict, whether we want to or not, is to keep our thoughts compartmentalized. I was reminded of Andrew Hacker's experience, related in his book *Two Nations*, in which his white students at Queens College said repeatedly that race wasn't important. However, when he asked them how much money they would need to be compensated for being changed from white to Black and living the rest of their lives as Black people, they answered that being Black was so much harder they would need millions of dollars. What tricks must we play on ourselves to hold two such contradictory pieces of information at one time? What can we do to make the connections that are essential to the understanding and therefore to the dismantling of systemic racism even in this time of economic upheaval?

The mood in the United States—already deeply undermined by 9/11, Iraq, and Katrina—turned to fear, even panic, with the narrowly averted collapse of our economy in 2008. Realistic fear, and fear-mongering, swept the country. The election of our first African American president encouraged some and further frightened or angered others. The threat of losing much that for many had seemed permanently in place has led to an interesting split among white people: those who elected right-wing social and economic conservatives in 2010, those who joined the Tea Party to "take back their country," and those who fueled the Occupy Wall Street movement in 2011. I say "white people" because my perception is that dark-skinned people, across class, never trusted that white folks would take them into consideration. They have always known that whites would throw them under the bus to save themselves. And that is exactly what is happening with the continuing mortgage crisis that disproportionately affects people of color and with the war against Latinos taking place in several states.

Many well-meaning white people are suffering civil rights burnout and delude themselves that racism ended in the '60s. A vice-president of financial affairs, potentially the one ally in senior administration, said to me in front of many of his colleagues and the people who reported to them, "Francie, you're living in a fifty-year time warp. There is no white privilege and there is no longer any racism." Meanwhile, over the last thirty years, our leaders have used systems of institutionalized white supremacy to create mass incarceration of young Black and brown men. There are now school-to-prison pipelines for dark skinned boys that begin in elementary school with highly disproportionate numbers of school suspensions and expulsions and a community-to-prison pipeline (facilitated by the "War on Drugs") of African American and Latino men and a growing number of women. For more about this, Michelle Alexander's *The New Jim Crow: Mass Incarceration in the Age of Colorblindness* is essential reading. Removing Black men from their communities, particularly those who are informal leaders, is nothing new; it began with the Jim Crow laws of the 1890s in the South. The extension of Jim Crow since the abolition of slavery can be tracked through three books, of which Alexander's is the third. The first is C. Vann Woodward's *The Strange Career of Jim Crow* and the second is Douglas A. Blackmon's *Slavery by Another Name: The Re-Enslavement of Black Americans from the Civil War to World War II*. Alexander claimed recently that "there are more African American men in prison and jail, or on probation and parole, than were slaves before the start of the Civil War....Black men reportedly make up 40.2 percent of all prison inmates." [1]

But our focus is being diverted from what is happening to the Black community. "Foreigners," particularly Arabs and Muslims, who before 9/11 were mainly considered white, are now presented as the dangerous people to watch out for. We are constantly fed a diet of fear of foreign terrorists and are not paying attention to the legislation that is passed that rolls back progress in civil rights, the whittling away of our individual rights, the deceitful people who are placed in powerful positions, and the on-going figurative and literal filibustering.

So what do we do in such a time? It is important to remain vigilant in the work to eliminate racism and to look for patterns in legislation and in decisions that move us backward instead of forward. We must constantly add to our knowledge and understanding of why it is in our personal and collective best interest to identify our blindnesses and work to eradicate what is at their roots. In Chapter 4, I quoted Charles Mills' concepts of "structured blindnesses, and opacities."[2] The *Random House Unabridged Dictionary* defines *opacity* as both "obscurity of meaning" and "mental dullness." Our first task is to begin to name what is being obscured and then to build new ways of seeing, thinking, and acting. What are our barriers to clarity?

First, we have very little awareness of social structures as separate from individuals so it is hard to see ourselves both as individuals and as members of a societal group at the same time. Being identified as white is both very personal and not personal at all—personal because white skin is part of my individual identity; not terribly personal because I am one of millions and millions of white people in the world. It's interesting to me that it is apparently so difficult to see ourselves concurrently as both members of a group and as individuals, because about other things we do it all the time. We are our grandparents' grandchildren; we are only children or oldest children or middle or youngest; we are teenagers or thirty-somethings or middle-aged or elders; we are poor or wealthy or getting by; we are even willing to place ourselves in gender groups—women, men, transgender. And yet we struggle with placing ourselves in the "white" group. Within all racial groups there are vast differences, including physical differences, personality differences, and differences in experience; it is not that all whites—or Asian Americans or Native Americans—are alike. Each of us is part of one or more racial groups, just as we are part of many other groupings into which we fell at birth or were placed as we grew up. Being a member of the white group does not make us good or bad; it is just what is true, based on the social constructs created by our European ancestors hundreds of years ago.

I believe that not seeing social structures is part of our anesthetizing ourselves. If I don't see patterns or structures or things beyond my personal experience, I don't have to deal with any of that. I don't have the responsibility to pay attention or to act. I remember seeing a photograph in the newspaper during the looting and burning that occurred in downtown Los Angeles following the acquittal of the police who beat Rodney King.

It was of two young white women, sitting at a bar in Santa Monica, twenty miles or so from downtown Los Angeles, looking out at the Pacific. When the reporter asked them how they felt about the verdict, they said they hadn't thought about it, implying that it didn't really have to do with them. It wasn't an important part of their experience. Perhaps the reporter happened to ask the only two individuals who felt so removed from what was going on in their large geographic area. Or it may be that, as part of their race and class privilege, the urban and judicial conflagration that was going on near them was simply not on their minds. An example of being removed from the Others' reality is the racialized response to Hurricane Katrina. While most Americans watched with horror the loss of lives and devastation of homes in New Orleans and on the coasts of Louisiana and Mississippi, the overwhelming racism—of the government's response, the press coverage, people's reactions—were seen very differently by whites and people of color. A September 10, 2005, press release from *Time* magazine confirmed that difference in a poll on "What Americans think about the government response to Katrina." One of the findings revealed that 73 percent of the Black people polled believed that race and class played a role while only 29 percent of the white people thought so. As is so often the case, white Americans in general see a situation very differently from African Americans. Not only do we have different perceptions, but we attach value judgments to our views and then develop beliefs about the world based on them. For example, having watched the news coverage for days, one of my family members said to me, "Weren't the white people smart to buy their houses on higher ground?" Her unexamined belief system was that everyone had the same real estate opportunities and the white people just happened to make the right decisions. The often-reported question, "Why did they wait so long to leave?" is based, at least in part, on the assumption that the poor, overwhelmingly Black victims chose to stay and ride out the storm. There was no thought that they didn't own cars to leave in. We are so removed from the Others' reality that we are kept from seeing the racism and classism involved in our assumptions.

There are many examples of the disparate perspectives; here are two more particularly clear ones. First, in its aftermath, the hurricane and its victims filled the news. Two pictures were published by news agencies on the same day; the Associated Press (AP) published one and Agence France-Presse (AFP) the other. The picture from AP was of a Black man wading through water and pulling a bag behind him. The caption: "A young man walks through chest-deep flood water after *looting* [italics mine] a grocery store in New Orleans on Tuesday, August 30, 2005." AFP's photograph was of two white people wading through the water, pulling what looks like a bag of bread and other items. The caption: "Two residents wade through chest-deep water after *finding* [italics mine] bread and soda from a local grocery store after Hurricane Katrina came through the area in New Orleans, Louisiana."[3] *Looting/finding.* Consider the images that spring to your mind and notice the race of the people in each image. Chances are good that, for those of us who are white, the *looter* is Black even though we know intellectually that looting is not a race-based activity. The person who finds something comes upon it by chance, and the implication is not that the item was taken illegally but rather that the finder was just lucky. The assumptions in each of the words feed the racial stereotypes that we already carry, and, if we are not paying attention, we don't even register the differences.

About a week after Hurricane Katrina struck, ex-first lady and mother-of-the-president Barbara Bush was touring the evacuee shelter set up in the Houston Astrodome. During an interview she said, "What I'm hearing, which is sort of scary, is they all want to stay in Texas. Everyone is so overwhelmed by the hospitality. And so many of the people in the arena here, you know, were underprivileged anyway, so this is working very well for them." Her comment was so like the rationale for the benefits of slavery for Black people, ("They're really happy here. We treat them just like family."), so based in racism and classism, that it was frightening. We are blind to others and we don't even recognize our blindness. Because we frequently don't see ourselves as part of a larger entity—a societal group—everything becomes personal. We feel personally criticized when white people are mentioned, even when the comment has nothing to do with us. On the other hand, we often seem able to separate ourselves from whites we judge as "bad" people. Similar to what Patricia Williams said about being seen as non-Black included into the group by white people and also being seen as Black and then excluded by white people from their group, so we are able to see ourselves as white and include ourselves in the white group when it benefits us—"We whites experience reverse racism"—or refuse to consider ourselves as white when we don't want to be connected to the larger group—"I'm not a member of a racial group. I'm just a person." The difference, of course, between Patricia Williams' experience and a white person's experience is that the inclusion/exclusion process is done to people of color at our whim. We who are white have the privilege to determine for ourselves when we want to be in the group and when we want to be out.

After getting comfortable with the awareness that we are always both members of a racial group (or groups) and also individual people, the next step might be to begin to think of white people as "your people." I am reminded of an important lesson provided by my friend Bill Bolden, an African American man who directed the residential life program at a college in Colorado. When we greeted each other at NCORE one year, he looked tired. I told him that and he said, "I *am* tired; I have spent the last two weeks hearing discipline cases. And do you know who most of those cases were about? White men. I'm sick of dealing with your people. You deal with them."

Mentally, I took a step back. It was what we used to call a "click!" or a "light bulb" experience—a sudden awareness. "White people as *my* people....Well, I never thought about it like that. If they are my people, then what kind of responsibility do I have for them?" Since that time I have thought a lot about Bill's comment, and I regularly talk about white people as "my people." I do it intentionally, both to continue to remind myself and to bring the notion to others' consciousness. When we begin to see white people as our people, we break through our dullness of mind. If they are our group, we see the connections between us and, therefore, our responsibility for their growth in understanding systemic white privilege and commitment to creating a fair world.

A second barrier to clarity in our understanding of racism is the assumption that it is an interpersonal problem. There is a belief that, if we could just be friends, everything would be fine. There is such a desire for this to be true. We have television programs and commercials, books, and stories that fly across the internet or that are printed in newspapers, all with the same message: "See, we're all friends, Black people and white people together. Everything's fine." We have deluded ourselves or been deluded that solving the racial problems in America is all about becoming friends, being kind to each other, "transcending race." In his book, *The Trouble with Friendship: Why Americans Can't Think Straight about Race*, Benjamin DeMott lays all of this out in ways that are so clear as to be uncomfortable. Television program after television program—"Cosby," "The Jeffersons," "Diff'rent Strokes"—movies from "Brian's Song" to "Guess Who's Coming to Dinner" to "The Shawshank Redemption" to "Sister Act," advertisements from McDonald's, Hallmark, and on and on reassure us that, in the end, we will all be fine together.[4] We are uncomfortable reading DeMott because we want to believe the myth of the personal fix. For those of us who are white, and maybe for some who are Black, the movies allow us to think it might be possible that all of this racial pain will end. Many of us remember Rodney King's plaintive cry, "Can't we all just get along?" after being beaten by the LA cops, and for a moment wonder that ourselves.

But that's not the problem. We could, potentially, all be friendly with one another, but, unless we change our laws, policies, practices, and culture in which racism and the superiority of whiteness is embedded, no significant progress will occur. My relationship with Marie, the woman who worked for us, is a clear example: No matter how much I loved her and wanted us both to have the same rights and opportunities, wishing wouldn't make it so. Only the intentional dismantling of institutional racism at the personal, interpersonal, institutional, and cultural levels could have changed that. Because we don't know how to make those changes, and we believe that it is not in our power as individuals, we become overwhelmed by the task, and we fall back on "getting along." In doing that we dismiss the power of history, politics, and the fact that things are as they are because many people, including those of us who are white, are benefiting from it. The only way around this is to engage in serious anti-racism work.

For some of us, there is extreme pain in looking at what was done to others by our ancestors in order to retain our privileged positions. We would rather ignore it or call it something else, for example, seeing slavery as an "economic" rather than a racial issue or viewing the taking of the West as simply our "frontier" spirit. We rationalize these acts as necessary for the health and strength of "our" nation. If we see ourselves as white, we have to deal with the guilt, shame, and confusion that comes up as we think of the treatment of African Americans, Latinos, American Indians, Japanese Americans, and so forth.

Many of us who are white don't know what to do with all of the information about what has been done historically in our names. Mills lays out what is required to be continually deluded, a model that we hold in our minds that "precludes self-transparency and genuine understanding of social realities. To a significant extent, then, white signatories [those of us who were not the creators of this contract but in whose names in perpetuity it was created] will live in an invented delusional world, a racial fairyland."[5] Because we won't, as a nation, look honestly at our history, it leaves those individuals who want to know little choice but to do serious searching for information and understanding of the intentional creation of "structured blindnesses and opacities."[6] I continue to quote Mills because his clarity about such a contract makes me feel less crazy—as though I have made up all of these connections that seem clear to me. It gives me something to hold onto rather than imagining that all white people are evil for not recognizing what is happening and putting a stop to it.

Even if we are willing to think of white people as "our people," we don't always know what to do. When we come out of denial or un-anesthetize ourselves, we often feel overwhelmed by white guilt or other feelings we aren't sure how to respond to, become uncomfortable, and return to denial.

During a monthly discussion group with white male managers and staff who were exploring what it means to be white on their campus, a few of the members began to speak at a more honest level than they had previously. The first two comments are ones that I hear often when I'm working with clients: "The mention of my race puts me on the defensive and implies that there is a problem that needs to be addressed. I feel like we are told by Black and Latino people that we, as individuals, have to take care of the problem or we're not good people," and "It's like it's all my fault. I had nothing to do with what happened to them. Why should I feel guilty?"

The next two were far more troubling to me: "I'm humiliated by those remnants of my family who are bigots, who are prejudiced and use the 'n-word.' So I try to be everything—this perfect white guy—to people of color, but occasionally I permit myself a racial epithet in private to get it out of my system," and "My discomfort makes me defensive and that leads to finding reasons to dislike the person of color. I act liberal and like a good white when that person is around, but I talk about him behind his back." In the first of them, several things caught me off guard: the notion that the man knew that he was holding racial epithets "in his system," that he was conscious of presenting a false self to people of color, that he had to deal with these two sides of himself—one that he felt was acceptable and one that he knew wasn't, but was part of him all the same. The pathology of compartmentalization. The final comment demonstrates additional mental unhealthiness to me. The defensiveness makes total sense, as does the discomfort; but, then, rather than looking at the feelings head on, this person intentionally places responsibility on the person of color to prove that he was accurate in his assessment. He also acknowledges the split between "good" behavior and what he knows is wrong, a conscious Dr. Jekyll and Mr. Hyde division.

In an odd way, I was fascinated by the fact that these men knew what they were doing and either didn't think the behavior troubling or didn't know what to do about it. For me, their behavior is a deeply enmeshed part of systemic white supremacy. Some of the basis of their ability to split themselves apart is guilt, I think, and guilt is one of the most complex barriers for white people who want to look honestly at systemic racism and our complicity in it. By exploring the ways that we hold collective guilt and shame individually and in the national psyche, we are better equipped to look at the role that these feelings play in our refusal to address our history genuinely and to understand how personal and collective guilt block us from moving forward. Our first task then is "To become comfortable with the uncomfortable and uncomfortable with the too comfortable," as my friend David Tulin says.

We avoid seeing or we cover up patterns of behavior in people who are like us, while we see them clearly in other groups. We do this in myriad ways. If we see three Latinos or African Americans talking, we think they are plotting; if we see three white men, they are having a business conversation; three white women are talking about babies; and three Latinas or African American women are causing trouble. Six women together, particularly a racially diverse group, are at least worrisome and often threatening to white men in the organization. The stereotypes are that white women whine; Asian American women are manipulative, but don't get visibly angry; Latinas and Latinos have short fuses. If Black females or males get visibly angry, then we talk about them as Angry Black Women/ Men; if three white men get angry, we who are white wonder what is wrong with them individually or make excuses for their behavior.

Outside of the workplace, Black males, whether they are in kindergarten or are adults, are seen as the most dangerous group in the country, and white people's response to them is fear. Think of how frequently we hear stories of white women crossing the street when a Black man is walking toward them, grabbing their purses when a Black man approaches, or locking their car doors in Black neighborhoods or when they see Black men on the street. A white man, generally speaking, is not seen as dangerous or as a potential criminal. A stunning example of this barrier to clarity is how the shootings at public schools have been reported. In Kentucky, Oregon, Washington, Mississippi, and Colorado, each of the incidents was reported as having been planned and carried out by "disturbed individuals." I remember police who were interviewed being baffled and not able to see a pattern in the perpetrators. They kept talking about how that kind of thing just didn't happen in their towns. And yet clearly there were race and gender patterns: the shooters were all white boys or young men. Had they been of color, the pattern of "racial violence" would have been central to the story.

More recently, there have been more mass killings, prompting *USA Today* to run a story with this headline: "Mass shootings are a fact of American life."[7] Among a random sampling that I looked at, six were carried out by white men (Omaha; Carnation, WA; Alabama; North Carolina; Santa Clara, CA; and at Northern Illinois University), three by Asian men (Binghamton, NY; Virginia Tech University; Oikos University, Oakland, CA), one by a Middle Eastern man (Ft. Hood, Texas), and one, a possible hate crime (Tulsa, OK). The murders in Tulsa might well be charged as a hate crime; two men (one white, one claiming to be white but perhaps actually Native) confessed to shooting five African Americans, killing three and critically wounding two others. As with the school murders, all of the shooters were men, most of them white.

As I said earlier, since September 11, 2001, Arab or Middle Eastern men have superseded Black men as "the most dangerous" people. As an indication of how dynamic and changeable whiteness as a category is, before that date they were usually considered white. They lost "white" status when a small group of men hijacked four airplanes. I remember hearing that African Americans, who themselves have been victims of racial profiling for many years, agreed with white people that Middle Easterners should be racially profiled—stopped by police without cause other than their appearance. It is important to note that, even at the extremely dangerous level of mass murder, we don't see patterns in white people. We ignore the potentially greater threat of home-grown terrorists, white males like Timothy McVeigh who bombed the Murrah Federal Building in Oklahoma City killing 168 people and injuring over 800.[8] His actions were based on his hatred of our government, yet he was spoken of by many as a deranged "individual." After that bombing, police did not stop all white men nor did that group suddenly come to be labeled as dangerous. The same continues to be true. We racially profile groups of color, but refuse to do the same kind of policing of white people. The "lone gunman," the crazy person— not a pattern of largely white male shootings and bombings.

Another way in which we obscure race is that we are keenly aware of the privileges that others get that we do not, because of socioeconomic class or membership in another target group such as gays or women. We generally compare up, not down. In other words, we are very conscious of what others have that we don't. We are much less likely to focus on the ways in which we have more unearned privileges than others.

The system of the supremacy of whiteness was created to serve white men who were heterosexual, able-bodied, Christian, wealthy landowners, to keep power and control in their hands. If we truly want to understand white privilege, the intersections of identity elements on which privilege systems are based and how each serves to support the others are an essential puzzle piece. If I miss those connections, I misread the supremacy of whiteness, and I am to unable to move toward dismantling it. The system is set up to pit one identity group against another, and we comply far too readily; that's part of where comments like "It is not about white privilege, it is about male privilege," or "I never think of myself as white, I just think of myself as working class," or "I'm not white, I'm gay" come from. Because the purpose of this book is to focus on white privilege, I will include only an introduction to the intersections of systems of oppression here.

Speaking very generally, each of us has several socially constructed elements of identity, based on race or races, gender, sexual orientation, physical ability, age, socioeconomic class, and religion. Because these constructs relate to our society's various systems of oppression, we either receive privileges or don't in relation to each aspect of our identities. For example, since I'm white, I receive the privileges that come with whiteness; people of color don't receive unearned racial benefits. Because I'm a woman and a lesbian, I get neither gender nor sexual orientation benefits, while a heterosexual Latino would. I do receive privileges in other categories, being able-bodied, Christian, and upper-middle class. I get the same white privileges that white men get. What I don't receive are gender privileges; adding my lack of sexual orientation benefits still doesn't change my race privileges. Part of what we need to consider is where we fall on each privilege/non-privilege scale and what unearned benefits we receive.

I list several privileges in each primary identity area to prompt your thinking. White people are presented in all forms of media as being the decision makers, the history creators, the ones who are, in the main, valuable individuals; we are the standards of beauty—with rare exceptions, mannequins in store windows have our skin color, people in commercials look like us, dolls look like us, and Miss America, the supposed paragon of beauty, is almost always white. Even the English language reflects white superiority and Black inferiority: "White lies" are not as bad as others, and we "whitewash" something to gloss over the problem. In European American cultures, brides wear white dresses and have white wedding cakes. On the other hand, black cats are dangerous; we talk about bad days as "black" days; in movies, good guys wear white hats and bad guys wear black hats; and the word "dark" almost always means something negative.

Men get privileges that women don't: being paid more than women are paid for comparable work; the ability to move about more freely and not worry about being raped; a statistically better chance of being elected to the United States Senate—even though they are roughly 49 percent of the population, as of 2012 they are roughly 70 percent of the House and 83 percent of the Senate. Heterosexuals get privileges that others don't: the ability to marry with its innumerable legal and financial advantages and to adopt children; the ability to identify your sexual orientation without penalty; the freedom to talk about your significant other, to express affection publicly, and to have her/his photograph in your office without fear of prying questions. Temporarily able-bodied people have privileges that those who have disabilities don't: the ability to move freely into all buildings without worrying about wheelchair access; being able to be hired for a job without the new employer feeling that "special accommodations" have to be made; being assumed mentally competent in ways that people with cerebral palsy, Parkinson's, or other diseases that have impact on physical but not mental acuity are not.

Wealthy and upper-middle class people have privileges that those in other social classes do not. Key among class privileges is the ability to choose—where you live, what you eat, where you go to school, what you study, if you work and what you do, having free time and what to do with it; backup resources like health insurance, auto insurance, and access to credit; being reflected in history, in media, in the culture at large—having your existence acknowledged.

In this country whose Constitution guarantees the separation of church and state, Christianity is a dominant institutional and cultural force. Christians have many privileges others don't. Christian and school and business holidays are synchronized so that celebrating them doesn't require taking vacation time. Christmas music, decorations, and paraphernalia are inescapable from late October into January, and the pretense is that it is a secular event, not a religious one. There is very little acceptance of things not Christian. The cultural assumption about prayer is that it is to a Christian god; there are many Christian radio and television stations; businesses like Clear Channel, Wal-Mart, and Blockbuster Video make organizational decisions based on their idea of "Christian values" (what products are sold, such as birth control pills; what scenes get edited from videos because they are sexual in nature; what programs are broadcast or not) without revealing their Christian bias to the customer. Fundamentalist Protestant values have been encoded in state and federal laws for quite some time. More recently, there has been an enormous push from the religious right to force their religious beliefs on employees and other stakeholders in their organizations. The argument focuses particularly on control of women's bodies: providing funds for birth control and/or abortion. Many are saying that it violates their religious freedom to have to sell, prescribe, or fill prescriptions for birth control, regardless of whether they are to be used for contraception or health purposes. Employers make the same claim of religious freedom in order to exclude contraception and abortion from the healthcare benefits granted to female employees. This movement, combined with concerted and often successful efforts to place new legal restraints on a woman's ability to obtain an abortion—waiting periods, forced ultrasound examinations, written consent of the man involved, murder charges, and so on—has been so overt that the mainstream press has named it the "War on Women." The sense of white male Christian entitlement to make those decisions and laws was reflected in House Oversight Committee Chairman Darrell Issa's all-male committee on contraception and health insurance from which the lone female witness, Sandra Fluke, was barred. How is this tied to race? We must remember that, generally speaking, what affects white women has an even greater impact on women of color.

I had never thought about hearing privilege until I began to consult at Gallaudet University, the national university for the deaf. Hearing privileges abound: I can communicate with all those who are hearing, talking around those who are deaf by speaking to other hearing people and the interpreters for the deaf; the journals in which deaf faculty have to publish are written in English, at least the second language after American Sign Language for deaf faculty, an issue that hearing faculty members don't have to deal with. Everything is geared to hearing people, without a thought that those processes might not work for everyone—announcements of airplane arrivals and departures, the notification on a computer that you have new e-mail, mechanized telephone systems with voice prompts, voicemail, and so forth.

Now here is the tricky part. Because we measure our own privilege by looking at what others have received that we haven't, rather than at what we have that others don't, frequently it is hard to believe that we have access to power and influence because we belong to one identity group when we are so clear that we don't have power and influence because of our membership in another. My experience is that there are two intersections that are the most difficult for people in the non-privileged position to separate: White working class people often aren't aware of the race benefits they receive, and straight African Americans often don't recognize their heterosexual privileges. The following stories reflect those difficulties. I was conducting a workshop with a group of female union workers in a steel mill in the Midwest. We had spent two days discussing gender issues at the mill; today we were going to talk about race. As they arrived for the meeting, the African American women sat on one side of the table, and all but one white woman sat opposite them. After some warm-up conversation, I asked them how they thought their race affected their experience at the mill. The white women said gender mattered, but race did not. The African American women told story after story of racial epithets, lost promotions, and being managed differently from white men and women.

One white woman was particularly adamant that gender had impacted on all of the women in the same way and that her being white had made no difference in her experience. She said that her struggles to make a living and a place for herself in an extremely hostile work environment had been so terrible that she couldn't believe that life would have been still harder if she had had to battle racism as well. "I am not white privilege!" she shouted, pounding her fists on the table. The visual image that came to me as I listened was of a rack holding gold stars that were to be awarded for pain. The white woman knew that she had earned two stars: one for socioeconomic class and one for gender. If she acknowledged that the African American women at the mill might deserve three—two such as she had been allotted, plus one for race—there might not be enough left on the rack to show what she had gone through. Somehow the recognition of her pain would be diminished.

What was most obvious to me at the time was the damaging effect of what I think of as the Pain Olympics, the process by which we downplay the pain and hardship in other people's lives and experiences because we believe we are playing a zero-sum game—if I win a star then there are fewer for you. There are not enough to go around because those with privilege have already reserved most of the constellations. And that puts those without privilege constantly in competition for the remaining stars.

The second incident took place in a group of about twenty-five women of color and white women—each of whom is in a decision-making position at a major university in the Midwest. I had been working with them for four years, ten days a year, on race and privilege and institutional change, and we had built a high degree of trust among us. One day I decided to separate the group along racial lines—white women in one group and women of color in another; on that morning it happened that all of the women of color were Black and straight, though that is not always the case. I said that I was going to work with the white women on whiteness and that I wanted the women of color to work on their heterosexual privilege. (All of our previous work had been on race, so this was a real shift.) There was much sputtering and denial—"What do you mean *privileges*? They are all taken away because I'm Black!" "I've never thought about being heterosexual. I don't have any privileges based on that." Because by that time I had spent more than fifty hours with the group, I didn't really have to say anything about the initial resistance. I just smiled, asked them to work on their assignment, and to report back in about two hours.

The resulting conversation was fascinating. What I watched was a group really grappling with having privilege when so much of their life is genuinely determined by lack of privilege. The Black women worked hard, identifying and examining their heterosexual privilege; for several of them it was the beginning of very deep work. In some ways it changed the course of what has turned out to be an almost eight-year endeavor at the institution; no longer was examining the dual roles of oppressor and oppressed the sole responsibility of the white women. Because of the shared conversation, they all became better institutional change agents, which remains the goal of the group. They were willing to step back and look at the intersections of oppressions rather than holding onto the African American woman lens through which they see the world most clearly.

I know I have barely begun to address a very complex issue—the intersections of privilege; however, it didn't seem responsible to leave this discussion out. In the end notes are the titles of books you might look at if you want to think more about this critical puzzle piece.[9]

Another barrier to our being able to see our whiteness and our privilege clearly is that we want to believe that we have achieved what we have based on our individual merits. "I was hired (admitted, honored) because I am good at what I do. It has nothing to do with the color of my skin." We are rarely conscious of how our race opens doors for us on a daily basis. As I was finishing my Master's degree at Bank Street College of Education, I began to look into doctoral programs. Because I am dyslexic, and because I don't believe in standardized achievement tests so my attitude about taking them is not great, my scores on the Graduate Record Examination did not meet minimum requirements for any of the programs I was interested in. (I was looking at Harvard, the University of Massachusetts at Amherst, and the University of North Carolina at Chapel Hill.) I had no grades because Bank Street used a pass-fail system then. Further, I was clear that the doctoral work I wanted to do was to create anti-racist curriculum. So not only did I not have grades or scores in my favor, but I was also openly preparing to challenge the current educational system. I did, however, have four aces in my pocket, each of which had to do with an area of privilege: First, I had gone to Bank Street and that would be very impressive to the schools to which I was applying. Second, I had a recommendation from one of the most esteemed child development theorists in the country. Third, part of the class entitlement I was born into involved being trained to be able to speak graciously to anyone about anything so I interview well. Fourth, and I believe most important, my whiteness made me more appealing and less threatening to all of the schools. I know that rules were bent on my behalf to admit me to three prestigious schools. I also know that, had I been a person of color proposing to do anti-racist work, the chances of my being accepted into two of those programs would have been slim.

This is a clear example that our educational system is not a meritocracy. I did not earn the right to be accepted to the doctoral programs—I didn't even meet their basic prerequisites. I'm not suggesting that I didn't have qualities and talents that a doctoral program would have been looking for; I did. But, while I had known intellectually that racism is ingrained in every American institution, this was the first time that the combination of my race and class privilege was so obvious to me. I had to give up my belief that we live in a world in which everyone is treated fairly, much less "the same." I had gotten something based on who I was, not on what I had done.

We believe that everyone has options that we do and that everyone is treated as we are, that we do not receive special treatment. We have the privilege of staying in denial about this, and, when someone disabuses us of that notion, we frequently say (or think), "Well, it just never occurred to me." However, our clarity can be obscured if our families were poor, or were recent immigrants, and we are very conscious that they had to struggle for everything they got. Some white people see themselves primarily as members of ethnic groups that have been oppressed in this country (Italian, Irish, Polish, Jewish) and so question why race matters. There is an unspoken belief that "If we can make it, you can. It just takes a little hard work."

Myths, particularly ones on which a nation is built, are very hard to counter or even question without being accused of being "un-American." One of the primary stories we tell is that, in the United States, if you try, you can succeed. That, of course, is based on another story, that everyone is equal. When the white ethnic immigrants arrived, many were treated horribly, called nasty names—*polak* (Pole), *dago* (Italian), *wop* (With Out Papers, that is, an illegal immigrant), *bohunk* (Bohemian and Hungarian)—and discriminated against in housing and work. That is what their descendants remember. Irish, Italians, and Eastern European Jews were all depicted as other than white; in fact, the Irish were drawn with black-tinted skin and Negroid features.[10] In the end they were allowed to become part of the white club; they worked hard and many were financially successful. For them, the myths proved to be true, at least on the surface.

There are, however, differences in how and why people came to America, and these differences had enormous consequences. The Europeans, for the most part, chose to come. Africans who were brought here as slaves had no choice. European immigrants were steered into a different category of jobs than those available to African Americans. Most white ethnics had access to manufacturing jobs—mills, clothing factories, and piecework jobs—which taught them skills that enabled them to create their own businesses. After Emancipation, African Americans generally were channeled into service jobs—train porters, waiters, doormen, domestic workers; Latinas/os were brought in to pick produce and do domestic work, and then often returned to Mexico, whether they were United States citizens or not. Not only did white people come into this country differently, they had very different experiences after they arrived. The situations are not analogous.

Finally, David Roediger, who has studied the intersections of race and class for many years, raises a profound question when looking at European immigration, considering "the extent to which gaining fuller humanity could require participation in inhumanity."[11] He goes on to affirm Toni

Morrison's belief that "becoming American required the European new immigrant to 'buy into the notion of American blacks as the real aliens.' "[12] Another cost of becoming white.

One of the tasks for those of us whose families immigrated from Europe between 1840 and 1920 is to hold two truths: First, the people who made those trips often left a homeland and a family they would never see again, came with little or no money, and struggled to establish themselves here, many against great odds. There is no need to minimize the difficulties. Second, their experiences were very different from those of African Americans. Many white immigrants were appreciated precisely because they were white, not Black—their human value was based on the determined lack of value of African Americans, whether they were enslaved or free.

Because we are the systemic power holders in the United States, we are able to frame everything (behavior, history, news, international analysis) from our perspective. In so doing, we keep ourselves in the central position of importance, and we are able to avoid any other perspective. This is an interesting barrier because it literally has to do with not seeing, with putting blinders on to block out other information. And, unless we are paying very close attention, the ways in which we do it are so subtle that we miss the behavior. Let me give you three examples.

I visited Border's Books three or four years ago. I went to buy a book of poems by Gwendolyn Brooks, an African American poet. When I couldn't find it in the poetry section, I went to the help desk and was told that it was in the African American section, two or three shelves near the front of the store on which all types of literature by Black people had been placed. In another part of the store, in a similar setup, was the Gay and Lesbian section—literature of all kinds written by gay and lesbian folks. (I forgot to check to see where they had shelved James Baldwin, who was both Black and gay.) I was upset for several reasons. First, I realized that my sister, for example, was unlikely to encounter anything written by someone gay or African American unless she purposefully searched for those shelves, so her learning was curtailed by Border's marketing approach. Second, by organizing books in this way, I think the store was assuming that a reader would want something specifically by a Black author as opposed just to reading a good novel that happened to be written by an African American. Third, and most pertinent to this barrier to clarity, the rest of the literature section was not labeled "straight white fiction." Seriously. So a customer could go to the literature section and look through the books, never aware that all she or he was seeing was fiction by white authors. The pernicious privilege is: Simply don't include the Other, and then act as though the picture is complete. In a sick way, it is brilliant. And I think we do it all the time, consciously or not.

Here's another example: *Publishers Weekly*, the magazine for the publishing world, puts out a list of bestselling fiction and nonfiction every year. In 2004, 132 hardcover works of fiction each sold more than 100,000 copies. Two of them were by Black authors: *Drive Me Crazy* by Eric Jerome Dickey and Alicia Keys' book of poetry, *Tears for Water.* One hundred thirty-one nonfiction books each sold more than 100,000 copies. Again, two were by African Americans: *Hallelujah! The Welcome Table: A Lifetime of Memories with Recipes* by Maya Angelou and *On the Down Low* by J. L. King.[13] People of color exist only marginally in our world, and we don't even stop to think about it.

Example three: In May of 2005, a young, attractive white woman from Georgia fled her wedding. When she got to Albuquerque, she called the police and lied to them, saying she had been abducted, and this news had 24-hour coverage on cable TV. Meanwhile, a similar series of events had taken place a year before and received no national coverage; that bride-to-be was Black.[14] Reporting on white people is the standard; the African Americans whose stories are reported are the exceptions.

These three stories are about African Americans. Is it any different for Asian Americans, Latinas/os, or American Indians? I don't think so. Given that we live in a multiracial nation, those of us who are white are surprisingly able to go through our lives learning very little about people of color; many of us don't notice that we're not seeing or hearing about people who aren't like us.

We consistently focus on isolated incidents, rather than looking at patterns of exclusion or blaming. For example, in exploring why there are no American-born tenured professors of color at a specific college, the senior administrators describe how each person of color who had taught at the institution had not really been qualified to be tenured. The question that should have been raised was (and continues to be): Are we scrutinizing the people of color differently than we are the white people who are up for tenure? Do people of color have an equal opportunity to be mediocre?

There is not much more that needs to be said about this. My purpose is to raise the question of whether we hold people of color to a different standard than we hold whites. I believe the answer is resoundingly "Yes!" Regularly, in corporate and academic settings, I hear people of color being identified as "not meeting our standards." When I ask if all of the white people meet those same standards, the answer is almost always "No," though it is cloaked in a variety of excuses. "Things were different when we hired John." "Back then people just hired their friends." "People called their friends at other organizations or schools and asked who was looking for a job." "We didn't go through such formal procedures." As if that explains why those folks are still at the institution/organization. And it's always "back then," as if it didn't happen the same way today. My response is this: As soon as you have evaluated all of the white men in your organization by these same standards, then talk to me about how the people of color aren't competent. Incompetence comes in all colors. If you are going to measure one group against that ruler, you have to measure them all, beginning with the people who have been there the longest.

This last barrier to clarity seems a fitting one with which to close the chapter. It's prevalent and insidious. We believe we are well-meaning, committed white people, so it is very difficult to accept that we, as individuals who have never purposefully done anything to hurt anyone, could be hated or feared. If we see ourselves and people like us only as individuals, we can't imagine people of color being damaged or offended by us. We don't want to face the fact that we are benefiting from our whiteness at the expense of our friends and colleagues of color.

Seeing ourselves as "well-meaning" and "good" as related to being white—or male, or wealthy, or heterosexual, or Christian, in other words a member of an oppressor group—serves several purposes, some intended and some perhaps not. For example, the person in the oppressor group, the non-target group (the federal government term for people who are not likely to be targeted for discrimination), is able to hide behind well-meaning-ness. "I didn't mean to do it," the person says, and the underlying assumption is that, since she didn't mean to, she's not responsible for the results. I often ask groups what happens if I inadvertently kick a person in the shin. I say, "I'm sorry," and, for me, the matter is over. Does the person's shin still hurt? Sure. Is the impact of the behavior still present, even if kicking him wasn't my intent? Sure. So the apology doesn't take away the pain. It just makes the kicker feel better and the one who was kicked look like a jerk if he continues to mention his hurting shin. Potentially, then, the ownership of the problem shifts to the one who is upset about being kicked. Seeing yourself as "well-meaning" removes responsibility for our actions. If no harm was meant, no offense should be taken.

Presenting ourselves as well-meaning is a classic way of playing our white race card. We've used our privilege to determine how others see us or at least how they talk about seeing us. We have positioned ourselves as above reproach, unable to be criticized. There is often a kind of arrogance that goes with "well-meaning," a piousness, a holier-than-thou tone. I heard it in a comment made by a white upper-middle class woman after a training on white privilege. It sounded so absurd to me that, in order not to laugh, I wrote it down on the closest piece of paper I could find—a napkin. She said, "If I raised a sexist, racist child, I would be crestfallen." *Crestfallen?* That's the feeling I get if the cake I'm making doesn't rise or if a surprise party I'm planning turns out not to be a surprise. It doesn't work in "If my daughter had a vicious character flaw, she's racist and sexist, I would be crestfallen," but maybe part of being "well-meaning" is that it's not so serious if your empathy and compassion don't develop well.

The same behavior and attitudes of well-meaning white people are talked about by other names: "goodwill whites,"[15] and "good intentions."[16] Joe Feagin talks about the "sincere fictions" that those of us who are white tell ourselves: "This self-definition involves the creation of 'sincere fictions'....In such personal characterizations, white individuals usually see themselves as 'not racist,' as 'good people,' even while they think and act in anti-Black ways."[17] Seeing ourselves as well-meaning presents a dilemma for us and for those people of color who interact with us. In my experience, it comes up like this: A person of color, fearful of criticizing a white person, will say in a telling tone, "Well, he *means* well." That's what's said. What's not said is that the person's actions don't match the person's sense of self: Meaning well doesn't equal doing well.

Naomi Wolf, author of *The Beauty Myth,* published a remarkable article in *Glamour,* titled "The Racism of Well-Meaning White People." Its perceptive honesty nails the behavior of what she calls WMWPs. She brings the discussion of barriers to clarity back around full-circle:

> Our racism has to do with how we see. It acts as a sort of shameful scrim, a dirty curtain woven of the fears and inequities that, in a racist culture, surround and envelop the fact of race....If one is dishonest and white, one pretends the scrim does not exist. But a white person in this country who claims to have no impediment of vision is not telling the whole truth.[18]

7

NOW THAT (I THINK) I UNDERSTAND WHITE PRIVILEGE, WHAT DO I DO?

During a break in a day-long session on white privilege that I was presenting at NCORE some years back, I was talking about my excitement at seeing an old friend. Before moving away, she had taught third grade at a private school in the Bay Area; she was the only African American teacher in a sea of wealthy white children and a few poor Latino and Black children that the school had recruited from another part of the city.

"I have always thought that if I had a child I would ship her or him off to my friend to raise, to be returned after adolescence. Then I know the child would be perfect," I said, only partly in jest. As fate would have it, a participant in my session—an African American woman whom I didn't know—overheard my comments. "Sounds like white privilege to me," she said as she walked by. "Oh," I thought as I listened again to what I had said, "that's exactly what it was."

I have long had a rule for myself: When I screw up, I have to talk about my mistake publicly and relatively quickly. This serves two purposes: First, it reminds me that I am always a beginner, no matter how much time I spend looking at my privilege; second, it provides a model for other white people that we're going to mess up regularly and that chances are good we won't die from it. If we use those times as learning opportunities, we might grow to be more like the person we want to be. So, after the break, I went back and told the story to a group of about 125 people. Not only did I not die, I learned again how tenuous my hold on "getting it" is, how quickly I am able to slip back into "structured blindness" while retaining the privilege of not looking incompetent to other white people.

Frequently, toward the end of a session on white privilege, a white person will ask, "So, now that I understand white privilege, what do I do?" And my response, after taking a deep breath that allows me to recover from my perception that the person is tired of listening to the painful reality, is almost always, "Not so fast." It took us a very long time to become so adept at using our privileges; it will take a great deal of work to learn how to use them differently—to remove barriers for people of color, not to erect them. As we move forward, I thought some concrete suggestions about joining learning and action might be helpful. I begin, as always, with the personal work, because it is the basis of everything else that we do. If we don't develop a practice of on-going assessment and exploration of our personal behavior, we are constantly at risk of undercutting the action we are involved in to dismantle white privilege.

One learning tool that I find helpful is the principles of dialogue as described in the works of Peter Senge[1] and David Bohm.[2] The three guiding principles are:

> ...listening with a willingness to be influenced, as though the speaker is really wise, and as an ally, to learn from others different from ourselves; suspension, the ability to notice and *temporarily* suspend one's reactions, feelings, opinions, and assumptions; and inquiry, to draw out inferences and assumptions (ours and others'), to uncover and reveal.[3]

I find listening to someone and being willing to "be influenced" and see that person as wise is a difficult task. Devoting that kind of energy to hearing someone with whom I disagree is really tough. And that is often what is necessary if we are to learn from and with people whose experience is very different from our own. One of my favorite examples of that sort of experience occurred relatively recently. Flying into work with a client for the first time, I was met by an older African American man, the limousine driver who took me to the hotel at which I was staying. The client is in Washington, and so I had been reading a copy of *The Washington Post* on the plane trip. One of the articles was about Jesse Helms, the then right-wing conservative Republican senator from North Carolina. Helms was long a foe of mine; I worked against his reelection many times, particularly when I was living in North Carolina. I began to talk about the article, and the African American man said, "I've worked with Jesse for years." At first I thought he was kidding, and then I assumed that I knew how he would feel, being Black and all. If I hated Helms' politics, surely this Black man would, I thought to myself.

Luckily a voice in my head said, "Get curious. Find out what he thinks." What proceeded was a fascinating conversation about his experiences with the senator over the years: how he feels truly welcome in Helms' house, he likes traveling with him, and he considers him a friend. The goal of listening and being willing to be influenced echoed in my head. I learned a lot in that conversation, about myself, this man, and Helms. While I will never respect Helms, during the conversation I did come to see him as more of a human being and less of a cartoon character. I have seen the limousine driver many times now. His main job is on Capitol Hill; his car service feeds his retirement fund. You never know when your assumptions will be challenged and you will hear something that will shift your perspective, if you are willing to listen.

The other two principles of dialogue are equally difficult for me; I think of working on them as building muscles. When we hear someone suggest suspending responses, opinions, and assumptions, even for a short while, it seems impossible and perhaps even undesirable. "Wait a minute—does that mean I'm not supposed to react, to show passion, to have an opinion?" a workshop participant asked. Actually it does, but not forever, just long enough to hear what the other person is really saying and to examine what that person's comments trigger in you.

Inquiry is also challenging for me, even though I have always been a relentless questioner. What is needed for genuine communication is often the information that the speaker leaves out because it is seems self-evident. Asking questions in a way that reveals the underlying meaning and talking about the unspoken is what inquiry is about. Most often, what you learn about are those aspects of a comment that are based on the speaker's history and context. For example, I don't have any idea, really, what a comment as apparently simple as "Isn't it sad that school lunchrooms are so segregated?" means. The person could be saying, "Isn't it sad that we've come such a short way since schools were desegregated?" or "How sad that the Asian American, African American, and Latina/o students segregate themselves from the white students," or "I wish we could all hold hands and sing 'Kum ba yah.'" Unless I take the time to search for what the speaker meant, I will probably project my biases about what I think he or she meant, make a judgment, and be off on another thought. All of that will happen in the blink of an eye. In short, no communication will have taken place.

I want to include one more piece about dialogue, written by Bill Issacs, a lecturer at Massachusetts Institute of Technology and director of The Dialogue Project there. Under the heading "A Safely Dangerous Setting," he brings up the very sensitive topic of "safety" in a dialogue and says, "People often express the desire to have a safe setting in which to explore difficult subjects and relationships. The safety of dialogue comes directly from the willingness to touch the dangerous. As one educator put it to me a while ago, 'Education is a process of endangering the soul in a spirit of enlightened discourse.'"[4] I have liked the mental image of a "safely dangerous setting" since I first read about it. I believe it is important to acknowledge the risk of conversations about race and systemically granted privileges and make an agreement to go ahead. I'll talk more about the concern about safety and how to address it in the next chapter.

It seems important to mention the phenomenon of guilt again as we talk about white people doing our on-going personal work. I continually hear people talking about it—either how they are made to feel responsible for all that "our people" have done and that makes them angry, or the genuine pain at hearing what other white people do to and about people of color and that makes them feel powerless. Guilt comes up about all different kinds of behavior, from the extreme and dramatic—the murders of Vincent Chin, James Byrd Jr.,[5] or Trayvon Martin—to the more mundane, daily experiences. Because guilt is cumulative, the last straw can come from some sort of horror story or a racial comment made in passing on TV; it almost doesn't matter in terms of its impact on us. Some examples: hearing a joke at the water cooler told by a white department chair in which he mimicked a Chinese accent and pulled the skin around his eyes to make them "slanted," forming an epicanthic fold; reading a list of some of the incidents in which nooses have been placed in schools or workplaces in which African Americans work—a New York City fire station, a Kansas City office of Consolidated Freightways, accompanied by racial slurs, a North Carolina transportation department maintenance shop, a school in Everett, Washington, in which a white student dangled a noose in front of a Black student;[6] hearing the story of a friend's biracial three-and-a-half-year-old daughter, half white, half Singaporean, who was told by three white nursery school playmates that she couldn't be the princess because there weren't any brown princesses—later, they told her she could be the dog; or listening to the story of the first week of school in a liberal Midwestern college town in which a white second grade teacher told her seven-year-old students that, given all of the shootings in schools around the country, she wanted them to watch out for people who might bring guns to school—particularly grownups or kids who were Black or Latino. A confused Latino boy went home and told his mom what the teacher had said, and the next morning the child's mother went to talk to the teacher and the principal. The teacher was surprised that the little boy had taken her warning personally. "I never meant to upset anyone; I just want the children to be watchful. We can't be too careful these days, with all the shootings in schools." (All the shootings the teacher was talking about were, of course, done by young white men.)

For this list, I deliberately chose recent incidents that, with the exception of some of the noose examples, were not headline grabbers. They are part of what Dr. Julianne Malveaux, the economist, and commentator, and college president, calls "have-a-nice-day racism"—daily occurrences for people of color at the hands of white people who are usually surprised that anyone took what they did seriously. The list of examples could go on for pages. This isn't about violent situations on a big scale. It is part of Patricia Williams' "spirit-murdering" category, and it is often invisible to white people. Pain or discomfort and guilt often come from hearing the stories, sensing the anguish that was caused, and either knowing what to do and not taking any action or not having a clue about what to do.

My belief about guilt, in general, is that it is not terribly useful. It often doesn't spur us to action, and, if it does, that response can be corrupted by our motivation—responding because we feel we have to rather than out of a generous spirit. White guilt, in particular, can become a quagmire of "Oh-I-wish-I-hadn't-done-that" or "If-only-I-had-said-something" or "I-never-know-what-to-say" or "I'm-so-disappointed-in-myself." Frequently what we're hoping will happen is that someone, and a person of color would be the best, will come to our rescue and tell us that "No one would have known what to do," "We all make mistakes," "Don't worry, you'll do better the next time" and reassure us that we're really good people after all.

For me, what is far more useful than getting mired in guilt is to understand that it is not about fault but rather about taking responsibility to do what you can to rectify the situation. When I asked her about white guilt, a friend of color said, "What good is white guilt to people of color....it is a useless expenditure of energy, and sometimes I find it more off-putting than some other white folks' behavior. It is, in my view, another way to not deal with present realities by feeling bad about past history....acknowledge it and move on."

On the other hand, I believe that there are lots and lots of white people who simply don't know what to do about the fact that so many horrible things have happened to people of color; they also don't know how to do something different. If they knew, they would try to do it. I also think that there are many people trying to make a difference and that all they know is how to work at an individual level because that is what we've been taught to do. I have spent my life working to move myself and others like me to a greater understanding of how our lives are shaped by whiteness. I have been blessed a thousand times over as guides and journey-companions, of color and white, have come into my life. They have been generous and forgiving of my lack-of-knowing, my insensitivity, and my inability to understand, while I have always been impatient with myself. Questions like "Why don't you do more? Why can't you better express your understanding in ways that communicate the urgency of doing things differently, more effectively?" fill my head on a regular basis.

It has often been incomprehensible to me that the white managers or administrators with whom I was working were in such denial about the pain they were causing the people of color who worked for them. Could they really not know the ramifications of the toxic environment, the differing expectations, and the regularity of vicious jokes that people of color were supposed to work in and through? And, whether they knew or not, didn't they understand their responsibility to make it right? I have gradually come to understand that, if I see and treat other white people as *they* instead of *we*, if I separate myself from the very folks with whom I say I am here to work, that I will never be as effective as I want to be. All of this has taken me to a bigger, more important question: What is the force that gets us to move ourselves into an unknown and uncomfortable place, to take our blinders off so that we are willing to see someone else's experience?

In order to put myself in other white people's shoes, I have begun to consider the nature of compassion and to say out loud, "I don't have very much compassion for myself or other white people. That is one of my challenges." For purposes of this exploration, I use a Buddhist definition of compassion expressed by Sharon Salzberg in her book *Lovingkindness*.

> Compassion…is the strength that arises out of seeing the true nature of suffering in the world. Compassion allows us to bear witness to that suffering, whether it is in ourselves or others, without fear; it allows us to name injustice without hesitation, and to act strongly, with all the skill at our disposal. To develop this mind state of compassion…is to learn to live, as the Buddha put it, with sympathy for all living beings, without exception.[7]

My hope is that, the more I explore, the more compassionate I will become; the more compassionate I am with myself and others, the better I will be at "bear[ing] witness" and "act[ing] strongly." For me, being compassionate means seeing all people as humans who struggle and suffer in their own lives. So being compassionate toward white people means my not minimizing or dismissing my own suffering or the suffering in other white individuals' lives in order to underscore the daily experiences people of color have because of racism. Taking the time and energy to meet people where they are and working with them to start there and move forward.

Remembering, as Rainer Maria Rilke said in his poem "Gratefulness": "If the angel deigns to come / it will be because you have convinced / her, not by tears but by your humble / resolve to be always beginning / to be a beginner."[8]

I am sure about one thing: I am not suggesting that only white people have work to do. However, because I am not of color, I don't feel comfortable proposing the nature of the work Latinos, African Americans, Native Americans, or Asian Americans should be doing about race. Further, I'm not asking people of color to have compassion or patience for white people as we grope toward understanding institutional racism, our privileges gained from it, or our complicity in it.

I have some fears regarding writing about focusing on compassion and thus implicitly suggesting that others do so as well. One is that, by my having compassion for myself or for other white people, we are somehow let off the hook for our participation in and collusion with the institutionally-held belief in white supremacy. That we hide in "All people suffer—we're all human beings under the skin" and "Their pain is no worse than mine." That, if we focus on each individual's suffering or the suffering in our own lives, those of us with privilege are less accountable for our behavior toward people of color as a group. In other words, our own suffering buys us out of having to take responsibility for the suffering we cause or are complicit in simply by belonging to a privileged class. Those of us who are white so frequently fail to remember that everything that happens in our lives occurs in the context of white supremacy—forgetting that fact is one of our most frequently used privileges.

I also have lots of questions. For those of us who do this work on institutional racism and white privilege and who are white, how do we deal with our feelings about those who fight directly or indirectly against us? If I hold them with anger and disdain, how can I connect myself enough to them to reach them? As a facilitator, how do I juggle the suffering of people who advertently or inadvertently cause suffering of others? Do we expect compassionate behavior from one group of people but not necessarily from others? Do we excuse those who have experienced a great deal of pain from being compassionate toward others? How can we be compassionate and challenging and fight for justice at the same time? But Salzberg's definition does not suggest being inactive. If I only am compassionate toward people who think like me or do not remind me of parts of myself I would like to ignore, how do I move to a place of forgiveness of my own shortcomings? In other words, do I have compassion only for those whom I deem to be "good" whites, thereby separating myself from other whites, from pieces of myself, and my discomfort with them? Our world is in such trouble that we have to use all the tools that we have, compassion key among them, to shift our direction. Clearly these ideas are a work in progress for me, but this thinking seems worth including. It might provide another opening to break through someone's defenses.

Moving from the heart to the head—balancing the need for the emotional intelligence required to think about guilt and compassion with the brainwork necessary to look at more subtle privileges—is the process of doing an inventory of our personal access to institutional power, resources, and influence based on race and socioeconomic class. This inventory is based on one created in 1970 by Sally Timmel[9] for use in the National YWCA. The original purpose of the exercise was to push white women to explore ways in which we had access to power, resources, and influence that had never occurred to us. By looking at the businesses we patronize, the organizations to which we belong, and the people and businesses that provide services to us, we began to see the daily systems of support to which we have access purely on the basis of our race and class. This access is most often the result of a combination of race and class, not one or the other. In most of my work on white privilege I have been careful not to talk about class because I see it as a way those of us who are white escape having to deal with our race. Far too often I have heard, "The issue is not really race; it's class." The implication is that all people within a certain class, regardless of race, receive the same privileges—that white privilege doesn't really exist. History and research are laden with evidence that this is simply not true, but many white people hold on to the myth. As we explore another layer of white privilege, it becomes crucial to examine the tangle of race and class. Always understood is that we do this in the context of the institutionalized dominance of whiteness.

Personal access to institutional influence, power, and resources is an aspect of white privilege that, even for those of us who have it, seems more amorphous than others. For those who don't have this set of privileges, they are almost unimaginable. These privileges are a combination of power and mindset. Access to power and resources is tangible. The mindset of entitlement reinforces the concrete privileges and holds them in place. This aspect of privilege reflects the entanglement of race and class, and it is hard to tease the pieces apart. Further, it seems to be extremely nebulous, hard to see, and hard to hold onto. The question to keep asking is, "In this situation is my access greater than that of other individuals because of my race or my class or both?"

We are so used to moving through the world in the ways that we do that often we are not aware of the shortcuts that are provided by this set of privileges. For those of us who are white or those people of color who are upper-middle class, part of this privilege appears to be personal and to apply to us as individuals, as opposed to us as members of our race or class group. The adage, "It's not what you know but who you know," reflects the privilege of having access to someone who can make things happen but also the sense that it is about me personally—I just *happen* to know so-and-so. It's "being in the right place at the right time." In the main, however, where we are and who we know has everything to do with the race, class, gender, sexual orientation, ability, and religious groups of which we are a part, although those of us who have these privileges usually see them as having to do with our personal good luck, intelligence, or social skills.

Until very recently, for example, African Americans, Latinos/as, American Indians, and Asian Americans were excluded (intentionally or not) from groups where the opportunity to know someone who might provide access was possible, such as, social clubs, expensive neighborhoods, or white sororities and fraternities. That is changing somewhat as we see a few African American men, for example, becoming CEOs of Fortune 500 companies. Part of the privilege of not understanding this personal access to power, resources, and influence is reflected in the comment of the former American Express CEO when he announced the current CEO of American Express, an African American man. "[Chenault] happens to be black. He could be green. It's a simply irrelevant characteristic."[10] If we see race or gender as irrelevant characteristics, we have to question why white men, with very few exceptions, head all of the major institutions in this country. Either race, class, gender, sexual orientation, and physical disability are relevant to an individual's ability to gain power and access to power, influence and resources, or all people of color, women, gays and lesbians, people with disabilities, and working class people are personally deficient. If 51 percent of the country's population is female and we believe that gender is irrelevant, how do we account for the fact that women hold a very small portion of the decision-making positions in American institutions? The same question could be posed about people of color as a group or people with physical disabilities as a group.

What are some specific ways in which these privileges function? By looking closely at experiences we have in everyday life, we become better at recognizing both the assumptions on which our behavior and that of others is based and when we are using race and class privilege. Because we cannot give our privileges back, our best options are to be clear about what they are, work actively not to employ them or to use them in a way that benefits those who do not have them.

At dinner one night, a friend told a few of us this story about an experience she had with her bank. It provides a model for understanding privileges on which experiences are based. Though she had earlier moved to Berkeley from the East Coast, she bought a house in an economically and racially diverse neighborhood in Oakland, California, a city with a large African American population. Her bank, Wells Fargo, has branches all over the Bay Area. She had opened her accounts at the North Berkeley branch years before, when she lived in that upper-middle class, predominantly white neighborhood. Perhaps naively, she assumed that the rules that applied to her account would be the same in all branches of the bank. Confident that the money would be credited to her account immediately rather than being held until it cleared, she waited to deposit checks that would cover her income taxes until April 14th. Then she deposited two checks, written by well-known corporations, to her account; she counted on their being credited immediately and thus covering her payments to the IRS. She made her deposit at the Oakland branch. On April 18th she received a note in the mail stating that her checks were being held until the bank received funds from the check writers to cover them, a fairly standard procedure for some customers in some banks. She was furious that the bank had put a hold on her checks and nervous that the IRS wouldn't be paid. Using her class privilege, she called the branch officer to find out what had happened and what they were going to do to remedy the situation. The officer explained that, because this Oakland branch had a much more "diverse" clientele than the North Berkeley branch, it was their policy to hold all checks over a certain amount. When she asked what he meant by more "diverse," he said that as they had so many African American customers that they, naturally, had to be more careful. She said that this sounded like a racist practice, and he responded that it wasn't racist; it was good business. She asked to speak to his superior, related the story, and asked what they were going to do to address this issue. The supervisor told her that they would look into the policy.

Taking this example apart, we find some of the aspects of my friend's race and class privilege. It didn't occur to her that the Oakland branch would treat customers differently than the North Berkeley branch did. She assumed that the bank would know her by her credit history, even though they did not know her personally, and would credit her account before the bank got paid. She believed that, due to her race and class, the senior officer to whom she was speaking would talk to her even though she was obviously angry. She was able to complain and then to let the matter go, since her access to resources hadn't changed because she had raised a ruckus.

The responses to the story around the dinner table revealed each person's race and class perspectives. Two people, one Latina and one white, both raised in the working class, rolled their eyes and laughed at the storyteller. Each said she would never have counted on the bank's clearing the checks so quickly and wondered why our friend had been so foolish. "Don't you know that the IRS doesn't take kindly to people bouncing their payments?" they asked in disbelief. A third, an African American man who worked for another bank, talked about how banks treat their customers differently, depending on their account histories. Given his assumptions about our friend's credit, he was mildly surprised that the bank hadn't covered the checks. What he was amazed at was the fact that the bank officer was so honest about the racial disparities in their practices. For him, the officer had made a foolish public relations mistake. A white man at the table, who also had his accounts at Wells Fargo, was so angry about the officer's assumptions about the Black people who lived in Oakland that he decided to move his accounts to a different bank and did so the next morning. As I listened to the story, I was particularly struck by the class arrogance on which our friend had based her assumptions: that the problem was the bank's and not hers, and that they would take care of their mistake. I said as much, and we talked about the level of privilege required for her to be able to rationalize her actions.

   I see the story and the discussion as a kind of model for how we might look at our actions better to understand our hidden assumptions. Everyone at the table had the opportunity to think about what they might have done in the same situation and what part of their own history would have been reflected in their behavior. They also shared personal information with each other that might prompt future conversations about privilege. Because of the gender, race, and class differences of the people in the conversation, everyone there was able to hear how those aspects of identity have influenced each individual's various perspectives, so there was learning on that level as well.

   As we know now, getting a loan for a house is not a "simple" process for anyone except for those who are the wealthiest, the one percent of the United States population. For others, the transactions are rife with race and class privilege. As I have talked about in several places and documented in Chapter 4, research has shown for years that people of color are less likely to get a housing loan than white people, given exactly the same financial background. A white person is assumed more worthy of getting a loan unless she or he proves otherwise, unlike people of color who are assumed *un*worthy until they are able to prove worthiness. Credit records are read differently depending on race (again, the assumption of qualified until one proves she or he is not versus the assumption of not qualified until she or he is able to prove differently). For a small reminder of what happens here, look back at Franklin Raines' speech at Howard University, mentioned in Chapter 4. The privilege of access to power, resources, and influence in buying a house is subtle and tied to race and class.

In a letter written to her white daughter and published in COLORLINES, a white mother said something I tend to forget.

> ...please remember that there was an unemployment crisis in the Black community long before there was an economic crisis in America as a whole. Black unemployment went largely ignored. It wasn't until the problems hit white America that the public and politicians took notice and even called it a crisis.[11]

In 1994 when I was buying my house, my realtor sent me to a loan broker whom she knew and with whom she had a good relationship. I met with him, talked about my financial situation, and filled out papers. I was asked for very few supporting documents. I didn't, for example, have to show him any tax returns even though I am self-employed and therefore considered a greater credit risk. When they ran a credit check, they found that in 1986 I had a late payment on a credit card. The loan broker called and suggested that I write a letter for my file stating that I had been out of the country at the time the payment was due. He was sure there wouldn't be any problem. If one is not paying attention, the interactions in this story could look personal, rather than having anything to do with privilege. My realtor wanted me to be able to buy the house so she took me to her friend the loan broker. I was an affable person, I looked like the people he knows and who live in his neighborhood, and I had been vouched for by someone he knew. Privilege smoothed my path. One of my challenges as a white person is to be realistic about all that went into my securing a loan. I must be clear that I did not get this loan purely on my own merits. My race and class opened doors beyond those that would have been opened for others—"beyond the advantages of most," part of the definition of *privilege*.

It is essential to note that, since the first edition of this book was published in 2006, the world's economy was put at risk. Government bailouts saved banks and industries considered "too big to fail," but millions of people lost their jobs or their homes or both. The whole conversation about loans and real estate has been reframed.

> The end of the housing boom in 2006 set in motion a vicious circle that led to disaster for millions of homeowners whose property has been seized or threatened, and for the lenders themselves, who have had to write off tens of billions in losses.

Foreclosures helped accelerate the fall of property values, helping spur more foreclosures....Tens of millions of others found themselves in homes worth less than their mortgages, unable to sell or refinance.

All told, roughly four million families lost their homes to foreclosure between the beginning of 2007 and early 2012.

In late 2010, evidenced [sic] emerged that the foreclosure process many have been deeply tainted by sloppy recordkeeping, cut corners and possible fraud, epitomized by high-profile cases of "robo-signing"—cases in which foreclosures took place based on forged or unreviewed documents. [12]

A study published by United for a Fair Economy in December 2008 reported that "people of color are more than three times as likely [as whites] to have subprime loans" and that high-cost loans account for 55 percent of loans to African-Americans and Latinos.[13] Further, a study by the Center for Responsible Lending found that "borrowers of color...were more than 30 percent more likely to receive a higher-rate loan than white borrowers, *even after accounting for differences in risk*." [14] [Emphasis added.]

So, while the housing and job markets have contracted significantly, another aspect of race and class privilege remains essentially unchanged. That privilege, frequently taken for granted by those of us who have it and glaringly absent for those who don't, is access to power and influence through personal contacts. This tends to correlate with wealth. It is the ability of the top five percent to place one or two phone calls to the top one percent, people with informal or positional power, and influence a decision. The privilege looks different for white people than it does for people of color, because usually people of color who have class privilege have to go through white people to get to decision makers; white people who have both race and class privilege go through their friends. Here's an example: A middle class young woman was accepted to a prestigious university. Because of a recent divorce and family money complications, the student applied for and received financial aid. Her mother wasn't satisfied with the amount of aid the university was giving her daughter, so she called a family friend, who *happens* to be a lawyer for the trustees of the institution. The lawyer called the president of the university, the president called a vice president, the vice president called the director of financial aid, and the young woman was given a second financial aid package, thereby denying another student aid.

Frequently, when people talk about race and class privileges, they describe them in terms of what those with privilege have access to and freedom from. Here's a short list: the privilege of access to privacy, space, relative safety (as in a gated community), relative quiet, abortions and other medical care, money at low interest rates, a career (interesting work), a sense of self-worth (based on race and class privileges for white people and on class privilege for people of color, although damaged by the supremacy of whiteness), good child care, good schools, access to fresh foods. And the privilege of freedom from: sharing inadequate living space with many people, a fifth-floor walk-up, the worst abuses of the legal system, a job that consumes your body, close supervision at work, and/or cleaning your own living space.

Obviously there are many other aspects of the privilege of having personal access to institutional power, resources, and influence based on our race and class. The ones listed above provide a starting—or continuing—place for exploring our privileged status. The inventory that follows offers us a second tool. Like the series of examples, it is designed to help us better understand the many ways in which access to power, resources, and influence are based on race and class, rather than our individual good luck and behavior. It is also meant to break through the denial of the fact that, purely on the basis of skin color, those of us who are white have institutional power and access to resources different from those who are not white. When we add socioeconomic class to the equation, upper-middle-class people of color become part of the privileged group, based on their class status, while skin-color privilege is still withheld from them.

First, think about the businesses you patronize—your banks, grocery stores, clothing stores, insurance companies, prescription drug stores, mortgage lenders. What contacts do you have in each business? Are you able to influence decisions? If so, how? How do the employees treat you, even if you are not a known and trusted customer? What do you do if you run into a roadblock with a junior employee? Do you have any way of influencing the outcome of a decision that affects you? Do you have friends in high places within that or an associated business? How were those relationships formed? Can you pull strings to get what you want? How did you gain the personal ability to influence decisions and behavior? How might your answers to these questions be attributed to "benefits...beyond the advantages of most"? In other words, could anyone, from any race or class group, be treated in exactly the same way or influence decisions in the ways that you are able to? If not, chances are very good that you are experiencing the effects of having racial or class privilege.

Next, think about the social, political, and religious organizations with which you or your friends or relatives are affiliated. For example, the Rotary Club, the YWCA or YMCA, Hadassah, the NAACP, sororities or fraternities, Links, the PTA, labor unions, the Junior League, the Knights of Columbus, the Lions' Club, and political parties. How did you become a member? Do you have friends or relatives who are or have been a part of this organization? In what ways are the other members similar to you by race and class? How might race or class subtly affect membership or leadership? What influence, power, or access to resources or power holders do you have? Do family members or friends have? Do you feel like you're able to say what's on your mind and have your ideas listened to in meetings or at organizational functions?

Once we become clear about the process of examining our access to power, influence and resources based on membership in our racial and class groups, we are able to see more clearly how our daily life is affected. For example, our experiences with service providers in education, healthcare, legal services, and our treatment by the judicial system are dramatically affected by our race and class. So are our experiences with the services provided by government, the fire department, police department, garbage collectors, street cleaners, tree trimmers, street repair people, and so on.

One of the nation's institutions where disparate experiences are most glaring is healthcare. What do your responses to the following questions tell you about your race and class privilege? What is your access to quality care? If your insurance company or HMO doesn't give you the answer you want, what is your response? How many phone calls do you make? Whom do you call to help you get what you need? The racial bias in healthcare is well-documented. At a more subtle level, how is your ability to influence decisions about care affected by your race, gender, and class? How many calls do you have to make to get a second opinion or see the top specialist in a field?

What is your experience with the educational system? What access do you have to influence the decisions made about your education or that of your children? Do you have the privilege to determine how your children are disciplined? If you attended a private school, how has that experience affected the networks to which you are connected? Consider the community in which you live. How does the tax base (socioeconomic class of residents) influence the public education available? Relative to higher education, how did you get into college? Did your access to influence play a part? What, if anything, did your family have to give up so that you could go to college? Were you admitted because of your parents' connection to the institution? If you work in a college or university, how many and what steps do you have to go through to influence a decision being made at the top levels of the institution?

Consider how treatment by the police or the judicial system is linked to your class and race. When you are driving, for example, when are you pulled over by the police? When you have broken the law or when you are DWB (driving while Black) or DWA (driving while Asian) or DWL (driving while Latino)? Our DWW (driving while white) is usually a very different experience. If you are stopped, how are you treated? If you are treated badly, what are your options for getting the lawyer of your choice? Do you have any (legal) power to assure that the police officer who treated you badly is penalized? Consider the phrase "Justice or Just us." Are you part of the "us" at any level, based on your race or class?

Finally, those who work in the academy or in the corporate world and have race or class privilege (faculty members, managers, and administrators) also have access to institutional power, resources, and influence that is not available to those who are not similarly privileged. Our task, if we are to continue to do the excavation necessary fully to understand, and therefore to alter, our privileged status, is to explore how class and/or race privilege affect our experience within the institution. Put succinctly, this privilege is the ability to interact informally, based on knowledge and relationships not included in our formal job descriptions—the ability and opportunity to pick up the phone to help a friend's son or your daughter get into college or to get a fellowship or to study abroad.

Here are situations in which race and class privilege are present and powerful. The task is to ask ourselves how, where, and when these opportunities present themselves with people who hold positional or informal power in academic and corporate settings. Where do we have connections that are not part of the narrow parameters of our jobs? A hypothetical example: I go to the grocery store in my neighborhood and run into the Vice President of Academic Affairs where I teach. As we both sort through the organic vegetables, I say casually, "Oh, I've been meaning to call you about Jeanine's tenure. Why don't you come sit on the deck and we can talk?" There are lots of ways that these kinds of connections occur: patronizing the same businesses, socializing at parties, seeing one another at weddings and funerals, visiting at the symphony or opera or jazz or salsa clubs.

Such connections often happen around children's activities: Your children go to the same schools, have the same dance teacher, the same piano teacher, are in school plays together. You and your partner and other couples go to the same church, travel together, play golf or tennis at the same place, belong to the same country club or swim clubs. Many times work-related activities that take place outside of work hours bring people together: belonging to or being advisors of sororities, fraternities, alumnae/i associations, social or political clubs, professional or academic organizations, Phi Beta Kappa, the MacArthur Fellows. Professional connections also provide opportunities that are privilege-based such as having the same publisher, being active in union leadership, serving on committees together, sharing a research assistant or project, being in the same department, or being in the same field but at different organizations or institutions. And that is just an initial list. My hope is that it will prompt you to look at the daily minutiae of your life to get clear about how institutionally bestowed race and class privilege play out in your personal experience.

If one is a change agent, these informal encounters also provide lots of occasions to influence conversations and decisions about how the organization deals with all sorts of issues that have racial implications. In fact, I would bet that that's the way most decisions are influenced, through interpersonal interactions among power holders. So we not only need skills in identifying the roles that white privilege plays, but we also need to get better and better at using our privileges to bring about institutional change. One of the ways to do that is intentionally to keep whiteness explicit in a conversation. Not central, but explicit. By doing that, we are bringing it into line with the way other races are dealt with.

Before discussing how to do this, however, let's look at the assumptions these strategies are based on. First, in the United States today, race is generally spoken of as something people other than white people have. There are "people," which often translates as white people, and then there are Asian American people, African American people, Latina/o people, American Indian people, and biracial and multiracial people. Second, in predominantly white institutions we talk about students' needs and then we talk about the needs of students of color. We don't often openly acknowledge that the reason students of color have needs different from those of white students is their experience of being seen and treated as "other" in the institution. Referring to students of color separately is itself an act of reinforcing their otherness, stating what occurs in a system which assumes the superiority of one racial group.

One of the ways for white people to take responsibility for our whiteness is to be explicit about the role that our race plays in our lives and in others'. Our goal is to work toward dismantling the perceived supremacy of whiteness on which all of our systems are based. To be most effective in dismantling systemic white supremacy, we need to be strategic about how we put whiteness on the conversation table. Doing this requires a delicate balance. On one hand, it is essential that we address the different needs of students or employees of color. On the other, we need to heighten the visibility of the racial component of white people's identity without keeping or moving ourselves to the center of the discussion. Increasingly, I talk about playing *my* "race card." I mention it casually, like a parenthetical phrase. "Of course, when I walk into a room I play my race card. I bring my whiteness with me. When Jill [another white woman in the room] and I sit down for a conversation, our whiteness is all over the table. It's not bad or good; it just is."

Here are three reasons for using the following strategies for keeping whiteness explicit. The first is to make those of us who are white conscious of how being white affects our experience daily. If we don't understand how we are complicit, intentionally or not, in keeping systemic white superiority in place, we cannot act to change it. The second is to name what frequently goes unnamed—whiteness—so that it becomes an open part of the conversation. The third is to shift to addressing the needs of white students *as a racial group*, while we continue to concern ourselves with the necessity of meeting the needs of students of color.

The first step in keeping whiteness explicit is a personal one. Begin looking at yourself in the mirror every morning or saying to yourself out loud, "What am I, a white person, going to do today?" The question doesn't mean, "What am I, a white person, going to do today about race?" Simply, "What is on the docket today for me—a person who is white?" The answer might be to go to the grocery store or to the beach. It might be to go to work or to take a child to the doctor. The purpose is to begin to be fully conscious that, whether you know it or not or feel particularly good about it, that's the reality in the racial context in which we live. And then you leave the house and begin to practice these strategies as you move around in the world.

Notice how often other races are named when, in similar situations, the white race is not. Many of us who are white are oblivious when this occurs, while most people of color are only too aware of this phenomenon. The practice of identifying others' races is particularly troublesome when the person's race is associated with a widely-held stereotype like African American men committing crimes or Asian Americans winning academic honors in the sciences.

Begin to document when race is identified and when it is not. Keep a small notebook and a pen with you. Make notes as you watch what happens in the media and in people's conversations. (This is not a time to criticize people around you who are not naming their whiteness.) For example, in 2001 when Shirley Caldwell Tilghman became the president of Princeton her gender was noted—she is the first woman to be Princeton's president—but neither the gender (male) nor the race (white) of the outgoing Princeton president, Harold Shapiro, was mentioned. I remember the morning after Chang-Lin Tien was named chancellor at UC Berkeley. The *Oakland*

Tribune had a front-page story about his being selected. With the story was a photograph of him, under which were the words "Qualifications impeccable." I was struck by how the (white) public had to be reassured, either because he was Chinese or because he was the only non-white leader the university has had. It is important to note here that race and gender are always potential factors. Not mentioning them does not mean that they are not at play.

If you are white, as you talk about yourself and your perspective on things, identify yourself racially to clarify that this is one of the lenses through which you see things. This is a tactic to shift away from business as usual, which is either that no race is mentioned or that only people of color verbally identify themselves. For example, "As a white person on this search committee, I feel that we don't have all of the voices necessary to make a good decision," or "I am conscious that my being white plays a role in our meetings, just as everyone else's race plays a role." This is something to do regularly but not constantly; if you do it thirty times a day, which you certainly could given how often whiteness is assumed but not acknowledged, it loses its meaning for those around you. It would be like all of the times I mentioned the Aunt Jemima posters on the wall in the restaurant in Chapel Hill that I talked about in Chapter 1. It wasn't an effective strategy.

If you are white, challenge yourself to identify everyone who is white as a matter of course, just as we often mention other people's race if they are of color. An exercise called the Race Game was created by an African American theologian named Thandeka. It is described in her book, *Learning to Be White*. "The Race Game...has one rule. For a week, the player, in all white settings, must use the word *white* whenever he or she mentions the name of a Euro-American." [15] One person playing this game reported:

> Every time I decided to play the game with someone new, I felt that I was about to be rejected, that the person would turn away, and that I would be shunned. I felt terrible....Before I said it, I'd hesitate as if I were about to stutter, and I don't stutter—ever! I am never at a loss for words. But now I couldn't pronounce the word. [16]

Thandeka believes that the feeling that is revealed while playing the Race Game is "shame—an acute sense of exposure, loss of trust, abandonment, and humiliation...." [17]

Obviously, what comes up when you do something like this is not only your internal uneasiness about race and being white but other white people's discomfort and unsettledness as well. We may think before we begin that it can't be that hard, when really what we're doing is breaking the agreement between us and other whites: "I won't mention this dreaded, taboo topic if you won't." Being shunned—literally treated as though you are not present—is an enormous penalty for saying something seemingly small. It reminds us again of our pathology surrounding the issue of race.

In conversations about students, while faculty and school administrators are appropriately focusing on the particular needs of those of color, they also need to look at white students and how best to serve them as members of a racial group. This, too, is a surprisingly difficult task to do. Many see that Black and Latina/o, Asian American and Native American students' lives are hugely affected by their skin color; that this is also true for white students as a racial group is not so clear. Too often we don't ask a critical question: "What do we need to be doing for white students to help them figure out what it means to be white in America and how to work effectively in a diverse environment with people who are different from them?" This is a conversation in which both white people and people of color should be involved. If done well, this strategy does not put white people back into the center; rather, it balances the task of addressing race and makes it clear that white students also need skills for living in a diverse world. The skills are different from those needed by students of color, but skill development is necessary all the same. The challenge for white students is to get them to identify with being white, acknowledge the importance that whiteness has in their lives, move them past feeling like they are victims of affirmative action and the attention paid to people of color, and help them to feel empowered to become change makers.[18]

Begin to challenge who is meant by "students" or "people." For example, is the Student Union as hospitable to various students of color as it is to white students? Does the Heritage Room of Central State University reflect the heritage of white people or of all people? Does the student newspaper feature stories about people of color similarly to the ways it does about white students, that is, are most of the sports articles about Black people while the student government and fraternity and sorority coverage is about white people?

This gets back to the very first story in the book, the one in which my airplane seatmate asked about "Balkanization" which is often code for people of color separating themselves from white people. What my seatmate and many others—both white and of color—miss is that there are reasons that people of color form their own groups. Often they are creating a place where they are comfortable and have power to influence and make decisions. The Congressional Black Caucus formed to create a greater power base in Congress because they felt their interests were not being represented, just as the Black Caucus of the American Library Association did. The librarians forming it believed that *white* was understood but not stated in the "American Library Association," as in so many other associations. The Black Student Unions at colleges and universities around the country are created for the same purpose, as are the multitude of student organizations for groups of color. They are generally formed in what are called PWIs—predominantly white institutions.

It is emotionally and perhaps intellectually hard for some white people to understand that there is a huge difference between a White Student Union and a Black Student Union. In PWIs, the student unions, like the schools, were built for white people, and then people of color were admitted. The schools didn't automatically change their culture when they brought students, faculty, and staff of color in, so organizations were formed to provide welcoming places. Please hear me clearly: This does not mean that all the white people at all the institutions are terrible people waiting to be inhospitable to people of color when they walk on campus. While there are probably some of those in every institution, given our nation's past and present, that is not what I'm talking about. But virtually all colleges, universities, and corporations in this country, with the exception of those institutions that were explicitly built for people of color—Tribal Colleges for American Indians, HBCUs (Historically Black Colleges and Universities), and a few institutions like the National Hispanic University—and corporations owned and run by people of color, were built by and for the people like those who framed our Constitution. This is not about all those folks being bad people. It is about maintaining power in the hands of those who run the nation: white, upper-middle class, heterosexual, Christian, able-bodied men.

As I said in Chapter 6, my friend challenged me, as a white woman, to see white people as *my people*. His push has produced a profound shift toward beginning to do that, but it is in no way easy. Here are my tactics so far: I consciously identify and read about white anti-racist activists. Having positive role models is essential for me: I need to see myself in an on-going procession rather than on a lonely walk, and I need an antidote to the actions of contemporary white people who activate my sense of shame at my people's actions. When I am dismayed by the behavior and decisions of our white male national leaders, I intentionally focus on how their—our—white privilege has contributed to their perceptions of what is acceptable and necessary. Rather than holding a model of good whites and bad whites, I concentrate on my conviction that being good or bad is an equal opportunity phenomenon that cannot be ascribed solely to one group. White people are white people. That is simply part of our identity.

And we have been given unearned privileges that affect each of our lives every minute of every day. Those privileges give us the responsibility, not the guilt, of taking action to dismantle the systems that give us privilege and power.

I close this chapter with one of my favorite stories about using our privilege to bring about change. During the spring of 1999, students in Ethnic Studies at the University of California-Berkeley held a hunger strike protesting the lack of institutional support for the department. While the details of the strike and its settlement are complicated, an individual's access to influence appears to have played a remarkable part. The following column was published in the *San Francisco Chronicle* on May 14, 1999:

> Here's a little back-channel talk about how that hunger strike over the ethnic studies cuts at UC Berkeley was resolved last week.
>
> Last Thursday, Assemblywoman Carole Migden [a white woman] got a call from an African American professor friend who teaches ethnic studies. The prof was distraught, telling the assemblywoman that hunger strikers were keeling over and that the chancellor wasn't budging.
>
> Migden—herself a former student activist who now chairs the Assembly Appropriations Committee—promptly called UC's Sacramento lobbyist and hinted that the students might not be the only ones starving if the impasse continued.
>
> Considering that UC had about $67 million in bills in front of Migden's committee, it must have been a very interesting conversation— because the next day, the chancellor met with the students.[19]

8
TALKING ABOUT RACE
What If They Call Me a Racist?

In a Human Resources department, the majority of the employees at all levels were white. There was, however, one African American middle manager, a woman. For several months, she watched the people at the front counter helping employees who came in to ask questions. She thought she saw a pattern of their spending a longer time with white employees, asking more questions to get at the roots of their concerns, and responding in a more professional yet caring manner. With people of color they were rude and gave their concerns short shrift. One front-line person, in particular, stuck out to her. She tried to talk herself out of what she thought she thought she was noticing, telling herself she was being too sensitive. She asked her manager, a white woman, to take a look, was told that everything looked fine. Finally, at a management meeting at which employee raises were being discussed, she lost it. "How can you talk about giving these people raises? They treat people of color very differently that they treat white people. It's just racist!" No one at the table spoke; there was quiet for about a minute, and then the meeting went on as if nothing had been said.

This story is symptomatic of what our conversations about race often sound like. For one person or another who's involved in the conversation, the blurt method is used—saying a great deal quickly without measuring words for impact—because people have so much to say and so few places in which to say it. Too frequently that is followed either by a total shutdown or a defensive response, and communication between the two people or within the group falters. In this instance, no one said anything, and six months later the employee was transferred. Not only was there no communication, but an enormous amount of white privilege and institutionalized racism was used first to silence the African American woman and then to determine her fate in the organization.

Rather than starting with what useful conversations about race might be like and how we as white people might address the "r" word (*racist*), which we will do later in this chapter, I thought it would be helpful to begin with some basic guidelines. My assumption is that few of us, regardless of color, find it particularly easy to have authentic cross-race conversations, and that all of us could use more skills. It is my experience and belief that we won't, as a nation, talk about race, and that, until we address racial issues in our country at the systemic, cultural, interpersonal, and personal levels, we will remain in racial conflict, stymied by our past, and unable to build a future that includes all of us.

Given that we want to communicate better with people who are different from us, and given that we want to use our unearned privileges to make systemic and personal changes, there are some things we need to remember. For example, we can't rely on old patterns or our own intuitions to keep us on the right track when we are talking to someone who is different from us. That's the platinum rule of diversity. The golden rule—Do unto others as you would have them do unto you—might be useful for people who are like us because we then have some sense of how we would like to be treated and can bet that they might like to be treated in that same way. There is much less assurance that people who are different from us will want what we want; they might, but, because they have different experiences, realities, and needs, we can't know that. So the platinum rule of diversity is: Do unto others as they would like to be done unto—treat other people as they would like to be treated, not necessarily as you would. Of course, in order to be able to do that, you have to pay attention to their needs and desires.

You have to move yourself from the center of your attention without losing sight of the place from which you are starting. This sounds much more complicated than it really is. Let me give you an example. As I said in Chapter 1, my father died when I was four. I have very few memories of him, but one is that when he would come home from work, after picking me up and giving me a hug, he would squat down on the floor, stick out his hand and say, "Now, look me straight in the eye and give me a really firm handshake." Consequently, I look people straight in the eye and have a strong handshake. What I want to communicate is "I am present, I am paying attention, I am pleased to meet you." Based on the golden rule, that would work universally. However, looking people straight in the eye has very different meanings culturally. People in some cultures believe that it is arrogant to look people squarely in the eye, and, in fact, it wasn't a safe thing, historically, for a Black man to do to a white person in the southern United States. In order to show respect, Black people were supposed to lower their eyes just as they were supposed to step aside for a white person to pass on the sidewalk.

Shaking hands, particularly firmly, is also problematic. For a white person to shake the hand of a person of color could communicate "I'm in charge," not "I am here with you." People in some American Indian tribes don't believe you should touch strangers, so I am using my white privilege to behave in ways that make me comfortable, without being told by the other person that it's okay. Hugging, of course, is another example. For a man, who by definition has gender privilege, to decide that he is going to hug a woman without first asking permission is using his male privilege. A similar thing would be true if a white woman hugged someone racially different without checking first. Checking isn't so difficult. "May I give you a hug?" or "May I shake your hand?" will do. People in the corporate world who work internationally are very clear that cultural differences or a show of cultural privilege can make or break a business deal.

There are things we need to know about ourselves in terms of communication style. I'm sure it won't surprise you to know that I communicate fairly straightforwardly and plainly. I am able to soften what I say in all sorts of ways, and my preference is to speak honestly and in ways that I can be best heard. My class and race privilege make that candor more possible. I value open communication, even if that means I hear things I would rather not hear. However, it's important to say that I feel that way based on my definition of *openness*; it means very different things to different people, depending on the amount of privilege one has, on culture, region of the country, and so on. So it is important to know as much as you can about the cultural rules of communication for the person with whom you are speaking (and for the organization in which you are working). In many cultures, for example, directly confronting someone is highly impolite, akin to calling the person a liar. What is personal information is, in large part, culturally determined, so be particularly careful if you are talking about money, family, politics, religion, or jobs. Even if you think you should be able to say how you feel, it may not be okay in that setting.

My experience in cross-race conversations about race is that most people, regardless of race, are cautious about what they say. People of color who work in predominantly white settings guard themselves carefully, knowing they have to survive in a system in which they are alien. White people, generally speaking, are publicly careful because they don't want to offend anyone, but privately, from stories I have heard, more and more racist language is being used in the workplace. I prefer to know and to say what I believe to be true, both personally and professionally. Part of my ability to do that, of course, comes from my race and class privilege. However, I do know that some of what I say, particularly about race and about organizational climate, has probably been somewhat "career limiting." I am willing to give bad news, as well as good, and then roll up my sleeves to help the institution figure out what to do about what they have been told.

Over the past ten years, I have noticed an increasing propensity in colleges, universities, and corporations to shrink from the truth about themselves. While they say they want to "create hospitable climates for diverse employees, students, and faculty," my experience is that they don't really know what that looks like, they often don't know where to start, and that most organizations don't have the backing of those in positions of power to carry out the long-term changes required. A great deal of leadership development is part of changing the institution. Given that, the "truth" that they want to hear is limited primarily to positive, superficial things. (I hurry to say that that is a generalization; there are some senior administrators who are extremely serious about creating an inclusive environment and will do all that they can to facilitate that.)

What "conflict" looks and sounds like is culturally determined, both in terms of ethnic culture and organizational culture. I grew up in a household in which raising your voice was considered conflict, so I have had to work hard to gain skills in using conflict effectively. Like anger, conflict is a very important tool that can be used to move a personal relationship or an organizational culture forward in ways that false niceness can't. However, again in my experience, conflict-averse organizational cultures abound, particularly where the issue of race is concerned. The prerequisite of "everyone"—which usually means those who have privilege—feeling "safe" in a conversation with those who aren't the privilege-holders stifles the honesty of hard truths, and institutional environments stay as they are or move backward. One way of keeping track of how conflict is seen in interactions is to use right-hand column (what was said) and left-hand column (what you were thinking) analysis to reveal what you and perhaps others are feeling or thinking but not saying.

Like a lot of other white Anglo-Saxon Protestants, I am not particularly comfortable with loud voices. I have learned, however, that, in many cultures and in some big families, raising your voice is simply a mechanism for being heard. When some of us WASPs hear loud, passionate feelings about an issue, we misinterpret the passion as anger, get nervous, and pull back. By doing that, we miss opportunities for real conversations about the feelings and perspectives of people ethnically or racially different from us.

It is very important for those of us who have both race and class privilege to explore continually our shifting biases toward people for whom English is not their first language, who speak Black English (Ebonics), or whose spoken English doesn't meet our standards. In working with clients, I find both subtle, covert biases and open righteous indignation toward people whose language and grammar don't measure up to the privileged person's criteria. The more subtle comments put the concerns about language off on other people—customers, students and their families, employees. "Well, we don't mind, but, you know, it's hard for others." "And they're good employees," is often added. Other comments are straightforward: "Give me someone who knows something, who speaks English." "Can't we just tell those people to go back where they came from?" These personal biases are also held by those who have the power to put their prejudices into legislation.

Many of us have preconceived notions about people's accents. We find western European accents—French, British, Castilian Spanish, Italian—relatively appealing while Asian and Mexican accents are experienced as unintelligible or offensive. Further, my experience in several organizations is that if someone speaks French at work, we aren't terribly bothered. However, if Filipinos, for example, speak Tagalog to one another at work, the assumptions are that they are purposefully excluding English-speakers, that they are not trying to learn English, and that they don't care. A mean-spirited quality is attributed to the behavior. I find similar attitudes about Mexicans and Mexican Americans who speak Spanish. There is a strongly negative "You're in America now. Speak English!" tone. That disdain is echoed in the anti-immigrant legislation in states around the country.

We judge people based on whether they speak English and, if so, how well, according to our standards. In a focus group I was facilitating for one of my clients, a woman supervisor said, "I'm Black and from Louisiana, and I'm told I'm not speaking 'proper' English." She went on to say that, because of that, she would probably not be promoted; she was not considered a good role model for those who worked under her. Part of that judgment connects assumed intelligence with speaking "standard" English; this is true to such an extent that there are courses, books, and on-line resources for people who want to learn to use bigger words, to "enhance" their vocabularies, and use upper-middle-class grammar and syntax. There is an obvious bias that sounding white and at least middle class is the goal for all, regardless of who they are or what their backgrounds are.

Sometimes people speak a different dialect even though we both speak English, for example, sports-speak (always talking in sports metaphors) or professional jargon (legal, education, medical, business). I remember working with a law school in which white men heavily dominated the faculty. They used lots of sports metaphors (doing an end-run, Monday morning quarterbacking, and so on), with legal jargon thrown in for good measure. I suggested that this was not a particularly welcoming trait in their school, that in fact it was sexist, but they paid little attention. I made my point by speaking for about five minutes straight in dressmaking terms: putting a dart in here, a gusset there, cutting the budget on the bias so that it would be more flexible, using a peplum to hide a course that might be controversial. The women in the room laughed; the men did not find it humorous. But a couple of them had some idea of what I had said. I had put sexism, power, and dominance squarely on the table, and, in fact, we had a good conversation about those issues at the school. Language is power; make no mistake about it. It is used to include and exclude and to keep people and systems in their places. Those of us with race and class privilege, and those of you with male and sexual orientation privilege, have the responsibility to change how language is used if we honestly want to create organizations that invite the skills and talents the institutions need to be successful.

We often have totally different experiences or realities, for example, whether we watch TV and, if so, what channels; whether we listen to the radio—AM, FM, jazz, classical, rap, rock 'n' roll, country, NPR (National Public Radio). I was working in Houston on 9/11/01 and I remember trying to get news. While there was a TV in the office in which I was working, what I really wanted was public radio and, in particular, Pacifica—America's only completely listener-sponsored radio—and I knew there was a station in Houston. When one of the women in the office asked what I was listening to, I said, "NPR," and she asked, "What's NPR?" I felt like I was wearing my race, class, and education privilege way too boldly, because I certainly had judgments about where the rest of the people were getting their information.

Frequently we go in with the expectation that we're not really going to communicate anyway, based on our fears or our judgments about what we hear people saying: men calling women "girls" or "chicks"; people telling jokes at a group's expense. We tell ourselves, "They aren't really going to listen to me because I am white or I am from Berkeley or I'm a lesbian or I'm Southern or I have gray hair," or "I'm not going to listen to them for the same reasons." To make communication work across race, gender, class, age, sexual orientation, and every other division, we must remember that we have very different realities depending on who we are. That is particularly true in terms of treatment in all of the major systems: housing, medicine, social services, media, education, and justice.

I'm reminded of one of my favorite lines from "West Side Story." Doc is talking to one of the gangs, the Jets. He says, "When I was your age…." and is interrupted by one of the Jets who says, "You was never my age, none a you!" Those of us who are white can never really know what it's like to be of color. We live under a contract that prohibits it. If we really knew, we would have to rise up against the system, and that we are not willing to do because it would put the comforts associated with our privileges in jeopardy. Short of that, the best we can do is to be as clear as possible about what it means to be us, about the lenses through which we see the world based on our membership in various groups, to consider actively another's reality, and then to change the systems that create those realities. To have genuine interaction with someone who is different from us, we have to think about what's going on in the world that would affect this person's life and, of course, what's going on in the immediate community that would affect our relationship and interaction.

Now, having said all of that, here are some suggestions about the specifics of talking with people who are different. Let's start with the basic active listening rules. Don't assume you know what the person is going to say. Stop and listen, turning off all channels in your mind except the listening one. Don't finish the person's sentences; the moment you do that you have switched from listening to her or him to listening to yourself. Don't use discussion-stopping language like: "Yes, but…." or "I know exactly what you mean…." or "But don't you think…?" or "Wouldn't you say…?" Whenever it's appropriate, use *I* messages. In other words, speak from your own experience, not from the general "Well, everybody knows" or "People say". Who's "people"? Who's "everybody"?

The next set of guidelines is more specifically geared to talking about race. Even though we are able to have calm conversations about all sorts of things, there are some topics that push our buttons—race is often one of them. First, be very clear about your motivation for the interaction. The purpose is to learn and share, not to teach, convince, or correct. One of the first questions you want to ask yourself as you enter into a conversation about race is "Why am I doing this?" Be sure that your impulse is "clean," that is, that you are really beginning the conversation for the reasons you say you are. Saying you want to hear the other's perspective when really you want to tell her or him what a bigot she or he is would not be a conversation destined for success. Identify your emotional investment in the conversation. What buttons has it pushed? Are you really having an old conversation with your relatives at Thanksgiving or are you fully present in the conversation that is taking place? Your goal is to act in as open a way as possible, unfettered by biases and assumptions, not to posture or prove the other person wrong. Listen "with your receiver turned up and your transmitter turned down," as I once heard someone say. Try hard to listen with the willingness to be influenced and not be defensive. Acknowledge out loud the risks of even having a conversation about race, gender, or sexual orientation in the first place. That's more than most of us do. After doing that, go ahead with the conversation, if both (or all) people are willing.

A cautionary note: It is essential to remember that we enter into interactions about our places where we are blind with enormous power and privilege imbalances. In a cross-racial conversation between a Latina and a white person, for example, the Latina is at greater risk because she has not been given the systemic privileges that the white person has. Unless that power and privilege imbalance is acknowledged and factored into the conversation, the interaction may cause more harm than good. Be willing to be wrong. Being blinded by our privilege often keeps us from being able to see or to hear clearly, especially if the person with whom we are speaking is different from us. Just by stopping really to listen to the person you change the dynamics of the situation considerably. There is even greater impact if you are willing to suspend judgment and consider that you may have mis-heard or mis-read what is being said or done.

As I have said before, remember that, even though you have good intentions, it is your behavior and the impact of that behavior that matter. Don't forget that you might do a really good job and the conversation might still be a hard one. The task is, again, to become "comfortable with the uncomfortable and uncomfortable with the too comfortable." That's particularly hard when you are responding to a difficult situation and you have to do it quickly. Give yourself the freedom not to have the answers immediately and to take some time for reflection. "I haven't really heard what you are saying in quite the way I'm hearing it now. I would like to take some time to reflect. Can I come back to you in a half-hour (or tomorrow morning)?" And that leads us directly to the next guideline.

Don't just do something; stand there. I have heard this attributed variously, from Dwight Eisenhower to Buddha, so take your pick. The point is just to stand and wait and think. Collect your thoughts, even for a couple of seconds, to get some clarity, especially in your heart, about the most effective things to do and say. Slow a potentially volatile conversation down. Very few "eruption" moments aid in building open communication. Before saying anything rash, take a deep breath. Stop to ask yourself if you are responding or reacting. Otherwise, we go back to the blurt method which is costly in terms of relationships and the after-effects of speaking before we think.

Expect suspiciousness from the person to whom you are talking, particularly if your conversation hasn't come up naturally. That concern is heightened exponentially when there is an even greater imbalance of privilege and power, such as in a manager-employee or faculty-student relationship. I find that it is often difficult for white people to accept that a person of color should be suspicious, by definition, of any white person they are talking to, just as someone who is non-privileged in other areas of identity would be—people with disabilities of able-bodied people, women of men, lesbian, gay, bisexual or transgender of heterosexuals, poor people of wealthier people. Because so many white people see ourselves as individuals and as relatively good people, we have a hard time imagining that we pose a threat to someone we work with or are talking to. We see ourselves as entering into conversations as just us; usually, the person of color sees us as a representative of our race and our gender.

One of the privileges granted to those of us who are white is permission to forget that all of us come into conversations bringing our history and our experiences with us. People of color generally bring their personal encounters, those they have witnessed, the stories they've read, and the history they know between white people and people of color, just as white people carry all that we've seen and been told about, our personal biases, and the unconscious and conscious beliefs about the superiority of whiteness. But we get to forget that we do this. We who are white walk into a conversation carrying all of the people in our race with us, whether we want to or know that we're doing it. And, while I personally may not count on an individual Asian American woman, for example, to be representative of the Model Minority—a role white systems have created and white people have colluded in enforcing for Asian Americans in which they are supposed to model for other races how to be a good "minority"—the person I'm talking to doesn't know that. Plus, while it might not be my intent to apply my stereotypes of Asian Americans to the person I'm talking with, I may well do that without thinking. A voice in my head might say, "How come you're so loud and boisterous? I thought Japanese American women were supposed to be dignified and quiet, seen but not heard." It's the impact of my behavior that they have to deal with. In order to protect themselves from spirit-murdering, they must expect the usual, not the exception. My task is to remember that that will probably be the expectation of many of the Chinese, Japanese, Vietnamese, Filipino, and Hawaiian Americans with whom I come in contact.

Most, if not all, Asian Americans have endured uncountable insensitive comments from well-meaning white people. Things that add up: A

Chinese American woman and the director of New Student Services at University of California at Berkeley was asked by a white parent at a new student program, "Why are there so many Asians here?" Asian Americans and their ancestors who have lived in the United States for generations have been denied rights, property, and treatment that those of us who are white have received as a matter of course. And all of that comes into play in a conversation. Though it might sound like a dramatic overstatement, America's racial history is present in all cross-race conversations. Actually, it is in all conversations, but we are not nearly so conscious of that when it's a white-on-white conversation.

The authors of *Taking It Personally: Racism in the Classroom from Kindergarten to College*, a remarkable book written together by a white woman and a Black woman (Ann Berlak and Sekani Moyenda), show why people of color might be wary of white people.

> Every day I see white people as loaded guns. I'm frightened of when they will take something from me that I have rightfully earned or deny me something I legitimately need. To protect myself I need to understand racism. I need to know what causes these guns to go off and how to dodge the bullets. Then I have to understand, when I get shot—and I will eventually get shot again—how do I get the bullet out and clean and heal the wound before the next one hits? [1]

Given those experiences, why wouldn't one be suspicious?

Don't take this personally, but take it very personally. This is an odd line to walk. I included Moyenda's comments because I have heard similar ones so many times it is impossible to count. As white people, what do we do with these comments? We can dismiss them as those of an angry Black woman, but that's way too easy. We can think, "Well, she doesn't mean me. She's talking about those other white people." That would be not taking it personally, in fact, not personally enough. We can think, "She means those other white people and she means me—she means all of us." That is both not taking it personally and taking it very personally.

To continue from *Taking it Personally*: "Kathy [a white student in Berkak's class] wrote in her journal, 'I am upset and enraged by the messages I heard from today's speaker [Moyenda]....I got upset and I was overcome with tears of rage.'" Berlak wrote back to her: "The goal is to be able to hear and feel Sekani's rage against racism and to be able to listen with empathy to an angry parent of one of your Black students...without taking it personally." [2] Later Berlak wrote: "Seeing themselves through Sekani's eyes revealed to them that they were not who they thought themselves to be. These changes of self-concepts as a result of seeing themselves as they were seen by Sekani are…what I mean by taking what Sekani was saying personally."[3]

Expect disequilibrium and cognitive dissonance on your part. In other words, expect to feel off balance in these conversations. You might well be learning things that turn your world upside down. If you have taken in Moyenda's words, this might be one of the times of disequilibrium. Certainly my client's comments in Chapter 2 about American Indians as school mascots made clear that her world had rotated 180 degrees. If you feel you are at a stuck point in a conversation about race or in your behavior, take a break and list your judgments and assumptions about the other person, about yourself, and about your expected outcome of the interaction. If you and the group are at the place of being able to do it, talk about some of your assumptions with the others so that there is more shared information about what is really going on. Remember, however, that revealing judgments and assumptions is a potentially dangerous move. If you don't know whether your group has the ability to talk about privately-held assumptions without getting defensive, move slowly. Just because everyone has good intentions doesn't mean that words, comments, or thoughts will come out in a non-hurtful manner.

Be honest about what you don't know. Don't try to pretend. Put yourself in the place of the other person, as much as possible. What would it be like to be her or him and talking with you? From David Tulin I have learned to make a distinction between ego function and role function. Ego function is that which we want to do, something that satisfies our ego. Role function is what we are supposed to do, our role in a conversation or an action. We are usually in ego function when we use the blurt method. We experience it as something we *have* to say. We can't not. I know my ego function is in charge when my stomach hurts or I am burning to say something, when I want to leap out of my chair to speak. At those times it is usually more prudent to stop for a moment to think if what I am going to say is going to add to the conversation or if I am just using my white privilege to take up more "air time"—public speaking space. Role function is what I should be saying or doing that is most effective in meeting my goals in the role I play. That doesn't mean that one wouldn't use the blurt method in role function; it means that you would plan an apparently emotional blow-up because it seems to you that using that approach would be the best tactic to help you reach your goals.

"Balancing advocacy with inquiry."[4] In *The Fifth Discipline Fieldbook*, Rick Ross writes that, particularly in conversations across difference where advocating a particular perspective might be what we are prone to do, inquiry is essential—really paying attention to the assumptions each person is making as she or he speaks. Bear in mind that there is often an imbalance of institutionally and systemically granted power between the two (or more) people involved in conversation about differences. That makes the advocacy/inquiry balance even more essential.

If you feel that your prejudgments and biases have kept you from seeing what is really going on, identify for yourself, and perhaps for others, the basis of your thoughts so that you are clearer about how and where you have been blinded. Ask yourself questions like: What made me think that? Do I really believe that now, or has that been my position for a long time and I just take for granted that that's still what I hope is true? What if I'm wrong? Check in with your self-critic to see if you are speaking from your insecurities. "She's probably going to think I'm dumb and racist anyway, so what does it matter what I say? Furthermore, she's probably right!" "I seem to be avoiding the really hard questions. It is my fears of what others will say about me that are keeping me from asking further and deeper questions."

Ask clarifying questions to re-hear what the person said. "Jean, would you mind saying that again? I'm not sure I understood what you were saying." Go back to the real words that were said, as opposed to the ones you thought you heard or what you were feeling. Work to sift and unravel, even if that makes the communication less clear for the moment or makes you feel more vulnerable. If it would be useful for the information you want and it is possible, set the boundaries for a response to your clarifying question. "Jim, I know this is really a lot to ask, but would it be possible to take off your dean's hat and speak as Jim as you tell me what you are thinking?" This setting of boundaries is most useful in separating out one's role and responsibility from one's personal perspective. However, one should never be expected to split apart the pieces of oneself. For example, don't say: "Margaret, it would really help me if you could stop being Chinese American and just speak to me as a woman."

The last three guidelines are not specific to racial conversations, though they are certainly useful there. These are overarching rules that we seldom think about until it's too late. First, don't ask any question you don't really want the answer to. "Marie, I want to check in with you. I fear I was really obnoxious at yesterday's meeting. I was running late and began to talk before I had caught my breath or slowed my mind. Was that your experience?" Second, don't make offers, promises, or bargains you can't keep. For example, don't offer to have a conversation that you are not genuinely serious about unless you have to (for example, it is your role function to do so). "Would you like to talk about why you think I am treating you differently than I treat others? I would be happy to do that." Don't promise something you can't deliver such as, "I will back you up in the meeting today." It is better to say nothing and do it if you can than promise support and not supply it. Don't make a bargain that you might regret, just because you think it will improve your relationship or you want to look like a good person. For example, "I really want to set up a relationship where you'll tell me exactly how you feel about me and I'll tell you exactly how I feel about you." Lastly, build support systems that encourage you to be your best self and that help you if you get off track. Because all of us are blinded in some ways but not in others, having a community in which you can talk honestly about what you are trying to see and to learn is vital. It is also crucial to be among people who will push us to work harder, even when we feel we are doing the best we can.

I was a participant in an intensive workshop that met periodically over a year's time. At one session I was talking about how painful it was to be a lesbian and not be able to count on straight people to back me up. I heard myself say, "I have supported African American women all my life. I wish they would support me now." Luckily for me, a white woman who had done a lot of work on race was in the group. She looked at me and said, "African American women don't owe you shit. You have worked on racism for yourself, not for them." I thought to myself, "Oh, yeah, I have been saying that for years, but I forgot. Thank God there was another white woman here to put me back on track."

Why don't they owe me? Because I choose to be an ally; I do it because it is in my interest, not in order to get support back. If that happens, it is a gift, but, if I ally myself for the purpose of getting support for myself, then I am betraying a genuine ally relationship. We'll talk more about allies in the last chapter.

"What if they call me *racist*?" One of the reasons that issues of diversity such as race, gender, and sexual orientation aren't discussed in the workplace, in classrooms, or at the dining room table, for that matter, is the fear that the conversation will "get out of hand"—that explosive questions will be asked, that people will be "disrespectful" of one another, and that people will leave angry and upset. One of the things I have always found intriguing is that among the greatest fears that prompts this hypothetical "out of control" conversation is white people's concerns about being called *racist*. Actually, someone's being called *racist* signifies that the meeting or interaction has blown up. That is all it takes. I thought about this for a long time, and then decided to create a workshop titled "What If 'They' Call Me a Racist?" The following was one of the experiences that moved me to pay attention to this.

Some years ago I was working with a university police department on issues of diversity. They were still upset about an incident that had occurred two years earlier when they had been accused of being a racist police force because they had brought in police back-up from across the state in preparation for a Black Family Day event at their college, an action that was different from their preparation for any other event on campus. One white officer said, "Call me anything you want. Call my *mother* anything you want, but don't call me a racist!" I was completely baffled by this officer's feelings. I had lived in and around enough different cultures to know that it is not smart to impugn anyone's mother. I began to ask questions: "What would seeing yourself as racist mean?" "What would it cost to incorporate 'racist' into your picture of yourself?" "Why is being called a racist so painful when, in fact, it doesn't change your privileged status at all?" They didn't have answers to any of my questions, and I think they were surprised that I didn't understand their feelings.

My definition of *racism*, and by extension, *racist* is not just about bigotry and prejudice. It's about having the power to put those prejudices into effect. A definition of *racism* that still works for me, that I probably first saw in Judith Katz's book *White Awareness*, is "prejudice plus power." For me, any of us who has race privilege, which all white people do, and therefore the power to put our prejudices into law, is racist by definition, because we benefit from a racist system. (I've identified many examples of putting bigotry into law—the early English-only in schools law in Texas, the anti-bilingual education legislation in California, the Three-Fifths clause in the Constitution.) So if somebody calls me a racist, my response is, "Yes, that's right, I am. Now tell me what's really going on." It took me a long time to come to that position, so I am not suggesting that is a response for everyone. But for me it is a given and it removes the sting of being called a racist. The question, then, is not whether or not I'm a racist, but what happened for the person with whom I am talking to make her or him say that? Terms like *racist, sexist, heterosexist,* and *homophobic* are words that people who don't have privilege use because they're so frustrated that they don't know anything else to say. And they believe it. In my experience, it generally has a basis in experience.

If you are white and don't define *racism* the way that I do, then the personal work about what to do if you're called a racist is different. Still, regardless of your definition, you need to know why you respond in the way that you do and to make sense of your response. If the term *racist* is a hot button for you then you need to know what that's about, do some work to desensitize yourself, and have the presence of mind to take a deep breath and to step back. I don't like to be called *racist*, but being able to ask a question is a lot more productive than getting into a power struggle. My perspective is that being called a racist doesn't have to do with me personally; it's about me as a member of my group. My behavior does have to do with me personally, and that is what I need to know more about. My question needs to be: "What have I done?" instead of being caught off guard and saying, "I can't possibly be a racist. I've never been racist. How can you say that?" And then we get into a power struggle over who's right and who's going to define what I am, and the ability to understand what's really happening is lost.

The strategies offered up to this point could be used in any number of settings. However, the following applications of them are specifically written for instructors and faculty. At virtually every college campus I have visited, there is an unspoken rule that volatile issues won't be discussed, particularly in the classroom. There is a great fear on the part of faculty, whether in community college classrooms or law schools, that a conversation will get out of hand and the professor will lose control. Most of us who went to school to learn how to be professors weren't taught to teach students, we were taught to teach subject matter, so many of us don't have the skills to handle conflict. One of your possible responses is, "We can't talk about these topics, they're too sensitive. I don't know what to do." My hope is that these suggestions will make it easier when the "r" word comes up.

First, as you prepare for a class you're teaching or a meeting you're in charge of, identify what your real fear is about being called a racist. Is it about being identified as a bad person? Is it about being caught out in some of your worst fears? You might be thinking, "Well, I know I have a lot of prejudices that I might admit to myself in the shower, but if I watch my words nobody else will know." You need to know what you're afraid of because we all know that our worst fears as professors will, inevitably, come up in class. If you're a man, regardless of color, do you feel the same about being called sexist? If you're heterosexual, do you have an extremely difficult time being called *heterosexist* or *homophobic*? Is your response on a par with being called a *racist*? If not, why not? Because they imply the same things—that we have biases and that we discriminate against people on the basis of them.

The second strategy is to think through your fear to its natural conclusion as opposed to your imagined one. What terrible thing will happen to you if somebody calls you a racist? There are some things that will probably happen. Perhaps your colleagues will look at you as a less good person. Perhaps they'll be grateful that it was you who put your foot in your mouth instead of them. Remember, we're talking about the natural conclusion, not the imagined or feared one. We need to sit down and ask: Am I worried about being called *classist*? Where do I sit with my own class stuff? How do I hold myself as an upper-middle-class person? What are my privileges? How do I express those privileges? What are the risks if I am called *classist*? Are they different and, if so, why?

Strategy number three: Think about the impact of your color, gender and position on how others hear what you say. How are we seen when we walk in? What weight do our words carry simply because of who we are and what we look like? Professors' words, for example, carry a lot of weight. Many times students have said to me, "I would say something to my professor, but he/she's going to give me grades." Or "I really need a good recommendation to go to graduate school, and so I'm not going to say anything about my concerns." The weight of the professor's words is, generally speaking, backed up by the institution in ways that corporations don't usually support managers, unless they are very senior.

A fourth strategy that I use a lot is to mention things first, before somebody else has a chance to. I talk about being white right off the bat because it's clear to everybody who's not white that I am. By talking about it, I open up the subject, model for others that you probably won't die if you talk about it, and make it clear to the group that I am willing to address thorny issues. It ceases to be a hot button. Introduce sensitive subjects yourself. You start out at the beginning of the class and say, "During the semester we're going to talk about some things that are sensitive." You're preparing your students to think about themselves as learners and asking them what kind of baggage they bring into that class.

I'm probably foolish in assuming that every professor is going to want to talk about how racism affects the institution; my hope is that professors will say, "Okay, I don't know what this means, but, if I'm going to be called a racist, I guess I better look at what racism is going on at this institution." One of the most useful strategies for professors is their willingness to say, "I'm learning here. I don't know. We'll have to find out together."

Strategy number five is probably one of the most important. If you are called a racist, don't say, "I am not," or "This has nothing to do with race." That alerts every person of color in the room to the fact that you don't have a clue about race and how it always has impact on us. The issue is not always race, but it is always a possible player. We take our whiteness with us everywhere we go. So saying this has nothing to do with race shows that we don't know what we're talking about. The fact is, whatever it was might not have been about race. But, by saying that, we've closed the conversation. And we're not going to be able to give the people in the room the clues they need to sort out whether or not it was about race. Those are conversation-stoppers, and what we're trying to do is get into conversation. There are, of course, other conversation-stoppers. "You're taking this too seriously." "Don't be so sure that everybody is out to get you." Those sorts of things essentially say that their perception is wrong. And, because faculty members have institutional privilege, what they say has great weight, whether it's accurate or not. The student of color is likely to say or at least think, "You don't know what you're talking about." But, because we're not in an equal dialogue, that's very likely not to be said out loud.

The goal is to find out what the other person's concern is by shifting the "I am not!" "You are too!" to "Tell me what's really going on." So what I need to do is be the researcher here. "Tell me what your concerns are." "Tell me what occurred; tell me what I said." "What did you hear me say?" "Tell me how it got to this point?" What you want is a dialogue. What you want is conversation in which each person is able to hear the other. We don't want to stop conversations. But, if we haven't done our homework about preparing for sensitive subjects, what we *do* want to do is stop conversations. So we pull rank, go to a power position, and say, "You don't know what you're talking about, and I'm the boss." We might as well be saying, "That's a really sensitive subject about which I know nothing. So we're going to move on whether you want to or not."

Finally, remember no one taught us about managing difficult issues in the classroom. We're all on a serious learning curve. However, if the goal is honest dialogue and relationship-building, then your behavior needs to reflect those desires.

There are three lessons I want to highlight from the strategies for talking about race. The first is that few white people have suffered serious job-related consequences from being accused of being a racist. Being called a racist doesn't remove any of my white privileges. I still live in a world that over-values me because of my skin color. That's not to say that it feels okay to be called a racist, particularly if we have made a commitment to do anti-racism work. If, however, we can use it as a gift that gets us to re-look at ourselves and the situations we're in, we've used some of that pain to move us to a different place.

Second, once I realized that generalizations about white people are both not very personal and very personal, I was able to figure out how to use what I had heard without becoming too defensive for too long, without becoming immobilized. Part of the "luxury" of being white is not hearing what people of color say about us. I put *luxury* in quotation marks because I believe that, without honest personal feedback and clarity about how my group is seen, I am not dealing with a full deck of cards. Even if it hurts, I need all of the information I can get.

Third, my bet is that it was difficult for some of you to read the strategy regarding people of color being appropriately suspicious of us. That information is painful, and it is also accurate for many, if not most, people of color. That doesn't mean that you should rush up to your friends of color and quiz them about whether they are suspicious of you. For now, read on to the next chapter where we'll look more deeply at talking about whiteness and being white.

9

TALKING ABOUT WHITENESS AND BEING WHITE

While preparing for a visit to a client in the Midwest, I had several conversations with people who work in that institution. Some of those calls focused on what topics I should and should not raise and how I could connect with those with whom I was working so that they would hang in for the conversation. Could I use the "d" word—diversity? No, they were sick of it. What about "inclusion"? That would be fine, but most of the people here don't really know what it means. And, most importantly, what about the "w" word—white? Finally the dean who had invited me, himself a person of color, said, "Be careful, Francie. Remember this is the Midwest, and we have to live here after you've gone."

It would be great if the Midwest was the only place where there is difficulty having straightforward conversations about systemic white supremacy. We who are racial justice educators could focus all of our attention there and make serious progress addressing social injustice. But that's not the case, of course. Had I been going to the Northeast, I might have been warned that New England and states to the immediate south are too "buttoned-down," too emotionally private and unwilling to have personal conversations in public, to talk about race. Someone once said to me that "The only thing that's black in Vermont are the black and white cows." In the South I might be told by white people that "Some of us are just not comfortable talking to Black people about race." And in the West many people—both of color and white—believe that there is no racism on the "liberal" coast, so there's no need to talk about race. "Didn't we deal with that already?" All over the country, there is always an excuse among white people about why today is not the day to have those conversations.

Meanwhile, of course, conversations about race go on all the time. White people talk among themselves about people of color, predominantly about Black people and Latinos. In parts of the country where there are large numbers of Asians—Asian Americans, Pacific Islanders, and Native Americans—white people talk about them, too. What almost never happens is white people talking with other white people about ourselves as white people. We particularly avoid conversations about our having systemically-granted privileges based on our skin color or that, by having and using those privileges, we collude in the maintenance of the systemic supremacy of whiteness.

Many of us had hoped that electing an African American president would place race squarely on the nation's table. That has surely happened, but not in the way we had wished for. Instead, the degree of anger and disrespect that has been displayed has been staggering, precisely because it has focused on President Obama's race: unending questions about whether he was born in the United States and could thus be a legitimate president; demonstrations at which white people wore placards depicting the President as an African witch doctor; political cartoons like the one in which the entire lawn of the White House was planted with watermelons. Less than nine months after Barack Obama was sworn in as the 44th president of the United States, at a joint session of Congress, a congressman from South Carolina interrupted the President's speech by shouting, "You lie!" To my knowledge, this was a first in American history.

This same kind of disrespect, and in some cases expressions of hatred, has spread to other officials who are members of marginalized groups: during a demonstration, white people chanted "nigger" at African American Civil Rights leader and Congressman John Lewis, spat on African American Congressman Emanuel Cleaver, and screamed "faggot" at gay Congressman Barney Frank. African American Congressman James Clyburn told *The Huffington Post*, "I heard people saying things that I have not heard since March 15, 1960, when I was marching to try and get off the back of the bus."[1] Some white people seem to have unleashed racial anger they have been holding in for decades. It has spread to legislation involving "illegal aliens" which is code for Latinas/os. Georgia and Alabama argue that they, not the United States, "have the sovereign right to protect their borders."[2] These stories help us understand the tenor of the current racial divide in the country. That divide has direct bearing on our work, for those of us who see ourselves as developing change agents. It increases the urgent need for us to get over our fears, start talking about being white, and bring that willingness to being the allies we profess we want to be.

At the 2011 NCORE I facilitated a day-and-a-half-long institute titled "If You Can't Talk, You Can't Act, and If You Can't Act, You Can't Change: Creating an Organizational Climate in which People Are Willing and Able to Talk about Hard Issues." I firmly believe that, until we who are white are able to have everyday conversations about our race or across race without being stopped by our fear of being called a racist or feeling saddled with individual guilt, we will not be able to move forward as a nation. Ta-Nehisi Coates, a senior editor for *The Atlantic,* wrote an editorial in *The Chicago Tribune* in August of 2010 titled "Conversation on race? Why we're just not ready."[3] His thesis is that America isn't qualified to have a nationwide conversation on race because white people are so willfully ignorant of the role that race—ours and others'—plays in our daily lives and in the history of our country. For example, the removal of books by and about Latinas/os and the dismantling of the Mexican-American Studies program in the Tucson, Arizona, Unified Schools[4] speaks to Coates' point. I think there were two real reasons for those actions: first, to undercut Latinas/os growing stronger by deepening the knowledge of their own history, and, second, to shield white people from knowing about the acts of theft, greed, and genocide—both literal and spiritual—that were carried out in their name.

So where do we go? It seems to me that we have to come at talking about race from two directions. As the Three Levels model in the Preface shows, we are all continually working at the personal, the interpersonal, and the organizational levels. While they are obviously not separable, the work that we must do at each level has distinct characteristics. In this chapter we will focus on the personal level and the organizational level, having focused predominantly on the interpersonal level in Chapter 8. Given my belief that all of us have personal work to do about the biases we hold and the identity-based privileges that are either systemically granted to us or withheld from us, how do we begin to make changes in ourselves?

People think about race. It might come up in a conversation with a friend or in a class at school; you might hear a person of color say something about white people and wonder if they are including you in their comment. You might feel angry that you have been placed in a group that you feel you have no real connection to. For example, on many occasions I have heard white gay men say, "I'm not white; I'm gay," implying that gayness was their only identity, rather than the one with which they most strongly identified. Regardless, the notion of having a racial identity has occurred to you—and probably to them, too.

Exploring the personal level is just exactly that: personal. At some point, if we want to change our racialized beliefs and behaviors, we each have to make a decision to begin to uncover the attitudes and biases that we hold. I have often said that each of us, across every kind of difference, has file cabinets stuffed with folders that are filled with stereotypes. When we have an encounter with a person, a thought, a perspective, a location, a food, an animal or whatever, we go to our file cabinets, pull out a drawer, and find the appropriate folder that connects to our experience. In a split second we are reminded of how we feel about whatever it is that we have encountered, and we move forward based on what we found. We rarely stop to ask if what we think is true, is helpful, or where the stereotypes came from. In his book *Whistling Vivaldi: And Other Clues to How Stereotypes Affect Us*, Claude Steele quotes Brent Staples, an African American columnist at the *New York Times*:

> I became an expert in the language of fear. Couples locked arms or reached for each other's hands when they saw me. Some crossed to the other side of the street. People who were carrying on conversations went mute and stared straight ahead, as though avoiding my eyes would save them....
>
> I tried to be innocuous but didn't know how....Out of nervousness I began to whistle and discovered I was good at it. My whistle was pure and sweet—and also in tune. On the street at night I whistled popular tunes from the Beatles and Vivaldi's *Four Seasons*. The tension drained from people's bodies when they heard me. A few even smiled when they passed me in the dark. [5]

Every time I read this story, I imagine myself on a dark street, already nervous because I'm alone, suddenly becoming aware that behind me is a 6′2″ Black man wearing an old military jacket. While I'm not sure what I would do, I am sure that I would be really afraid. I know that Black men carry the stereotype of being the most dangerous people in the United States. Despite massive amounts of data that this is, in fact, not the case, because of the way that media regularly report crimes that stereotype is burned into my mind. Only the Black men whom I count among my close colleagues and friends prevent that knee-jerk reaction.

In my head I go to that dark street, conscious of an African American man walking behind me. He suddenly starts whistling, and he's whistling Vivaldi! I am positive my entire body would relax. I might turn around and smile. Three things have happened in those few seconds. First, I dug into my racial stereotype file and pulled out the fear of unknown Black men. I was taught that fear in my Southern childhood, and it has been re-taught over and over again. Second, I pulled out my socioeconomic folder and instantly assigned the man a class. Relying on another of my biased beliefs, this one about who is familiar enough with the *Four Seasons* to whistle them, I see this man as being from the same class as I am, the upper-middle class. A third stereotype pops into my mind: Surely someone who whistles Vivaldi (someone of the upper-middle class) can't be a rapist or a murderer. And then I realize how much work I have left to do based on how quickly those stereotypes came up. Both those that I classify as negative and those I see as positive are absurd and dangerous. They are a disservice to the person being prejudged and to me.

Before you say to yourself, "But this is about safety...." or "Don't you know the statistics about rape—that one in every six women has been or will be raped in her lifetime (while the statistic for men is one in thirty-three)?"[6]—take a deep breath. The point of using this emotionally-loaded example is that it gives us the opportunity to untangle a set of stereotypes that most of us carry, particularly those of us who are women. In the safety of the place where you are now, think about how your racial stereotypes might, in fact, make you less safe. If I have bought the myth that most rapists are African Americans and so I am less careful if I turn around and see a white man following me, I could be making a huge mistake.

Obviously we need to look at ourselves. How *does* personal work take place? I turn back to Chapter 1, "Beginning with Ourselves."

> When we set out to do intentional personal work, as we must, and to turn ourselves inside out, we have to first know where we want to get to in our understanding and behavior. Then we have to identify honestly where we are now and how we got there, being conscious of how our racial, ethnic, and cultural roots have shaped our perceptions.[7]

As I read it now, the prescribed steps feel too intellectual. I remember my friend Hugh Vasquez standing up in a packed session at NCORE and asking, "Francie, that all sounds great, but where is your heart?" He stopped me cold. I drew a deep breath and went to an entirely different place in my body—out of my head and into my feelings. Here and now, if I speak from my heart, what would I say?

> This work is vitally important. It's not something to do because you want to be like your friends or you want to look good. In fact, this work might separate you from your friends. But it will connect you to others around the world who are working toward building a community in which all of us are honored and can be productive, in which all of us share the goal of being equally valuable. This is what we do because we

want to be the best humans we can be and to get our privileged selves out of the way of others doing the same. I only have one life that I'm sure of, and as I am leaving it I want to be able to know that I did all I could do to bring about racial justice.

This may sound idealistic and abstract. However, what I'm talking about requires courage, will, and determination. It is not simple. Yet, genuinely experiencing and treating as your equals those who are different from you in terms of privilege is not as impossible as it sounds. You start small and move step by step. That's all we can do. It's not about putting on your Crusaders for Social Justice cape and flying off to fix everything. It's not about taking care of others. It's all about taking care of ourselves and building the community we want to live in.

Imagine what would change if all men saw it as their responsibility to stop other men from committing acts of sexual violence. Imagine what could happen if all wealthy people decided to give ten percent of their income so that others might have food, housing, and quality education. Or if all of us, regardless of class, gave ten percent of our time to organizations such as food banks, house-building projects, literacy projects. Even if we started with five percent, think of the changes it would make. It's about heterosexuals stepping up as allies to the LGBTQ (lesbian, gay, bisexual, transsexual, and queer) communities, across race and class. Or paying attention as we casually walk up the stairs to get in a building, knowing that the staircase accessible to me is keeping others out. It is about Christians not allowing other Christians to burn others' holy books like the Koran or demean others' religions or lack of religion. The motivation comes from the heart, and then the head plans strategically and concretely.

It's difficult for me to explain thoughtfully and heart-fully how to begin the process of owning whiteness and talking about it. It's so much part of my DNA now that I have trouble separating it out. And that would be my process, anyway, not yours. Remember, I grew into serious thought about race in my mid-teens and early twenties, 1963–1972, in the South, during the height of Civil Rights activity and the war in Viet Nam. My first stage for battle—and it was a war for me—was my family, then my home in Texas. My "preferred intervention strategy"[8] was angry, harsh and combative. Against my family and my culture, I was fighting for my sanity, my integrity and my life. More than anything, I didn't want to be like them. I know it sounds dramatic, and it was. It was also reflective of what was happening in the country, particularly in the South. There is a gospel song that I learned in the YWCA that is still deeply resonant for me:

We are soldiers in the army.
We got to fight, although we have to cry.
We got to hold up the blood-stained banner,
We got to hold it up until we die.

I took on the role of warrior. I am still a warrior in my heart, though now I am more seasoned and have found more useful intervention strategies. Your own on-going awakening will fit your environment and your personality, at least initially. Based on what you discover and the experiences you have, your strategies will probably alter over time as mine have.

Here are some questions and processes that might be helpful in moving you to take the next step. (Step one was picking this book up, even if it was assigned reading.) First, bring to full consciousness the fact that elements of your identities have profound impact on your experiences, whether you're white or straight or male or Christian or upper-middle or upper class or temporarily able-bodied or some or all of the above. All of those identities give you privileges, whether you want them or not. You can't not get them and you can't give them back. How you recognize them and use them can make life- and institution-altering differences. You can either continue to use them as though they were due you or you can use them to bring about institutional change.

Next, ask yourself questions that prompt you to connect with how you're feeling about doing all this necessary work. Keep a journal of your responses. I suggest you write it by hand; like many others, I find that I remember what I write better than what I type into my computer. There's one less mechanical barrier between you and what you're trying to discover.

How is it that you want to see yourself as a white person?

What kinds of specific actions would you take to become who you believe you are or want to be?

In *The Artist's Way*, Julia Cameron asks questions that can be applied to many emotionally difficult endeavors. Here are four that seem particularly relevant to getting through resistance to owning privilege. List any resentments (anger) you have in connection with this project.

1. Ask your[self] to list any and all fears about the projected piece of work and/or anyone connected to it….It does not matter that they are groundless to your adult's eye. What matters is that they are big scary monsters to [you].

2. Ask yourself if that is all. Have you left out any itsy fear? Have you suppressed any "stupid" anger?
3. Ask yourself what you gain by not doing this piece of work.
4. Make your deal....Sign your deal and post it.[9]

You don't have to do anything with what you have uncovered. Just sit with the information and feelings, letting them slowly suffuse your consciousness. You might want to investigate where they all came from; some of what comes up will be familiar and some of it will baffle and embarrass you. At this point, if you haven't read it or want to reread it, you could look at Picca and Feagin's *Two-Faced Racism: Whites in the Backstage and Frontstage*.[10] My hunch is that, if you have been truly honest, you will see yourself reflected in these journal entries. This is an early turning point in your process. Because of all the racial hatred embedded in our national history and culture, you're bound to find racist thoughts in your head. It's possible that you will feel so bad about the words that come from your unconscious that you'll consider abandoning self-examination. I urge you to move ahead anyway. Stopping now would be a clear example of using your privilege of remaining ignorant and believing that "We're all human beings; everybody is the same." At this point it's very important to remember that you are responding to these questions because you want to be part of changing the environment of the institution to which you are connected. It's hard and painful work. But, as Robert Frost said, "The only way around is through."

Next, get a notebook to carry with you all the time. Start writing down what you observe about being white and where you see yourself reflected. What do you notice on television and in the movies? Who do you see and in what roles? How many white people are in the crowd scenes and how many people of color? What is the racial breakdown of those pictured in newspapers? Count to make sure you're not kidding yourself. What is reported about white people? Is their race mentioned or are they presented as generic people while people of color have their racial identity named? "Police arrested a Black man as he was robbing a convenience store" as opposed to "Police picked up a suspect thought to be connected to the robbery of a convenience store." In the second example it is certainly possible that the suspect was a person of color, but, because race wasn't identified, you wouldn't know unless you were shown a photograph. White is the default. In books you read, what is the race (or are the races) of each of the characters?

Our social lives are often a place where the story we tell ourselves and the reality are very different. Well-meaning liberal white people regularly report that their lives have many more people of color in them than they do. I think they believe it's true. I was staying at a cousin's house in a trendy area of a city I don't know well. I asked him what the racial composition of the neighborhood was. He replied, "Oh, it's pretty mixed." "Where does the closest person of color live?" I asked. He stopped and thought. "Well, there's an Asian family about three blocks away."

Who lives in your neighborhood? Who comes to the social events you attend? How is your immediate response different from reality? Whose history did you learn? Whose history was excluded? And so on. The point of this initial exercise is to develop your conscious awareness, not to judge or to take action. Just notice. Keep your list daily for a week. At the end of that time, think about what you saw. Does it bring you closer to being able and willing to describe those experiences, identifying everyone's race?

Let's talk again about an exercise that for me is a starting place for white people. I've tried many approaches to it—from assigning the task to cajoling to threatening—but nothing has worked. The behavior I'm looking for seems simple to me: It begins with white people identifying themselves and other white people as white just as we often mention the race or skin color of individuals of color when we talk about them. As you read this you might be thinking, "Didn't she already talk about this?" Yes, in Chapter 7, "Now That (I Think) I Understand White Privilege, What Do I Do?" I described a game that theologian Thandeka created and talked about in her book *Learning to Be White*. As I quoted earlier, "The Race Game...has one rule. For a week, the player, in all white settings, must use the word *white* whenever he or she mentions the name of a Euro-American." Thandeka reported that none of the people in her class could do this task for a day, let alone a week. I had difficulty believing her results so I decided to try it myself.

In a K-8 private school I ran a year-long group for white teachers and staff on white privilege. Following Thandeka's lead, I gave the group the assignment. When we met a month later, no one had been able to bring her- or himself to say the word "white" publically in reference to white children or adults. My hunch is that they each hoped that if they came back and reported their experiences that I would drop the request and move on. But I reassigned the Race Game, moving the time to winter vacation and assigning the task for only one day to address some of their excuses. A month later only one person had tried the experience, and it had turned out to be productive. Identifying one of her niece's friends as white prompted a long conversation with her sister, her niece's mother.

I have thought about this assignment in the years between the first and second editions of *Understanding White Privilege*, and I'm still mystified that it is such a difficult thing to do. Why is there so much more reluctance to identify white people than to identify men? Perhaps this question would be the start of a conversation moving us closer to thinking about being white. Over time I become increasingly clear that, while it may be personally hard to deal with being white, the naming process is vital. Until we can talk about whiteness and our common experience of that, we will be unable to make essential changes in our relationships with people of color and in the systems of which we are a part, from our family to our workplace to our country.

If we look again at the Three Levels (Figure 9.1), we see that what we carry at the personal level in some ways defines the people with whom we build relationships, the groups with whom we build affiliations, and what we believe is appropriate individual and group behavior. If all the leaders I have experience with are white men who look sort of like me, when I am in a position to interview and hire chances are good that those are the people who will look qualified to me. An example: I worked with the Board of Deans at a very prestigious university. Well into the discussion, one of the few women in the group said, "Francie, go look at the coat rack. You'll see a collection of men's jackets, all size 40 or 42. We [women] have often said, 'Why don't we do our hiring that way? It would be so much quicker than going through all of the candidates and determining that, in the end, white male suit jacket number three is best.' " Now did the people on the search committee decide ahead of time that a white male would be the person they would choose? Maybe; maybe not. What I would bet my ranch on, as we said in Texas, is that there was little or no open conversation within the committee about the white candidates *as white*. In colleges that are heavily male-dominated, such as many STEM [science, technology, engineering, and mathematics] fields, maleness probably wouldn't be mentioned, either. It would be silently—perhaps unconsciously—assumed.

Let's look at another example of stereotypes about people of color: that they are, as a group, not qualified for jobs in higher education. The other side of that bias is that white men, as a group, are qualified. As I've said, white men are considered qualified until they prove that they aren't, and people of color and white women are seen as *un*qualified until they prove that they are. Many don't get that chance. I recently heard again a story I have heard many times before: In a search for a provost, the leadership team, all of whom were white, determined that the candidate with institution-wide support, an African man, was not a "good fit" based on his accent and on the institution from which he had gotten his doctorate. The team was so concerned about his inability to "fit in" that they called the search a failure and hired no one. The next year they hired a white lesbian for the position.

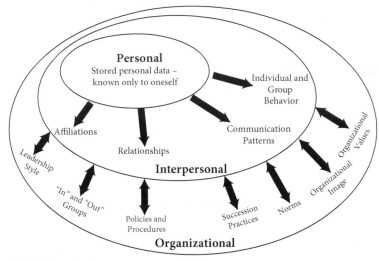

Figure 9.1 The Three Levels

This example shows the direct connection between the personal level, where attitudes sit, and the organizational level, where decisions based on those biases are made. It underscores the necessity for those of us who are "leading while privileged" to be aware of the values, biases, and belief systems that we carry around, either consciously or unconsciously. Claude Steele is clear that not only are identity-based stereotypes personally damaging, but that also they are societally dangerous in that they negatively affect "our ability to fix some of the bad ways that identity still influences the distribution of outcomes in society."[11]

While we continue essential personal work, we must remember that personal change is not the real goal of a person committed to bringing about racially just relationships or systems. That commitment requires a body of knowledge that many of us overlook or simply don't have. Our task as institutional change agents is to learn about how systems work, in particular the system we are trying to change. In order to be an effective change agent, one must never underestimate the centrality of power—getting it, holding it, and extending it—in the behavior of the organization and individuals in it.[12] It is rarely mentioned. Change agents have to ferret out the basic and on-going role of acquiring and maintaining power by observing, keeping notes, and connecting the dots.

The conversations and decisions, or lack of them, about the provost search took place in an institution that has its own climate and culture, just as every system or organization has. As racial justice organizational change agents, it is these we study, rather than the individual personalities of the major players. Climate and culture, though related, are different from one another. Organizational climate can be discovered by observing what is going on: listening to people and exploring the organization's history, its employee composition, ways of doing things, formal and informal rules, leadership style, and so on. Take a snapshot, look for patterns, form hypotheses about what will continue to happen.

Examining an organizational culture tells us more about *why* an organization functions as it does. Exploring it reveals the way things are done that are subtle, invisible, and often unconscious—the "forces underneath" that "guide and constrain the behavior of members of a group through the shared norms that are held in that group."[13] Organizational culture is context-specific, nuanced, and ambiguous. Studying the culture of an organization leads us to the assumptions on which life in it is based. They are not necessarily ours, even though they might look similar on the surface. "'Culture' refers to those elements of a group or an organization that are most stable and least malleable."[14] Discovering an organization's culture helps us formulate the most effective change strategies.

We are committed to moving people and systems forward, believing that many people want equitable and inclusive schools but don't know how to achieve them. Before we can bring about change, we need a specific vision of what we want our organization to become. We need an overall long-term strategy to achieve our goals, and each action we take must be carefully considered. In order to be effective, we have to know how our institutions think and work.

To understand your school's climate and culture in terms of race, start with a set of simple questions. Even though you may feel like you know all this, take the time to write down your answers. Look for patterns that give you clues to the best approach to moving forward with talking about whiteness.

1. How serious would you say your school is regarding addressing issues of diversity and inclusion? What information and experiences do you base your assessment on?
2. Where is your school in the process of addressing diversity and inclusion? Does it have an overall plan for how it will create a diverse and inclusive institution or are there several uncoordinated plans in various departments or offices? How will leaders and parts of the organization be held accountable for following the plan? Where are the resources for funding the plan coming from?

3. Where does the institution talk about "inclusion" and how? In the president's speeches? In departments as an integrated part of curriculum? In recruiting, hiring, tenure, and promotion? In classrooms? In conversations about policies and practices?
4. What language does your school use to talk about race? For example, does it still use the term "minorities" (with its implication of "less-than") and who does that include? "People of color" and "white people"? "Diverse" students? "Affirmative action hires" and "affirmative action students"?
5. Are white people in the institution explicitly talked about as a group in the same ways that students, faculty, and staff of color are? For example, "white faculty, administrators, students, staff"? If so, by whom and in what situations? A few people of color who are seen as renegades? A few white people who are seen as renegades?
6. Is there a history of trying to open conversations in which white people were identified explicitly just as people in other racial groups were? Who opened the conversations, who was involved in them, and what happened? Did it happen again?
7. If you were to do a cost-benefit analysis of beginning to talk about whiteness, what would you discover? What would the costs be for you individually? For the academic community? What would the benefits be for you individually? For the community?
8. How would you encourage people—faculty, staff, students, administrators—to begin including whiteness in their thoughts, their conversations, and their decision-making?

How might you set up these conversations about race at your school? Start with something that is uncomfortable for you, but doesn't push you over the edge. For example, practice a conversation like this with a white ally:

White person A: "We hired a new secretary in our department."
White person B: "Really? Tell me about the person [avoiding assumptions about gender]."
White person A: "Well, she's a Japanese American woman who's worked in the physics department for years. She was needing a change, and we were looking for someone."
White person B: "Oh, great."

Let's say the person hired was white.

White person A: "We hired a new secretary in our department."

White person B: "Really? Tell me about the person [avoiding assumptions about gender]."

White person A: "Well, she's a white woman who's worked in the physics department for years. She was needing a change, and we were looking for someone."

White person B: "Oh, great."

End of conversation. In each case her race was identified. (So was her gender, but that's another book.) Nothing was said about the woman's qualifications, her skills, or her value. All we know in each case is the person's racial identity and gender. Yet moving white people to talk about themselves as white or to identify a group of white people or a white individual *as white* is almost impossible. So step out and lead. When people ask you why you are naming "white," begin the conversation.

There are several books that are helpful for those about to have difficult conversations. Each suggests a different approach. Spend some time looking at each of them, see which you think most fits your organizational environment, read it, and ask people to participate in a dialogue. You might decide to use one of these with a diversity council or a group that addresses incidents on campus.

Crucial Conversations: Tools for Talking When Stakes Are High by Kerry Patterson, Joseph Grenny, Ron McMillan, and Al Switzler.

Fierce Conversations: Achieving Success at Work & in Life, One Conversation at a Time by Susan Scott.

Courageous Conversations about Race: A Field Guide for Achieving Equity in Schools by Glenn Singleton and Curtis Linton.

Difficult Conversations: How to Discuss What Matters Most by Douglas Stone, Bruce Patton, and Sheila Heen.

How the Way We Talk Can Change the Way We Work: Seven Languages for Transformation by Robert Kegan and Lisa Laskow Lahey.

To underscore again the need for these conversations, I close with an email I received from a white male student at a liberal arts college in the Northeast, one that is considered among the most liberal and socially just.

X College, in its short history, has built a strong tradition of breaking down socially constructed norms through activism....However, this history does not come without its own unique set of complications. In regards to race, a significant setback we face here at X College is the overwhelming number of white students who identify personally and politically as "liberal" and/or "progressive" and who either see themselves as exempt from their white race or [as] a member of a "super-race," what I have read Dr. Kendall refer to as "good-white-people."

Unfortunately, I see that a lot of white students here generally stay away from critically and reflexively thinking about race, resistant to engaging with their white identity or acknowledging the implications of its subsequent privileges. I wish to attend and graduate from an institution that is actively committed to anti-racism; we must make a priority of addressing our white-based racial problems.

Together we must go forward and work until we attain racially just relationships and systems, remembering that "[h]ow we set up the terms for discussing racial issues shapes our perceptions and response to these issues."[15] Talking about whiteness is a crucial part of that stepping up and stepping out. To quote Rabbi Hillel, "If not now, when?"

10

BECOMING AN ALLY AND BUILDING
AUTHENTIC RELATIONSHIPS ACROSS RACE
The Challenge and Necessity of Making Race Our Issue

At a small liberal arts college in which there is at least spoken support for working on "diversity," a white professor asked an African American colleague to teach a course on issues of diversity and multiculturalism with her. The professor was a woman who frequently spoke out about feminism and race and was seen as one of the liberal leaders and allies to people of color on campus, so the African American woman said yes.

As they began to design the class, the white woman said that she believed they should leave the "sensitive" issues (that is, race) until the end of the semester. The African American woman was disturbed, but, because she didn't have a doctorate, she felt she could say nothing. However, she was clear that, by not acknowledging her whiteness and by asking that race not be discussed, the white professor negated the presence of race, and therefore of people of color, in the room; the white woman was acting as if she herself was not affected by race and that none of the other white people in the room were, either. Based on the white professor's comments, the African American decided to speak theoretically rather than personally about various kinds of privilege. She decided against talking straightforwardly about racial dynamics on campus.

And still, at the end of the semester, a white student complained in class that the African American woman had made him feel uncomfortable and that she had attacked him by even mentioning whiteness and race. The white professor, who had always identified herself as an ally to people of color and as someone who could be counted on, was silent as this confrontation took place. By saying nothing publicly to the offended student, the white woman confirmed by implication the belief that it is the responsibility of people of color to deal with racism. Addressing racism was left to the one who was most negatively affected by it and most professionally vulnerable, and those with privilege, the white students, missed an opportunity to be shown models of how to be an ally.

This chapter is about relationships—some that are across race, some that (for those of us who are white) are same-race relationships. It is about how to be an ally if you are a person with privilege, and it is about what is required to have authentic relationships with someone who is racially different from you. This is not a chapter about friendship. While it is certainly possible that friendships will develop over years of doing racial justice and anti-racism work together, that is not the goal. It is, as my mother used to say, *lagniappe*—a Creole word meaning something extra you didn't expect to get. The conversations here, like those in the rest of the book, are viewed from the contexts of organizational change, racial justice, and the institutionalized supremacy of whiteness. My hope is that, through the examples and skills identified in the discussion about each kind of relationship, you'll feel better equipped to address the racism and white privileges in the institutional communities of which you are a part.

One way to work for social justice is as an ally. The gay and lesbian community realized many years ago that, without the help of straight allies, gays and lesbians don't have the clout needed to fight heterosexist and homophobic legislation. Gradually the call for allies has spread to other communities for which discrimination is systemic. What it means to be an ally varies greatly from person to person. For some, it means building a relationship of love and trust with another; for others, it means intentionally putting one's self in harm's way so that another person remains safe. Each type of alliance has its own parameters, responsibilities, and degrees of risk. For example, being an ally to someone who is in a less privileged position than I am requires different work than is necessary if the person has privileges like mine. There is also a variety of styles that an ally can use. Some of us are bold and audacious; others are more reserved. The common element is that we align ourselves with a person or people in such a way that we "have their backs."

Being an ally is integral to my work for social and racial justice: I ally myself with an individual or group for a common cause or purpose. I see myself as an ally of people whom I don't know, individuals who are members of groups with which I align myself as a matter of principle. One of the most effective ways to use our privilege is to become the ally of those on the other side of the privilege seesaw. This type of alliance requires a great deal of self-examination on our part as well as the willingness to go against the people who share our privilege and with whom we are expected to group ourselves. For me and, I think, for many others, choosing to be an ally to a person or to an issue (I will say more about that distinction) is a very serious commitment; it is a choice to put oneself on the line, both publicly and privately. It is not something you can just sign onto because it sounds like a good thing. People of color and people in other target groups want potential allies to consider a commitment seriously before making it. It is better not to sign up than let the target group members down. *Target group* is the federal government term that refers to those who, because they are at greatest risk of being targeted for discrimination, are federally protected.

The story at the beginning of this chapter is connected to what it means to be an ally and occurred at a school at which I was asked to speak. The African American woman who had invited me told me this story and, even though it was a year later, she was still very upset about it. I spent the day visiting classes and going to a faculty meeting. During the meeting, one white woman in particular said all the right things. She talked about the vision and mission of the school, which is social-action based, and how the faculty had no choice but to revamp their curriculum. I talked with her after the meeting and liked her; she complimented me on a piece I had written on allies; her commitment seemed believable. After the meeting, I went out to dinner with the African American woman. She asked me if I had had an interesting conversation with the white woman, I said yes, and then she said, "She's the one I team-taught with." I was furious. Angry at the woman for being such a horrible representation of white women, but probably most infuriated at myself for allowing my ego to be so massaged that I had not seen the clues about who she really was. I spent my trip home writing many of the examples of how to be an ally that are presented later in this chapter. I thought that, if she had missed the point in the earlier version of these thoughts, I would be as concrete as I could about what ally behavior does and does not look like.

Being an ally always occurs in the context of being a good change agent; this is not something one does to help someone else or to help a group. A person who wants to be an ally intentionally chooses to be a change agent at both the personal and institutional levels. You have to be absolutely clear that you are doing this because it is in your interest or for the greater good. Before identifying yourself as an ally, much time should go into exploration of how your life is influenced by having white privilege and what being an ally means to you.

First, think about how you define *ally*. What you see as being an ally might be very different from how someone else sees it. For example, *ally*: "a person [who] is associated with another or others for some common cause or purpose," *advocate*: "a person who pleads for or on behalf of another; intercessor," *coalition*: "a combination or alliance, esp. a temporary one between persons, factions, states, etc.," *connection*: "a circle of friends or associates or a member of such a circle."[1] Do you understand the difference between being supportive and being an ally? I can be supportive of someone and want her or him to be successful without committing to stand with that person publicly. Next, be clear about why you want to be an ally to this person or to this particular issue. What is your motivation? Often we want to be allies because we feel guilty about the privilege we have, and we either want to get rid of it or act as if we don't have it. Our hope, sometimes unconscious, is that if we work with someone they will like us and that will make us feel better about who we are. As understandable as this desire is, avoid falling into that trap. Working on ourselves and our guilt or shame is personal, internal work. That work has to be well begun before we connect ourselves with others working for racial justice and institutional change.

It is essential that you know what your expectations are about being an ally, what you think you are signing up for, and what the expectations are of the people to whom you are allying yourself. If you're not clear about that, harmful misunderstandings can occur. Also, you need to know what you expect from them. If it's thanks and much open appreciation, you're working toward the wrong goal. As I have said over and over, we have to do this because we are clear that it is in our interest. We also need to communicate clearly about our boundaries in terms of time and commitment, actions and behavior. I remember an important interaction between a colleague and friend, a heterosexual Japanese American man, and me. A gay rights march was coming up and I had asked him participate. In response, he said, "I'm just not there yet. I would like to say I will go, but I know I won't." I told him I was sorry he wouldn't go, but that I was really glad to know what to expect. I also said that I appreciated his being honest about his own limits and that that made me trust him even more.

Assuming that you have a shared goal with the one or ones to whom you are allying yourself, do you have agreement on appropriate means to reach that goal? What do you need to know to be a useful ally on this issue? Educate yourself about the issue in general and about the specific situation on which you want to act. An ally needs as complete an understanding of what is going on as possible. How much of the big picture do you understand? What else do you need to know to understand how systems of oppression work, in the world in general and in the context of your institution? Do you understand the varying roles that people with privilege can play? Those of us who are white can *choose* to be an ally on an issue, but we cannot decide further. This last point is important: We must be asked or accepted as an ally. We can't choose to be someone's ally and then move ahead with what we think we should do. *If we are someone's ally, that person calls the shots.*

Another useful part of the work before becoming an ally is to consider the characteristics of various types of relationships that might potentially be confused with alliances, but, in fact, have very different qualities.[2] A reminder: I am describing each of the relationships in the context of the work- or school-place. A colleague or peer is the least personal of relationships. It is professional and limited, and usually it is institutionally based and recognized. Sometimes you work toward mutual goals on a project or on research, or you work in the same office or department. Often colleagues are competitive with one another, vying for the same position or recognition from the same person with power.

A friendship is personal, even in a school or work setting. Rather than being competitive, friendships are supportive, with each person wanting the best for the other. We get to choose our friends, rather than having them chosen for us as is the case for peers and colleagues. There is trust between friends and sometimes open conversation. Other times we don't say all that we are thinking because we want to protect our friend from our thoughts, particularly if they are critical. Usually, friendships are based on things you have in common—interests, passions, activities, children who are the same age. And most often they are with people who share our same privileges—same race, approximately same socioeconomic class, same sexual orientation, same religious perspective, same physical abilities, and same gender. My hunch is that generally we are able to see our friends' perspectives; their experience is fairly well known to us.

Most of us have relationships across privilege: those between men and women most frequently. From the large body of literature on female–male relationships, including bestsellers like John Gray's *Men Are from Mars, Women Are from Venus* and Deborah Tannen's *You Just Don't Understand: Men and Women in Conversation*, it is clear that, after centuries of interactions, power and privilege continue to be divisive factors between men and women. It appears, even though many women report that they desire it, that there are relatively few male–female interactions in which gender is honestly part of regular conversation and the men are consistently working to remove the barriers that their gender power puts in place. But few women are willing to face the reality that their primary relationship is with someone from their oppressor group. I get sharp responses when I bring it up: "My husband is an exception. He and I have a wonderful relationship," "That's easy for you to say. You're a lesbian," "Well, men just can't help being like they are. What can you do?" It's clear that men are conscious of their institutionalized power and privilege and like it. One only has to look at the statistical differences in income between men and women or at humor that degrades women to be clear that we live in a culture that does not value women, much as it does not value people who are not white. But that's another writer's book.

Authentic relationships across privilege are another situation entirely, because in those both people are self-aware and willing to keep channels of communication open about power and privilege differences. My experience is that consciousness and determination to deal with those differences are relatively rare. Authentic relationships across racial privilege involve the risk of losing social and cultural capital: Your value in social groups and in the culture in which you work is endangered. When a white person "gets it" and begins to speak honestly about racism and the supremacy of whiteness and how they play out in the organization, she or he becomes a threat to other white people and is seen as a potential danger to keeping things the way they are. When a person of color enters into an authentic relationship with a white person, she or he is often seen as betraying her or his race. So there's not always a lot of support for authentic cross-race relationships. Mutual respect is obviously essential, as is the determination not to make assumptions about one another and about the relationship. Each step toward deepening has to be tested to be sure that both people see it the same way. Bonding in such relationships is intentional; it doesn't just happen. The same is true as the two share their personal worlds. I remember a close friend of color saying to me as we were driving toward his house, "Do you have any idea what a big thing it is for me to take you to my home—to let you into my private world?" I thought to myself, "Well, I guess I don't, really. I invite people to my house all the time. My race and class privilege are showing up." Later we talked about what the experience was like for him and for me.

I'm reminded of a similar situation in which the personal perspectives were defined by race and culture, and I totally missed the impact of my behavior. A Latino friend and colleague invited me to his Christmas party year after year. Every time I said I thought I could come and, at the last minute, cancelled. He lives an hour and a half away, and it seemed like too much of a trek in the midst of holiday preparations. And I spend my work life interacting with large groups of strangers and prefer smaller groups in my personal time. One day he said to me, "Every year I invite you to our Christmas party, and you never come. Why is that?" "Well, I don't like big parties." "Do you realize that when I send you an invitation, I am inviting you to become a part of our family?" "No, I never thought about it like that. I'm really sorry." From then on I made the effort to go and, of course, enjoyed myself immensely. Authentic cross-race relationships are risky and challenging; they require paying serious attention to nuances of behavior that we might otherwise take for granted. In the work setting, this would involve purposefully paying attention to the public interactions between the two of you, because you can be sure that others are keeping a close watch. It means, for the white person, being invested in providing support to the target group person, particularly countering comments made by unthinking white people.

And now we get to ally relationships. As I have thought about what it means to be an ally if you have privilege, I have come to make a distinction that I didn't initially. During a conversation with a colleague, one of my own unconscious assumptions about allies became clear. As he was talking about being an ally to *people*, I realized that I am basically an ally to *issues*. He was talking about supporting another African American man at his institution; I was looking at addressing the supremacy of whiteness there. I always identify myself as an ally on issues of race; I am not always an ally to individual people of color as individuals. Do I think anyone should be a target of racism? Absolutely not. Do I think some people of color are enormous jerks who, from my perspective, do a lot of things wrong? Of course.

Focusing my alliance on a person leads me to relationship and friendship. I make certain decisions and act in specific ways because I am in relationship with her or him. Concentrating my alliance-building energy on issues pushes me to a very different place: I have to study, to learn, to refine what I know and what I need to know so that my actions and behavior move us closer to the social and institutional change we, as allies, are striving for. Allying myself with an individual, then, occurs because of who that person is in relation to the issue to which I have an allegiance. Obviously I am making a somewhat artificial distinction because it is impossible to separate people and issues totally, but here's an example of how my thinking and my actions might differ depending on the direction of my focus. A white woman is hired as a new department chair and becomes one of two women on the senior management team. I am pleased because I believe that, until there is a diversity of voices among decision makers, our university will not be able to make the changes necessary to ensure the possibility of success of all students. I know how hard it is for women to be successful on our campus, and I want to do all I can to help. If I see myself as allying with people, my energy goes into building a relationship with her as an individual. I support her publicly and privately and do the things I perceive that an ally must do. When she begins to make decisions about curriculum change and tenure and promotion with which I disagree, I do not tell her how I feel because I fear it will have negative impact on our relationship. If my alliance is clearly concentrated on the issues of social justice on campus, truth between us is pivotal. I am more likely to be concerned about moving our agenda forward than protecting either her or me from the conflict that might arise because of my opposing ideas.

As an ally to a person, I am willing to do deep personal introspection about my role and experience as a person with privilege. I see that as part of my alliance. I respect the other's interpretations of an action or situation as accurate, instead of doubting them based on my own privileged perspective. This does not mean that I take everything the person says as true, but rather that I believe her or his description is real to her or him. I am willing to get into trouble with the person to whom I have allied myself; if a stink needs to be made about a particular incident, I have committed to hang in rather than leaving when it gets dangerous. Finally, I act as a spokesperson on the issue in the marginalized person's absence. This does not mean that I speak for someone else, as though I am part of that person's group. I will never be that. It means that, if there is no one speaking up, I will not let the opportunity pass. Different from a friendship, when I am an ally to a person I act in support of that person's ideology.

Here's another example of the difference between being an ally to a person and an ally to an issue. I was working closely with a faculty at a university when a new senior administrator, an African American man, was hired. Knowing that he was coming, I spent a great deal of time talking with the faculty about ways that they might support him. Initially, he seemed to be doing a good job, from the perspective of the people of color. He was enthusiastic and creative, and he appeared to have the senior administrator's ear. As time went on, I thought he made decisions that were more in the president's and trustees' interest and less in that of the faculty, staff, and students of color. He wasn't good on gender issues, either. Obviously, other African Americans in the institution struggled with what to do. They could see what was happening, yet there are so few African American scholars in senior positions around the country that to challenge one, even privately, is very difficult. Those of us who are white aren't ever in that dilemma; because we take a critical mass of leaders with us everywhere we go—that group of people who run corporations, colleges, and universities—and because our criticisms aren't read as being about a whole group, we can speak up far more easily.

As I've said, there is no equal opportunity to be mediocre. We who have white privilege run the gamut from smart to not-so-smart, skilled to inept, just like every other group of people. However, our privilege puts us in the position of being seen as competent until we prove ourselves incompetent while people who do not have privilege, particularly race, gender, and ability privilege, are viewed as incompetent until they prove themselves competent. Sometimes that's impossible to do, if they are seen, by definition, as incompetent. Think about how often you have seen job descriptions that say something like, "Qualified minorities encouraged to apply." How many have you seen that say, "Qualified white people encouraged to apply?" "Qualified" is assumed; there's no need to state it. And, when people of color or women are hired, we are assured that they are actually able to handle the job. Further, if they aren't successful, chances are good that the company or institution of higher education won't hire another person from that category for a long time, because failure is attributed to that person's gender or race, not to her or his personal lack of skills. So criticizing the African American man was dicey, and it only happened behind closed doors. He was extremely competent, but he was, in many ways, working against the best interests of people of color and white women there. Allies to an issue had to act strategically so as not to undermine the man but his actions instead.

If my alliance is clearly concentrated on the issues of racial justice, truth between allies is essential. I am more likely to be concerned about moving our agenda forward than protecting my personal ally or me from conflict between us. I support a person who has less privilege than I do until her or his actions become indefensible, and then I decide to speak, both personally and publicly, about what is going on, using well thought out strategies. I consistently examine my decisions and thought processes through the lenses of white privilege and social justice as opposed to simply through the lens of a particular person's experience, as I might if I were supporting an individual. And, while it is desirable in a personal ally situation to be consistently on top of the context (experiences in the rest of the institution, of other people of color, of what is happening at other institutions and in the world, of intersections between various aspects of privilege, of current writings and research), when I make a commitment to be an ally to an issue understanding the context is integral to my ability to fulfill my promise. My responsibilities as an ally to an issue are much broader and deeper.

As an ally with privilege, I have to ask constantly: Do I think I am doing charity work—helping those who, from my perspective, are unable to help themselves and so allying myself to *help* someone else, or am I doing this for the greater good of us all? The first is offensive and racist because it assumes that people of color are not fully capable. During the question and answer part of an event, a white person asked the speaker, who was a Latino, what white people could do to help? He said, "We can take care of ourselves if you will take care of your people and remove the barriers you put in our way every day." It is not about helping; it is about working with them and using our privilege, power, and access to influence and resources to change the systems that keep people of color oppressed.

Allies work continuously to develop an understanding of the personal and institutional experiences of the person or people with whom they are allying themselves. If the ally is a member of a privileged group, it is essential that she or he also strives for clarity about the impact of privileges on her or his life. I must consistently ask myself what it means to be white in this specific situation. How would I be experienced now if I were of color? Would I be listened to? Would I be getting the support I am getting now? How would my life in this organization be different if I were not white/male/heterosexual/tenured/a manager? I must closely observe the experiences of people of color in the organization: how they are listened to, talked about, promoted, and expected to do additional jobs. For example, members of target groups counsel all the people in the organization who look like them even though that is not a part of their job description and they have to speak for all members of "their" group or serve on a disproportionate number of committees so that there is "racial input." Few of us who are white ever have to be "professional whites," asked to speak for our race, represent our race, or offer support to people purely because their skin color is the same as ours.

Allies choose to ally themselves publicly and privately with members of target groups and respond to their needs. This may mean breaking assumed allegiances with those who have the same privileges as you. It is important not to underestimate the consequences of breaking these agreements and to break them in ways that will be most useful to the person or group with whom you are aligning yourself. You could step into a situation in which a person of color is being overrun by someone who looks like you: "John [a white man], I think Eugene [a Filipino] is making an important point. Would you hold your comment for a second so I can hear what Eugene has to say?" Or speak out about a situation in which you don't appear to have a vested interest: "Jean, there are no women of color in this pool of candidates. How can we begin to get a broader perspective in our department if we continue to hire people who have similar backgrounds to ours or who look like us?" You could interrupt a comment or joke that is insensitive or stereotypic toward a target group, whether or not a member of that group is present. "Lu, that joke is anti-Semitic. I don't care if a Jewish person told it to you; it doesn't contribute to the kind of environment I want to work in."

This is not about rescuing or grandstanding or making a show of our support so that we will look good or progressive or liberal. Other white people may perceive our stepping in as betraying our same-race relationships. Comments such as "Who made you the political correctness police?" or "Don't you have a sense of humor?" or "Can't Chong take care of himself?" alert you to the fact that you have broken the unspoken code about criticizing another white, broken what Aida Hurtado calls the "unspoken rules of privilege."[3] While we may choose to take this risk ourselves, it is important to work strategically so as not to put the person with whom we have aligned ourselves in greater jeopardy. The example above about the unbalanced pool of candidates is worded to make it clear that it is in the department's interest to interview and hire people who bring different experiences and points of view to the table. The white person could have covered himself by implying that his concern was for the lonely woman of color already present. ("Jean, there are no women of color in this pool of candidates. I know from talking with her that Aurora is sick of being the only Latina in our department.") Instead, he made it clear that a mostly white staff was not good for him or for the institution.

Allies believe that it is in their interest to be allies and are able to talk about why this is the case. Talking clearly about having the privilege to be able to step in is an important educational tool for others with the same privileges. I regularly preface what I am about to say with, "As a white person, I think or feel or understand or am not able to understand...." I let others know that I am clear that being white has an impact on how I perceive everything. We choose to make an issue of a specific situation, acknowledging that our whiteness gives us the privilege to speak with impunity. "As white women, because of our race privilege, our promotions are at far less risk than those of the women of color. Let's speak to the women of color and see what their suggestions are about dealing with the harassment we have all been experiencing."

Allies are committed to the never-ending personal growth required to be genuinely supportive. If both people are without privilege it means coming to grips with the ways that internalized oppression affects you. If I am privileged, uprooting long-held beliefs about the way that the world works will probably be necessary. We always have to face the intentionality of white people's treatment of people of color, both historically and currently. In order to be an ally, I must hold in my consciousness what my racial group has done to keep us in positions of power and authority. This is not about blaming myself or feeling guilty. In fact, I think guilt is often self-serving; if I feel guilty about something, I can get mired in those feelings and fail to act to change the situation. Staying conscious of our behavior as a group moves me to take responsibility for making changes. It also gives me greater insight into the experiences of those with whom I align myself.

Allies are able to articulate how various patterns of oppression have served to keep them in privileged positions or to withhold opportunities they might otherwise have. For many of us, this means exploring and owning our dual roles as oppressor and oppressed, as uncomfortable as that might be. I need to see how my whiteness opens doors to institutions or opportunities that most probably would not have opened so easily otherwise. To understand that as white women we are given access to power and resources because of racial similarities to and our relationships with white men. And we often receive those privileges at the expense of people of color, both male and female. While we certainly experience systemic discrimination as women, our skin color makes us less threatening to the group that holds systemic power.

Allies expect to make some mistakes but do not use that as an excuse for inaction. As a person with privilege, it is important to study and to talk about how your privilege acts as both a shield and as blinders for you. Of necessity, those without privileges know more about what those privileges look like than those who are privileged and can take them for granted. We need to remember that each of us, no matter how careful or conscious we are or how long we have been working on issues of racism, is going to say or do something dumb or insensitive. Our best bet is to acknowledge our mistakes openly and learn from them. We should consistently question how our perceptions might be different if we were not members of a privileged group. For example, what might it be like to be the only woman of color in a group of senior decision makers who are all white and male? Would you read situations and conversations differently than one of the white men? What things might you say or how might you make your comments? What kind of support might you want if you were other than white and male?

It's useful to keep a filter in your mind through which you run your thoughts or comments. Remarks such as "If I were you...." or "I know just how you feel...." are never very helpful in opening up communication, and, in conversations in which there is an imbalance of privilege, they take on an air of arrogance. People with privilege can never really know what it is like to be a member of the target group. While I can sympathize with those who are of color, it is not possible for me truly to understand the experience of a person with different skin color because I am never going to be treated as they are. The goal is to show someone you are listening, you care, and you understand that being white causes you to be treated differently in the world. Much more useful comments would be "Because of my white blinders I don't always notice how he or she responds to you" or "Obviously, as a white person, I have never had your experience, but I would like you to tell me how you're being treated."

Allies know that those on each side of an alliance hold responsibility for their own change, whether or not people on the other side choose to respond or to thank them. They are also clear that they are doing this work for themselves, not to "take care of" the Other. Although it is difficult to remember that, it is essential. We must continually examine the institutional and personal benefits of hearing a wide diversity of perspectives and building different points of view into the work we do. Also, interrupting less-than-helpful comments and pushing for an inclusive work environment is important. We do it because we, as well as others, will benefit. We do not step forward because we think we should or because the people of color can't speak for themselves or because we want to look good to the people of color around us. We are allies because we know that it is in our interest.

Allies know that, in the most empowered and genuine ally relationships, the persons with privilege initiate the change toward personal, institutional, and societal justice and equality. I don't mean doing it all or taking over. Sharing power of decision-making about what will happen is essential. Assess who will be at least risk when stepping into a situation to initiate change, confer with others who are at greater risk about the best strategies, and move forward. Being an ally is like performing a dance. Our moves should be carefully designed to have the greatest effect. We understand that this is not an opportunity to take charge, to ride in to fix everything. Ally relationships are just that: relationships. Together with the people who aren't privileged, we choreograph who makes which moves and when they will be made. On many occasions, people of color have looked at me and said, "You help her understand what's going on. She's your white sister." They were clear that it is not their job to educate white women and that, because of my privilege, I am less likely to suffer from speaking straightforwardly than they would.

Allies promote a sense of inclusiveness and justice in the organization, helping to create an environment that is hospitable for all. Clarity that expecting people of color to address racism, women to take care of sexism, and gay men and lesbians to "fix" heterosexism in the organization is racist, sexist, and heterosexist, respectively, is crucial. Instead, an ally chooses to become the point person for organizational change on these issues. Clues that this assumption is operating: The Diversity Committee is composed predominantly of people of color and white women, while those with greater positional and informal decision-making power are on the "important" committees. Or the senior manager reroutes all announcements of "diversity" conferences to a person of color with an attached note that says, "Thought you might be interested," implying that addressing issues of diversity is not his or her concern. Or men joke on the way to a sexual harassment seminar that they don't know why they have to go since they "already know how to harass." Or the majority of people pushing for domestic partner benefits are gay or lesbian. Pay attention to the days and times meetings are scheduled so that no one group bears the brunt of exclusion. For example, be sure that meetings are not regularly scheduled on Saturdays or Jewish holidays or before or after the regular work day so that parents have difficulty with childcare.

Allies with privilege are responsible for sharing the lead with people of color in changing the organization; they hold greater responsibility for seeing changes through to their conclusion. *Sharing* the lead is very different from *taking* the lead. When we take the lead we get to keep ourselves central and see ourselves as riding in on a white horse (a color chosen intentionally) to take care of everything. Sharing the lead requires that we are in alignment and partnership with people who are working to change the institution for the good of all of us. People who have committed themselves to being allies involve themselves in building a strategic diversity plan for the organization, tying it to the organization's business plan, and resting their personal credibility on the implementation of the plan. They find ways to secure funding for scholarships so that an economically and racially diverse student population is guaranteed, push for an assessment of current policies and procedures in the organization, and work to change them so that they don't have impact on various groups of people differently. They intentionally use their access to power, resources, and influence to help those who might be able to bring about change to do so.

Allies are able to laugh at themselves as they make mistakes and at the real, but absurd, systems of supremacy in which we all live. As many oppressed people know, humor is a method of survival. But those with privilege must be very careful not to assume that we can join in the humor of those in a target group with whom we are in alliance. We appreciate that there are times when laughing together is the only thing we can do short of throwing ourselves off a tall building. As Cornel West, an African American scholar, has asked on numerous occasions, "What could be more Theater of the Absurd than being Black in America?" We must pay attention to the boundaries of who-can-say-what-to-whom: While it may be okay for a person of color to call me his "white sister," it would be presumptuous for me to call him my "Latino brother." In some communities, African Americans call white men "white boys" to lessen the feeling of white men's power. It would be insensitive, on the other hand, for a white male ally to call African American men "Black boys." This is because of the history of that phrase and the implication that a person with privilege is ignoring the impact of race and believes that we are really all the same under the skin.

Allies understand that emotional safety is not a realistic expectation if we take our alliance seriously. For those with privilege, the goal is, to quote David Tulin again, to "become comfortable with the uncomfortable and uncomfortable with the too comfortable" and to act to alter the too comfortable. Allies must be willing to step in and take risks. It is not good enough just to know the right things to say. In fact, knowing all the right things to say, saying them in public, and not backing them up with actions is really playing on your privilege. It is worse than not saying anything at all because then the person without privilege believes she has backup and is left out there on the limb. We must be alert to our desire to create a "safe" environment for an interracial conversation. My experience is that when white people ask for safety they mean they don't want to be held accountable for what they say, they want to be able to make mistakes and not have people of color take it personally, and they don't want to be yelled at by people of color. Those of us who are white are almost always safer and freer from institutional retribution than people of color. That knowledge should help us remain in uncomfortable situations as we work for change. We should also identify committees, decision-making teams, and departments that are "too white" and work to bring a critical mass of people of color and white allies into those groups. We do this because the current composition is less able to make wise decisions due to its narrow vision. While discomfort is certain to follow, the benefits of inclusiveness far outweigh the discomfort.

Allies know the consequences of their not being clear about the experience of being Other: not being seen as trustworthy, lacking authentic relationships, and working without the foundation for coalition-building. For allies with privilege, the consequences of being unclear are even greater. Because our behavior is rooted in privilege, those who are in our group give greater credence to our actions than they might if we were members of groups without privilege. Part of our task is to be models and educators for those like us. We understand that, because we don't see a colleague of color being mistreated, doesn't mean that daily race-related experiences aren't occurring. I often hear white people make comments such as, "Well, my friend is Black, but he's beyond all this race stuff. He is never treated poorly." Or "I'm sure she doesn't have any problems with white people. You'd hardly know she's Hispanic." Or "He *is* Black, but he's really like a *white* Black person. He's treated better than I am." Comments such as these alert a person of color to the fact that we don't have those experiences, we can't imagine other people having them, and therefore put little credence in the stories that people of color relate. If we are to be genuine allies to people of color, we must constantly observe the subtleties and implications of other white people's comments and behavior just as we observe our own. We must take the risk of asking, "What if I am wrong about how I think people of color are being treated in my institution? What can I do to seek out the reality of their experiences? How will I feel if I discover that people I know, love, and trust are among the worst offenders? What will I do?" We should remind a colleague who says, "She's always whining about race. This is not about race," that as white people we simply can't know what it is like to be of color. We will never be treated as if we were. While not everything is about race, there is always the possibility that it is an element in any situation. To deny that reality signals people of color and other white people that we can't be trusted as allies or as members of a coalition.

We become barriers instead of allies when we want to maintain control. Allies can become enemies, or those who seemed to be allies can turn out to have been enemies (or just well-meaning white people) all along. Some time ago, I began collecting examples of this phenomenon. Often they are about well-meaning white people. As in this case: "You know I am one of the greatest proponents for this initiative [changing the institution in order to be able to attract and retain more faculty and students of color], but we would be doing our employees a terrible disservice to suggest that there is institutional racism in our system." Month one: "We need to design this so that it will work on our campus." Month two: "Let's have the consultant redesign her approach." Month four: "This is such an important and long-needed effort that we can't afford to have it go poorly. We have some big issues on our plate at this point, so I want to put off inaugurating this project so that the diversity initiative isn't tarred with the same brush. Let's wait until after the upcoming governing board meeting." Month eight: "As soon as the governing board signs off on our strategic plan at the end of next month, we will be set to go." It never happened.

Another example: "Just wanted to let you know that we actually encountered some obstacles from the administration in forming our reading group on white privilege. When I forwarded our intended message to the Provost, he sent it on to the Vice Provost and the Dean of the Faculty. Both of them had major objections to the fact that, as an administrator, I was trying to dictate to the campus community what a topic for reading groups would be. 'Too political,' was the comment. We've started an interesting conversation on this, but it did show me that our work really is never done."

And another: "We're all doing the work and we're all good white people so what's the problem? We're better anti-racists than those people in other parts of the country, so we don't need to work with them. We'll just do our own thing." Again: "What you're saying doesn't really apply to us. We're in a different generation; we don't need to talk about this. The real problem now is that white kids in predominantly Black city schools feel like victims." And: "All we're supposed to do here is 'diversity lite.' Don't upset anyone, don't raise any real issues, don't ask us to look at our history as an institution. What can I do?" This was from a woman of color who is head of the diversity effort.

Another example: After I publicly criticized Morris Dees, the white man who is head of the Southern Poverty Law Center, for his arrogance of requiring the presence of armed police officers and putting all conference participants through security screen and search before his speech at a conference held in a college gym in Pella, Iowa, a woman of color said to me, "I can't afford to yell at you or at Morris Dees....each of you is helpful in different settings. If you white people want to fight among yourselves, go ahead. I'm not going to weigh in—we just need the outcomes." What was it that I, the queen of allies, missed? How did my ego function rule when I so clearly needed to be in role function? What happens when we who are "experts" get fooled by the compliments of others and blinded by our alleged "brilliance"? As Tim Wise said to me, "We have to continually remind ourselves that we don't know shit. I actually do think we know more than we say, but, if we do know, we then have to deliver." There is absolutely no time for resting on our laurels.

From another consultant, a Latina: "Look at how white people sabotage because of wanting to maintain control. They turn on us instead of doing their own work. They say, 'You're not X, you're not Y, you're not Z, so we'll get someone else—who's more edgy, who's not as edgy, who understands us better, blah, blah, blah.' Or 'This work is too soft, a waste of time, mental masturbation.' And, as an outside people, we crumple because we want to be doing a good job. They come in and say, 'Tell us what we can do.' We give them ideas and they go, 'No, no, no, that won't work.' Or 'Yes, but....' The white woman says, 'Don't question me as a white woman because I've done this before; I always work with women of color, so therefore I know.' We're in a no-win, heads you lose, tails I win, cycle of frustration. And then the institution gets left out there hanging, and we as change agents get discouraged.

"Often, we want to retreat. And then we feel bad, and the system stays the same. We need to have a time where we really stay in the conversation, through the discomfort, say things as we see them, and ask what we should do about it. At least name it out loud. The pattern is that we feel we're becoming less and less competent and less and less effective, and so we do softer work and don't say what we know to be happening.

"There's a sense of entitlement in many long-time white allies. They say, 'We've done so much serious work that you owe us.' We're so busy trying to change our institutions that we forget to continue our own personal excavation, and then the unresolved issues between us get in the way of our *doing* the work."[4]

Comments from an African American woman as she reflects on the white people she is working with in her institution: "White folks who claim to be your allies just continue to be who they are—they haven't shed who they are.... They're still working in that same realm—they don't think they have privilege. I want to say to them, 'You have not progressed toward anything. You haven't shed that old skin like a snake to create a new one. You say, 'That's so terrible that these things are happening,' and yet you are a part of those things. Behind closed doors you become a white person again. And, if you decide to go against the grain, to go against what your people have created, that will affect everything you love.' There is a lot of fear in doing that."

Once, during a break in a meeting with the Women, Race, and Privilege group, I was complaining about my Irish terrier, Bailie, and how I had not really trained him. When we started again, one of the women of color said, "No matter how much training they get, white people will always be Bailies; they will always revert back to who they are and what they know—how to be white." "Are you saying white people are dogs?" I asked. "Well, I guess I am. This is your life's work. It's my *life*. You can leave or take a break. You can put on your Crusader for Social Justice capes, go out and do good things, and then come home, hang your capes on the coat rack, and go out to dinner. We can't ever take ours off."

Being a genuine ally is some of the hardest and riskiest work we can do. It requires those of us with privilege consciously to move ourselves into the battle so that members of target groups can more easily move out of the line of fire. Being an ally is lonely and frightening as well as enriching and rewarding. If I am serious about this work, I must strive to remove the layers of blinders that my privilege places over my eyes. One of the reasons that being an ally is so difficult is that, the less I protect my eyes from the world around me, the more I see and understand. Often the determination to keep things as they are pushes me to despair. I have many ways of keeping myself buoyed up—others' wise words are among the most useful. This quotation from Dr. Martin Luther King, Jr., is one of the most helpful to me.

I am convinced that the universe is under control of a loving purpose. And that in the struggle for righteousness man has cosmic companionship. Behind the harsh appearance of the world there is benign power.[5]

This need not to be alone—to have companionship—in this work is very real. I think it's part of the reason that people of color are willing repeatedly to risk believing that white people will show up when they say they will and do the personal and institutional work to deal with their people. I began to get curious about authentic conversations and relationships across race many years ago. Repeatedly, in meetings and at conferences, the descriptions of cross-race interactions divided along racial lines— white people describing one experience, people of color another. For many men and women of color in corporations and academia, white women are seen as the primary barriers to promotion and tenure. They frequently form a broad band in the middle of the organizational hierarchy as middle managers and associate professors, making it very difficult for people of color to break through and move up. Most white women, on the other hand, see women of color as sharing their same oppressive experience of being women and don't recognize the role race plays in their respective experiences. (See Chapter 5, "How White Women Reinforce the Supremacy of Whiteness.")

There are some things of which I am sure: that race alters each group's needs and expectations around an authentic conversation or relationship; that white people and people of color face different risks as they enter into a relationship, whether it be as colleagues, friends, or allies; and that the context of institutionalized white privilege, in which we all live, is a primary barrier to our ever meeting as "just people," as white people often desire. I know that there are things white people need from people of color: the willingness of people of color to begin to establish trust *again* and even consider moving into another relationship; the good will of people of color, having decided to move forward, to give the new potential relationship the benefit of the doubt, in case this person is different; the clarity on the part of the person of color that there is something in it for her/him; and the commitment of people of color to do their own personal work on biases, prejudices, and assumptions about white people as well as their work on class, sexism, and heterosexism.

There are many more things that people of color need from white people in order to work to create authentic relationships: the pledge to observe with open eyes the experience of being of color in the context of the institutionalized superiority of whiteness; clarity about what one gets from an authentic conversation or relationship, understanding one's own interest; the humility not to have all the answers or not to be central, not the focus; and the strength to be vulnerable. People of color need us always to see ourselves as white; to listen to anger about others like ourselves without taking it totally personally or getting defensive and thinking, "She's not talking about me when she says *white people*"; the assurance that we will get curious and ask, "What if it *is* me?" And the firm resolve to talk together about difficult questions such as: the risks for people of color in cross-race relationships; the risks for white people in cross-race relationships; and the risks involved in cross-race, cross-gender relationships.

Even in conversations with people you don't know or in meetings with people from other parts of the organization, there are ways to acknowledge awareness of your privilege and open doors to deeper conversations. For example, you might hear, "As a member of my particular privilege group (white, Christian, heterosexual, male), I know that I will always have work to do to understand better the effects of privilege on my life." Or "Race, gender, sexual orientation, religion, and class are not always the main issue, but they are always in the mix." Another clue would be, "I recognize that my privileges, granted to me because I am white/straight/upper-middle class/ a manager/ a professor sometimes blind me to the experience of others," or "The issues of systemic discrimination—racism, sexism, classism—should always inform what we do. For example, this committee's task is to plan a meeting, but it is essential that we determine how race and gender influence the planning process." Finally, "After listening to what you have said, I realize that my perspective has been affected by my privilege. I need to go away for a while and think about this before returning to the conversation. When might we get back together?" Acknowledging awareness of our privilege and using it to change systems would look like this: "…white people's responding to every manifestation of white supremacy as if it were directed against them." [6] Imagine.

Margaret (Meg) Wheatley, a white woman who is an internationally-known organizational consultant, provides other ideas about the possibility of creating authentic relationships across race and privilege. Her first book, *Leadership and the New Science,* was a runaway bestseller. Most of the Fortune 100 companies brought her in to consult and then, she realized, went on with business as usual. No longer willing to collude, she put that work aside and began to work with others building leadership in communities. Initially, her newer books, *Turning to One Another: Simple Conversations to Restore Hope to the Future* and *Finding Our Way: Leadership For an Uncertain Time,* made my skeptical mind nervous. "This is too simple," "What she's suggesting will never work," "Your mind has gone soft," and so on. But then I read a series of her questions that stopped me. I don't even remember where I found them; I just know that I keep coming back to them, over and over again: What if we truly believed in the humanness of each person? What if we understood that each of us is connected to all others; that, if others aren't able to thrive, we won't either? What if we saw all others as valuable as ourselves? I repeat these from Chapter 2 because I want to put them back into the forefront of our minds. I think they are the type of question that many of us read, focus on for a couple of minutes, and then go about our too-busy days. I think they deserve far greater attention and implementation.

Wheatley says that, if we have the power to be seen and heard, we can heal ourselves. I believe that, if we held her questions as the template for our behavior and acted on it daily, authentic relationships would become part of our everyday experience. If we genuinely felt others to be as valuable as ourselves, we would be forced to dismantle the systems that keep us separate, giving all of us fair and equitable access to the tools to create healthy lives. If we really understood our connections to all others, we would know that the world we save would be our own. It's not that it's too simple. In some ways it's that it is too profound a shift. I am convinced, though, that, if we believe something is in our best interest, we will do whatever is necessary to achieve it.

Time's running out, and we've got work to do. Here's what we need to remember: There is no magic bullet. As Audre Lorde reminds us:

> There are no new ideas still waiting in the wings to save us as... human. There are only old and forgotten ones, new combinations, extrapolations and recognitions from within ourselves—along with the renewed courage to try them out. And we must constantly encourage ourselves and each other to attempt the heretical actions that our dreams imply, and so many of our old ideas disparage. [7]

We have only ourselves and our courage to roll up our intelligent, emotional, and physical sleeves and do what we know, in our unanesthetized selves, is right. And the truth is that we have nothing to lose by doing it and lots to gain. Imagine a world, even a workplace, where we really did use all the talent, all the skills, all the gifts that people bring. Imagine the additional energy that would be poured into our institutions if each person was genuinely valued for all that she or he is, not in spite of their color, class, orientation, religion, ability, or gender, but because of them. Imagine. And let's get to work.

NOTES

PREFACE

1 Drum, "Rand Paul and Civil Rights."
2 Private interview with author, 2/16/2012.
3 www.foxnews.com/politics/2009/08/31/phoenix-pastor-draws-protests-telling-church-prays-obamas-death/
4 http://www.newser.com/story/80996/baptist-pastors-prayed-for-obama-death-on-presidents-day.html
5 http://12160.info/video/multiple-people-carry-assault
6 Andersen, "Whitewashing Race," 26.
7 Senge, *The Fifth Discipline*, 42–3.
8 Attributed to Donald Berwick, MD, to W. Edwards Deming, and to Paul Batalden, MD.
9 Perea, Delgado, Harris, and Wildman, *Race and Races*, 265–266.
10 Headden, "One Nation, One Language?"
11 Braden, *The Wall Between*, 339.

1 BEGINNING WITH OURSELVES

1 Braden, *The Wall Between*, 339.
2 Bennis and Thomas, "Crucibles of Leadership," 40.
3 Timmel [writing as Sarah Kimmel], *White on White*, 1–3.
4 Teachers College Press published the guide in 1982 as *Diversity in the Classroom: A Multicultural Approach to the Education of Young Children*. The second edition, *Diversity in the Classroom: New Approaches to the Education of Young Children*, came out in 1996.

2 WHAT'S IN IT FOR US?

1 Kotter, "Leading Change: Why Transformation Efforts Fail," 7.

2 US Commission on Civil Rights, 1970.
3 McIntosh, "White Privilege: Unpacking the Invisible Knapsack."
4 Mills, *The Racial Contract*, 20.
5 Terry, "The Negative Impact on White Values," 120.
6 Schmidt, "New Research Complicates Discussions of Campus Diversity—in a Good Way."
7 Braham, "No You Don't Manage Everybody the Same," 28.
8 Cose, *The Rage of A Privileged Class*, book jacket.
9 Comment from Pat Lowrie, 6/5/2005.
10 Hubbard et al., *How to Calculate Diversity Return on Investment*.
11 Segrest, *Born to Belonging*, 165.
12 Mary Chesnut, *A Diary from Dixie*, 25–6, as quoted in Segrest, 165–6.
13 Segrest, 165.
14 Ibid.
15 Notes from a keynote speech given by Heidi Beirich, head of the Southern Poverty Law Center's Intelligence Project, at the White Privilege Conference, 3/29/2012.
16 Segrest, 162.
17 MacDonald, *All Souls: A Family Story from Southie*, 51.
18 Hanh and Berrigan, *The Raft is Not the Shore*, 1.
19 Ibid., 2.

3   WHAT DOES IT MEAN TO BE WHITE?

1 Gould, *The Mismeasure of Man*, 64.
2 Ibid.
3 Ibid.
4 "Race: The Power of an Illusion," California Newsreel, 2003.
5 Painter, "Why Are White People Called 'Caucasian'?" 12.
6 Ibid., 22.
7 As quoted in Roediger, *Black on White*, 188.
8 McKinney, *Being White: Stories of Race and Racism*, 1.
9 Van Ausdale and Feagin, *The First R: How Children Learn Race and Racism*, 187–8.
10 Williams, *Seeing a Color-Blind Future*, 6.
11 Perea, Delgado, Harris, and Wildman, *Race and Race*, 103.
12 Harris, "Whiteness as Property," 1753.
13 López, *White by Law*, 42–3.
14 Perea et al., 124–5.
15 Harris, 1747.
16 Ross, "The Rhetorical Tapestry of Race," 93.
17 Ibid.
18 Lopez, 44.
19 Perea et al., 124.
20 Lopez, 5.
21 Zia, *Asian American Dreams*, 26.
22 Perea et al., 376.
23 Ibid.
24 Ibid., 382–3.
25 Ibid., 398–9, 407.
26 Ibid., 376.
27 Martinez, "Mexican-Americans and Whiteness," 211.

28 Ibid., 210.
29 Perea et al., 313.
30 Perea et al., 316–17.
31 *The New York Times,* "Texas Conservatives Win Curriculum Change," 3/12/2012.
32 *The Nation* on-line, "How One Georgia Town Gambled Its Future on Immigration Detention," 4/12/2012.

4   UNDERSTANDING WHITE PRIVILEGE

1 Kaiser Family Foundation, http://facts.kff.org/chart.aspx?ch=364
2 Kochhar, Fry and Taylor, "Wealth Gaps Rise to Record Highs Between Whites, Blacks, and Hispanics."
3 This Nation.com, American Government and Politics Online.
4 Bureau of Labor Statistics, Current Population Survey, unpublished data, 2010 (2011).
5 Zia, *Asian American Dreams*, 27.
6 Vernellia R. Randall, University of Dayton School of Law, http://academic.udayton.edu/health/
7 "Washington Post/Kaiser Foundation/Harvard University Racial Attitudes Survey," *Washington Post*, 7/11/2001.
8 hooks, *Talking Back*, 113.
9 hooks, *Feminist Theory: From Margin to Center*, ix.
10 Johnson, *The Gender Knot*, 149.
11 For more about the ways that race was used to manipulate working class and poor whites to be satisfied with low wages see Roediger, *The Wages of Whiteness* and Harris, "Whiteness as Property."
12 Williams, "Spirit-Murdering the Messenger," 128.
13 hooks, *Talking Back*, 113.
14 Mills, *The Racial Contract*, 19.
15 Raines, "40 Acres and a Mortgage."
16 Harris, "Whiteness as Property."
17 Williams, *The Alchemy of Race and Rights*, 9–10.
18 Ibid.
19 Lorde, *Sister Outsider*, 128.
20 Mills, *The Racial Contract*, 19.

5   HOW WHITE WOMEN REINFORCE THE SUPREMACY OF WHITENESS

1 The DiCE Group, *The Diversity Calling: Building Community One Story at a Time.*
2 Bennis and Thomas, "Crucibles of Leadership," 40.
3 Chodron. Quoted from a Pomegranate calendar, 2008.
4 Rich, "Resisting Amnesia," *Blood, Bread, and Poetry: Selected Prose, 1979–1985*, 145.
5 Ibid.
6 Rains, "Is the Benign Really Harmless?," 88.
7 Ibid., 78.
8 Ibid., 81.
9 Ibid., 86.
10 Ibid., 90.
11 Ibid., 91.

12 Williams, *The Alchemy of Race and Rights*, 64.
13 King, "Dysconscious Racism: Ideology, Identity, and the Miseducation of Teachers," 133–46.
14 Loewen, *Lies My Teacher Told Me: Everything Your American History Textbook Got Wrong*, 142–143.
15 Beck and Clowers (as cited in Loewen, 138).
16 Ibid., 145.
17 Ibid., 144.
18 Bartlett, "Penn State, Motivated Blindness, and the Dark Side of Loyalty."
19 Covey, *The Speed of Trust: The One Thing that Changes Everything*, 135.
20 Ibid., 160.
21 Wheatley and Frieze, *Walk Out Walk On*, 4–5.
22 Rich, 145.

6 BARRIERS TO CLARITY

1 "Michelle Alexander: More Black Men Are In Prison Today Than Were Enslaved in 1850," *Huffington Post*, 4/10/2012.
2 Mills, *The Racial Contract*, 19.
3 Salon.com, http://www.salon.com/news/feature/2005/09/01/photo_controversy/index_n.p.html
4 DeMott, *The Trouble with Friendship*, 12–13.
5 Mills, 18.
6 Ibid., 19.
7 *USA Today*, "Mass Shootings are a Fact of American Life," James Alan Fox, 1/10/2011.
8 Sheryll Shariat, Sue Mallonee and Shelli Stephens-Stidham (December 1998). "Summary of Reportable Injuries in Oklahoma."
9 Other writings about intersections: Harris, "Finding Sojourner's Truth: Race, Gender, and the Institution of Property," Hurtado, *The Color of Privilege*, Kissen, *The Last Closet: The Real Lives of Lesbian and Gay Teachers*, Moss, *The Color of Class*, and Roediger, *The Wages of Whiteness*.
10 Jacobson, *Whiteness of a Different Color*, pictures inserted between 200–1.
11 Roediger, 34.
12 Ibid.
13 JBHE [*Journal of Blacks in Higher Education*] Weekly Bulletin, 4/28/2005.
14 Tucker, "Media Frenzy isn't Color-blind."
15 Jones, "The Impairment of Empathy in Goodwill Whites for African Americans," 66.
16 Bush, *Breaking the Code of Good Intentions*.
17 Feagin, Vera, and Batur, *White Racism*, 186–7.
18 Wolf, "The Racism of Well-Meaning White People," 249–50.

7 NOW THAT (I THINK) I UNDERSTAND WHITE PRIVILEGE, WHAT DO I DO?

1 Senge, *The Fifth Discipline*.
2 Bohm, *On Dialogue*.
3 Toni Wilson, "Dialogue as a Process," handout from workshop on dialogue, The Women's Circle, October, 1996.
4 Senge et al., *The Fifth Discipline Fieldbook*, 375.

5 Vincent Chin, a Chinese American man, was beaten to death in 1982 by two white men who had been laid off from Chrysler. They blamed the Japanese auto makers for their loss of work, believed Vincent Chin to be Japanese, and killed him. James Byrd Jr. was a Black man who was chained to the back of a pickup by two white men and dragged to death in Jasper, Texas, in 1998.

6 DeWayne Wickham, "Photo Prank using Leashes Stirs Chilling Memories," *USA Today*, 5/23/2005, 11A.

7 Salzberg, *Lovingkindness*, 103.

8 Rainer Maria Rilke, "Gratefulness," in Muller, *Sabbath*, 128.

9 Timmel [writing as Sarah Kimmel], *White on White*.

10 *USA Today*, 4/27/1999, pages 1-2B.

11 Sally Kohn, "'The Talk' With My White Daughter: Don't Be Like John Derbyshire," *COLORLINES*, 10/4/2012.

12 *The New York Times*, "Foreclosures (2012 Robosigning and Mortgage Servicing Settlement)," 4/4/2012.

13 http://www.faireconomy.org/files/StateOfDream_01_16_08_Web.pdf, Key Findings

14 Debbie Gruenstein Bocian, Keith S. Ernst and Wei Li, "Unfair Lending: The Effect of Race and Ethnicity on the Price of Subprime Mortgages." Center for Responsible Lending, 2006. Accessed at http://www.responsiblelending.org/issues/mortgage/research/page.jsp?itemID=29371010

15 Thandeka, *Learning to Be White*, 14.

16 Ibid.

17 Ibid.

18 For information about work with students, see Beverly Tatum, Karyn McKenzie, and Melanie Bush.

19 *San Francisco Chronicle*, 4/14/1999, A21.

8   TALKING ABOUT RACE

1 Berlak and Moyenda. *Taking it Personally*, 169.

2 Ibid., 156.

3 Ibid., 158.

4 Senge, 387.

9   TALKING ABOUT WHITENESS AND BEING WHITE

1 *Huff Post Politics*, 4/20/2010, http://www.huffingtonpost.com/2010/03/20/tea-party-protests-nier-f_n_507116.html

2 http://www.npr.org/2012/03/01/147752410/appeals-court-defers-on-ala-ga-immigration-laws

3 Ta-Nehisi Coates. "Conversation on race? Why we're just not ready," *Chicago Tribune*, 8/26/2010.

4 "Rejected in Tucson," *The New York Times*, 1/21/2012.

5 Steele, *Whistling Vivaldi: And Other Clues to How Stereotypes Affect Us*, 6.

6 National Institute of Justice & Centers for Disease Control & Prevention. *Prevalence, Incidence and Consequences of Violence Against Women Survey*, 1998.

7 Kendall, *Understanding White Privilege*, 2–3.

8 Bennis, Benne, and Chin, *The Planning of Change*.

9 Cameron, *The Artist's Way: A Spiritual Path to Higher Creativity*, 159–60.

10 Picca and Feagin. *Two-Faced Racism: Whites in the Backstage and Frontstage*.

11 Steele, 4.
12 Grusky and Miller, *The Sociology of Organizations: Basic Studies*, 104–5.
13 Schein, *Organizational Culture and Leadership*, 8.
14 Ibid., 11.
15 Cornel West, *The New York Times*, 8/2/1992.

10 BECOMING AN ALLY AND BUILDING AUTHENTIC RELATIONSHIPS ACROSS RACE

1 *Random House Unabridged Dictionary*, 2nd edition, 1993.
2 The ideas for both the pre-work to being an ally and the qualities and characteristics of relationships came from discussions with the women in the Women, Race, and Privilege group at Michigan State University.
3 Hurtado, *The Color of Privilege*, 128.
4 This conversation was with Jackie Reza and is used with her permission.
5 Dr. Martin Luther King, "Pilgrimage to Nonviolence," 1958.
6 Garvey and Ignatiev, "Toward a New Abolitionism," 346–9.
7 Lorde, *Sister Outsider*, 38–9.

BIBLIOGRAPHY

Adams, Maurianne, Lee Anne Bell, and Pat Griffin, eds. *Teaching for Diversity and Social Justice*, 2nd ed. New York: Routledge, 2007.

Adams, Maurianne, Warren J. Blumenfeld, Rosie Castaneda, Heather W. Hackman, Madeline L. Peters, and Ximena Zuniga. *Readings for Diversity and Social Justice: An Anthology on Racism, Antisemitism, Sexism, Heterosexism, Ableism, and Classism*, 2nd ed. New York: Routledge, 2010.

Alexander, Michelle. *The New Jim Crow: Mass Incarceration in the Age of Colorblindness*. New York: The New Press, 2010.

Allen, Theodore W. *The Invention of the White Race*. Vol. 1, *Racial Oppression and Social Control*. New York: Verso, 1994.

Allen, Theodore W. *The Invention of the White Race*. Vol. 2, *The Origin of Racial Oppression in Anglo-America*. New York: Verso, 1997.

Ancheta, Angelo. *Race, Rights, and the Asian American Experience*. New Brunswick, NJ: Rutgers University Press, 1998.

Andersen, Margaret L. "Whitewashing Race: A Critical Perspective on Whiteness." In *White Out: The Continuing Significance of Racism*, edited by Ashley W. Doane and Eduardo Bonilla-Silva, eds. New York: Routledge, 2003.

Andersen, Margaret L., and Patricia Hill Collins. *Race, Class, and Gender: An Anthology*. Belmont, CA: Wadsworth Publishing Company, 1995.

Anzaldua, G., ed. *Making Face, Making Soul: Haciendo Caras, Creative and Critical Perspectives by Feminists of Color*. San Francisco: aunt lute books, 1990.

Applebaum, Barbara. *Being White, Being Good: White Complicity, White Moral Responsibility, and Social Justice Pedagogy*. Lanham, MD.: Lexington Books, 2010.

Aptheker, Herbert. *Anti-Racism in US History: The First Two Hundred Years*. Westport, CT: Praeger Publishers, 1993.

Baca Zinn, Maxine, Pierrette Hondagneu-Sotelo, and Michael A. Messner, eds. *Through the Prism of Difference: Readings on Sex and Gender*. Boston: Allyn & Bacon, 1997.

Bartlett, Tom. "Penn State, Motivated Blindness, and the Dark Side of Loyalty." *Chronicle of Higher Education*, 11/11/2011.

Beck, Warren, and Myles Clowers. "'Gone With the Wind': The Invisibility of Racism in American History Textbooks," in *Lies My Teacher Told Me: Everything Your American History Textbook Got Wrong*. New York: Touchstone Simon & Schuster, 1995, pp. 137–171.

Bell, Derrick. *And We Are Not Saved: The Elusive Quest for Racial Reform*. New York: Basic Books, 1987.

Bell, Derrick. *Faces at the Bottom of the Well: The Permanence of Racism*. New York: Basic Books, 1992.

Bell, Ella L. J. Edmondson, and Stella M. Nkomo. *Our Separate Ways: Black and White Women and the Struggle for Professional Identity*. Boston: Harvard Business School Press, 2001.

Benjamin, Rich. *Searching for Whitopia*. New York: Hyperion, 2009.

Bennett, Lerone. *Before the Mayflower: A History of Black America*, 8th revised ed. New York: Viking, 2007.

Bennis, Warren G., and Robert J. Thomas. "Crucibles of Leadership." *Harvard Business Review* 80, no. 9 (2002): 39–45.

Bennis, Warren, Kenneth Benne and Robert Chin. *The Planning of Change*, 3rd ed. New York: Holt, Rinehart and Winston, 1969.

Berger, Maurice. *White Lies: Race and the Myths of Whiteness*. New York: Farrar, Straus, & Giroux, 1999.

Berlak, Ann, and Sekani Moyenda. *Taking It Personally: Racism in the Classroom from Kindergarten to College*. Philadelphia. Temple University Press, 2001.

Blackmon, Douglas A. *Slavery By Another Name: The Re-Enslavement of Black Americans from the Civil War to World War II*. New York: Doubleday, 2008.

Blaut, James M. *The Colonizer's Model of the World: Geographical Diffusionism and Eurocentric History*. New York: Guilford Press, 1993.

Bohm, David. *On Dialogue*. New York: Routledge, 2004.

Braden, Anne. *The Wall Between*, 2nd ed. Knoxville: University of Tennessee Press, 1999.

Braham, Jim. "No, You Don't Manage Everybody the Same." *Industry Week*, Feb. 6, 1989, 28–30, 34–35.

Brooks, Roy L., ed. *When Sorry Isn't Enough: The Controversy Over Apologies and Reparations for Human Injustice*. New York: New York University Press, 1999.

Brown, Cynthia Stokes. *Refusing Racism: White Allies and the Struggle for Civil Rights*. New York: Teachers College Press, 2002.

Bush, Melanie E. L. *Breaking the Code of Good Intentions: Everyday Forms of Racism*. Lanham, MD: Rowman & Littlefield, 2004.

Cameron, Julia. *The Artist's Way: A Spiritual Path to Higher Creativity*. New York: Penguin Putnam, 1992.

Cose, Ellis. *The Rage of a Privileged Class*. New York: HarperCollins, 1993.

Covey, Stephen M. R. *The Speed of Trust: The One Thing That Changes Everything*. New York: Free Press, 2006.

Cox, Taylor, Jr. *Creating the Multicultural Organization: A Strategy for Capturing the Power of Diversity*. San Francisco: Jossey-Bass, 2001.

Cox, Taylor, Jr., and Ruby L. Beale. *Developing Competency to Manage Diversity: Readings, Cases & Activities*. San Francisco: Berrett-Koehler Publishers, 1997.

Crenshaw, Kimberlé, Neil Gotanda, Gary Peller and Kendall Thomas. *Critical Race Theory: The Key Writings That Formed the Movement*. New York: The New Press, 1995.

Cross, Elsie Y., Judith H. Katz, Frederick A. Miller, and Edith W. Seashore, eds. *The Promise of Diversity: Over 40 Voices Discuss Strategies for Eliminating Discrimination in Organizations*. Chicago: Irwin Professional Publishing (co-published with NTL Institute), 1994.

Cushing, Bonnie Berman, ed. *Accountability and White Anti-Racist Organizing: Stories from Our Work*. Roselle, NJ: Crandall, Dostie & Douglass Books, Inc., 2010.

Dace, Karen L., ed. *Unlikely Allies in the Academy: Women of Color and White Women in Conversation*. New York: Routledge, 2012.

Delgado, Richard, and Jean Stefancic, eds. *Critical White Studies: Looking Behind the Mirror*. Philadelphia: Temple University Press, 1997.

Delpit, Lisa. *Other People's Children: Cultural Conflict in the Classroom*. New York: New Press, 1995.

Delpit, Lisa. "The Silenced Dialogue: Power and Pedagogy in Educating Other People's Children." *Harvard Educational Review* 58, no. 3 (1988): 280–98.

DeMott, Benjamin. *The Trouble with Friendship: Why Americans Can't Think Straight about Race*. New Haven, CT: Yale University Press, 1998.

DiCE Group, *The Diversity Calling: Building Community One Story at a Time*. Joe-Joe McManus, Ph.D., ed. Xlibris Corporation, 2011.

Diversity Inc. *The Business Case for Diversity*, 4th ed. New Brunswick, NJ: Allegiant Media, 2003.

Drum, Kevin. "Rand Paul and Civil Rights." *Mother Jones*, May 20, 2010.

Dyer, Richard. *White*. New York: Routledge, 1997.

Dyson, Michael. *Race Rules: Navigating the Color Line*. New York: Vintage Books, 1997.

Evans, Sara M., ed. *Journeys That Opened Up the World: Women, Student Christian Movements, and Social Justice, 1955–1975*. New Brunswick, NJ: Rutgers University Press, 2003.

Feagin, Joe, Hernán Vera, and Pinar Batur. *White Racism,* 2nd ed. New York: Routledge, 2001.

Frankenberg, Ruth, ed. *Displacing Whiteness: Essays in Social and Cultural Criticism*. Durham, NC: Duke University Press, 1997.

Frankenberg, Ruth, ed. *White Women, Race Matters: The Social Construction of Whiteness*. Minneapolis: University of Minnesota Press, 1993.

Friere, Paulo. *Pedagogy of the Oppressed*. New York: Herder & Herder, 1972.

Fries, Kenny, ed. *Staring Back: The Disability Experience from the Inside Out*. New York: Penguin Putnam, 1997.

Fulbeck, Kip. *Paper Bullets: A Fictional Autobiography*. Seattle: University of Washington Press, 2001.

Garvey, John, and Noel Ignatiev. "Toward a New Abolitionism: A *Race Traitor* Manifesto." In *Whiteness: A Critical Reader*, edited by Mike Hill. New York: New York University Press, 1997.

Giddings, Paula. *When and Where I Enter: The Impact of Black Women on Race and Sex in America*. New York: Bantam, 1985.

Goodman, Diane J. *Promoting Diversity and Social Justice: Educating People from Privileged Groups,* 2nd ed. New York: Routledge, 2011.

Gould, Stephen Jay. *The Mismeasure of Man*, rev. ed. New York: Norton, 1996.

Grusky, O., and George A. Miller, eds. *The Sociology of Organizations: Basic Studies*, 2nd ed., New York: Free Press, 1981.

Hacker, Andrew. *Two Nations*. New York: Scribner's, 1992.

Hale, Frank W., Jr. *What Makes Racial Diversity Work in Higher Education: Academic Leaders Present Successful Policies and Strategies*. Sterling, VA: Stylus Publishing, LLC, 2004.

Hanh, Thich Nhat, and Daniel Berrigan. *The Raft Is Not the Shore: Conversations Toward a Buddhist-Christian Awareness*. Maryknoll, NY: Orbis Books, 2001.

Harjo, Joy, and Gloria Bird. *Reinventing the Enemy's Language: Contemporary Native American Women's Writings of North America*. New York: Norton, 1997.

Harris, Cheryl. "Finding Sojourner's Truth: Race, Gender, and the Institution of Property." *Cordozo Law Review* 18 (1996): 309–409.

Harris, Cheryl. "Whiteness as Property." *Harvard Law Review* 106 (1993): 1709–91.

Headden, Susan. "One nation, one language?" *U.S. News & World Report*, v. 119, Sept. 25, 1995, pp. 38–42.

Herbst, Philip H. *The Color of Words: An Encyclopedic Dictionary of Ethnic Bias in the US*. Yarmouth, ME: Intercultural Press, 1997.

Hill, Mike, ed. *Whiteness: A Critical Reader*. New York: New York University Press, 1997.

Hitchcock, Jeff. *Lifting the White Veil: An Exploration of White American Culture in a Multiracial Context*. Roselle, NJ: Crandall Dostie & Douglass Books, 2003.

Hitchcock, Jeff. *Unraveling the White Cocoon*. Dubuque, IA: Kendall/Hunt, 2001.

hooks, bell. *Feminist Theory: From Margin to Center*, 2nd ed. Cambridge, MA: South End Press, 2000.

hooks, bell. *Killing Rage: Ending Racism*. New York: Holt, 1995.

hooks, bell. *Talking Back: Thinking Feminist, Thinking Black*. Cambridge, MA: South End Press, 1989.

hooks, bell. *Teaching to Transgress*. New York: Routledge, 1994.

Howard, Gary R. *We Can't Teach What We Don't Know: White Teachers, Multiracial Schools*, 2nd ed. New York: Teachers College Press, 2006.

Hubbard, Edward E., Dolores Gillium, and Kathexis Design. *How to Calculate Diversity Return on Investment*. Las Vegas, NV: Global Insights Publishing, 2008.

Hurtado, Aida. *The Color of Privilege: Three Blasphemies on Race and Feminism*. Ann Arbor: University of Michigan Press, 1996.

Ignatiev, Noel. *How the Irish Became White*. New York: Routledge, 1995.

Ingraham, Chrys. *White Weddings: Romancing Heterosexuality in Popular Culture*. New York: Routledge, 1999.

Jacobson, Matthew Frye. *Whiteness of a Different Color: European Immigrants and the Alchemy of Race*. Cambridge, MA: Harvard University Press, 1998.

Johnson, Allan G. *The Gender Knot: Unraveling Our Patriarchal Legacy*. Philadelphia: Temple University Press, 1997.

Johnson, Allan G. *Privilege, Power, and Difference*. Mountain View, CA: Mayfield Publishing, 2000.

Jones, Charisse, and Kumea Shorter-Gooden. *Shifting: The Double Lives of Black Women in America*. New York: HarperCollins, 2003.

Jones, Janine. "The Impairment of Empathy in Goodwill Whites for African Americans." In *What White Looks Like: African American Philosophers on the Whiteness Question*, edited by George Yancy. New York: Routledge, 2004.

Katz, Judith H. *White Awareness: Handbook for Anti-Racism Training*. Norman: University of Oklahoma Press, 2003.

Kegan, Robert, and Lisa Laskow Lahey. *How the Way We Talk Can Change the Way We Work: Seven Languages for Transformation.* San Francisco: Jossey-Bass, 2001.

Kendall, Frances E. "Diversity Issues in the Workplace." In *Valuing Diversity,* edited by Lewis Griggs and Lente-Louise Louw. New York: McGraw-Hill, 1995.

Kendall, Frances E. *Diversity in the Classroom: New Approaches to the Education of Young Children,* 2nd ed. New York: Teachers College Press, 1996.

Kendall, Frances E. "Frances E. Kendall." In *Journeys that Opened Up the World: Women, Student Christian Movements, and Social Justice, 1955–1975,* edited by Sara M. Evans. New Brunswick, NJ: Rutgers University Press, 2003.

Kendall, Frances E. "A White Woman to White Women." In *Unlikely Allies in the Academy: Women of Color and White Women in Conversation.* New York: Routledge, 2012.

Kim, Elaine, Lilia V. Villanueva, and Asian Women United of California. *Making More Waves: New Writing by Asian American Women.* Boston: Beacon Press, 1997.

Kincheloe, Joe L., Shirley R. Steinberg, Nelson M. Rodriguez, and Ronald E. Chennault, eds. *White Reign: Deploying Whiteness in America.* New York: St. Martin's Press, 1998.

King, Joyce E. "Dysconscious Racism, and the Miseducation of Teachers." *Journal of Negro Education,* No. 2 (1991): 133–46.

Kissen, Rita. *The Last Closet: The Real Lives of Lesbian and Gay Teachers.* Portsmouth, NH: Heinemann, 1996.

Kivel, Paul. *Uprooting Racism: How White People Can Work for Racial Justice,* 2nd ed. Philadelphia: New Society Publishers, 2002.

Kochhar, Rakesh, Richard Fry, and Taylor Paul. "Wealth Gaps Rise to Record Highs Between Whites, Blacks, and Hispanics," Pew Research Center, July 26, 2011.

Kotter, John. "Leading Change: Why Transformation Efforts Fail." In *Harvard Business Review on Change.* Boston: Harvard Business Review, 1998.

Lawrence, Charles R. III, and Mari J. Matsuda. *We Won't Go Back: Making the Case for Affirmative Action.* Boston: Houghton Mifflin, 1997.

Lerner, Gerda, ed. *Black Women in White America.* New York: Vintage Books, 1992.

Lerner, Gerda, ed. *Why History Matters: Life and Thought.* New York: Oxford University Press, 1997.

Lipsitz, George. *The Possessive Investment in Whiteness: How White People Profit from Identity Politics.* Philadelphia: Temple University Press, 1998.

Liu, Eric. *The Accidental Asian: Notes of a Native Speaker.* New York: Vintage Books, 1998.

Liu, Meizhu, Barbara Robles, and Betsy Leondar-Wright. *The Color of Wealth: The Story Behind the U.S. Racial Wealth Divide.* New York: The New Press, 2006.

Loewen, James. *Lies My Teacher Told Me: Everything Your American History Textbook Got Wrong.* New York: Touchstone Simon & Schuster, 1995.

López, Ian F. Haney. *White by Law: The Legal Construction of Race.* New York: New York University Press, 1996.

Lorde, Audre. *Sister Outsider.* Freedom, CA: Crossing Press, 1984.

MacDonald, Michael Patrick. *All Souls: A Family Story from Southie.* Boston: Beacon Press, 1999.

McIntosh, Peggy. "White Privilege and Male Privilege: A Personal Account of Coming to See Correspondences through Work in Women's Studies." In *Race, Class, and Gender: An Anthology,* edited by Margaret L. Andersen and Patricia Hill Collins, 2nd ed. Belmont, NY: Wadsworth Publishing, 1995.

McIntosh, Peggy. "White Privilege and Male Privilege: A Personal Account of Coming to See Correspondences through Work in Women's Studies." Working Paper 189, Wellesley, MA: Wellesley College Center for Research on Women, 1988.

McIntosh, Peggy. "White Privilege: Unpacking the Invisible Knapsack." *Peace and Freedom* (Philadelphia, PA: Women's International League for Peace and Freedom) July/August 1989.

McIntosh, Peggy. "White Privilege, Color and Crime: A Personal Account." In *Images of Color, Images of Crime: Readings,* edited by Coramae Richey Mann and Marjorie S. Zatz. Los Angeles, CA: Roxbury Publishing Company, 1998.

McIntyre, Alice. *Making Meaning of Whiteness: Exploring Racial Identity with White Teachers.* Albany: State University of New York Press, 1997.

McKinney, Karyn D. *Being White: Stories of Race and Racism.* New York: Routledge, 2005.

Martinez, George A. "Mexican-Americans and Whiteness." In *Critical White Studies: Looking Behind the Mirror,* edited by Richard Delgado and Jean Stefancic. Philadelphia: Temple University Press, 1997.

Miller, Frederick A., and Judith H. Katz. *The Inclusion Breakthrough: Unleashing the Real Power of Diversity.* San Francisco: Berrett-Koehler Publishers, 2002.

Mills, Charles W. *The Racial Contract.* Ithaca, NY: Cornell University Press, 1997.

Moody, Joann. *Faculty Diversity: Problems and Solutions.* New York: RoutledgeFalmer, 2004.

Moss, Kirby. *The Color of Class: Poor Whites and the Paradox of Privilege.* Philadelphia: University of Pennsylvania Press, 2003.

Muller, Wayne. *Legacy of the Heart: The Spiritual Advantages of a Painful Childhood.* New York: Simon & Schuster, 1993.

Muller, Wayne. *Sabbath: Finding Rest, Renewal, and Delight in Our Busy Lives.* New York: Bantam, 2000.

Okun, Tema. *The Emperor Has No Clothes: Teaching About Race and Racism to People Who Don't Want to Know.* Charlotte, NC: Information Age Publishing, Inc., 2010.

Ong, Paul M., ed. *The State of Asian Pacific America: Transforming Race Relations: A Public Policy Report.* Vol. 4. Los Angeles: LEAP Asian Pacific American Public Policy Institute and UCLA Asian American Studies Center, 2000.

Painter, Nell Irvin. "Why Are White People Called 'Caucasian'?" Paper presented at the Fifth Annual Gilder Lehrman Center International Conference, New Haven, Yale University, Nov. 7–8, 2003.

Patterson, Kerry, Joseph Grenny, Ron McMillan, and Al Switzer. *Crucial Conversations: Tools for Talking When Stakes Are High.* New York: McGraw-Hill, 2002.

Perea, Juan F., Richard Delgado, Angela P. Harris, and Stephanie M. Wildman. *Race and Races: Cases and Resources for a Diverse America.* American Casebook Series. St. Paul, MN: West Group, 2000.

Pharr, Suzanne. *In the Time of the Right: Reflections on Liberation.* Berkeley, CA: Chardon Press, 1996.

Pharr, Suzanne. *Homophobia: A Weapon of Sexism,* 2nd ed. Berkeley, CA: Chardon Press, 1997.

Pheterson, Gail. "Alliances Between Women: Overcoming Internalized Oppression and Internalized Domination." *Signs: Journal of Women in Culture and Society* 12 (1986): 146–60.

Picca, Leslie Houts, and Joe R. Feagin. *Two-Faced Racism: Whites in the Backstage and Frontstage.* New York: Routledge, 2007.

Pommersheim, Frank. *Braid of Feathers: American Indian Law and Contemporary Tribal Life*. Berkeley: University of California Press, 1995.

Raines, Franklin D. "40 Acres and a Mortgage." Charter Day Speech, Howard University, Washington, D.C., March 8, 2002.

Rains, Frances V. "Is the Benign Really Harmless?: Deconstructing Some 'Benign' Manifestations of Operationalized White Privilege." In *White Reign: Deploying Whiteness in America*. Kincehloe, Joe L., Shirley R. Steinberg, Nelson Rodriguez, & Ronald Chennault, eds. New York: St. Martin's Press, 1998.

Rich, Adrienne. *Blood, Bread, and Poetry: Selected Prose 1979–1985*. New York: W.W. Norton & Company, 1986.

Robinson, Randall. *Quitting America: The Departure of a Black Man from His Native Land*. New York: Dutton, 2004.

Robinson, Sally. *Marked Men: White Masculinity in Crisis*. New York: Columbia University Press, 2000.

Rodriguez, Nelson M., and Leila E. Villaverde, eds. *Dismantling White Privilege: Pedagogy, Politics, and Whiteness*. New York: Peter Lang Publishing, 2000.

Roediger, David, R., ed. *Black on White: Black Writers on What It Means to Be White*. New York: Schocken Books, 1998.

Roediger, David, R., ed. *The Wages of Whiteness: Race and the Making of the American Working Class*, rev. ed. New York: Verso, 1999.

Roediger, David, R., ed. *Working Toward Whiteness: How America's Immigrants Became White*. New York: Basic Books, 2005.

Ross, Thomas. "The Rhetorical Tapestry of Race." In *Critical White Studies: Looking Behind the Mirror*, edited by Richard Delgado and Jean Stefancic. Philadelphia: Temple University Press, 1997.

Rothenberg, Paula. *White Privilege: Essential Readings on the Other Side of Racism*. New York: Worth Publishers, 2002.

Roy, Beth. *Bitters in the Honey: Tales of Hope and Disappointment across Divides of Race and Time*. Fayetteville: University of Arkansas Press, 1999.

St. Jean, Yanick, and Joe R. Feagin. *Double Burden: Black Women and Everyday Racism*. New York: M.E. Sharpe, 1998.

Salzberg, Sharon. *Lovingkindness*. Boston: Shambhala Publications, 1997.

Santiago, Roberto, ed. *Boricuas: Influential Puerto Rican Writings—An Anthology*. New York: Ballantine Books, 1995.

Schein, Edgar. *Organizational Leadership and Culture*, 3rd ed. San Francisco: Jossey-Bass, 2004.

Schmidt, Peter. "New Research Complicates Discussions of Campus Diversity—in a Good Way," *Chronicle of Higher Education*, January 31, 2010.

Scott, Susan. *Fierce Conversations: Achieving Success at Work & in Life, One Conversation at a Time*. New York: Berkley Books, 2002.

Segrest, Mab. *Memoir of a Race Traitor*. Boston: South End Press, 1994.

Segrest, Mab. *Born to Belonging: Writings on Spirit and Justice*. New Brunswick, NJ: Rutgers University Press, 2002.

Senge, Peter. *The Fifth Discipline*. New York: Doubleday/Currency, 1990.

Senge, Peter, Art Kleiner, Charlotte Roberts, Richard R. Ross, and Bryan J. Smith. *The Fifth Discipline Fieldbook*. New York: Doubleday/Currency, 1994.

Singleton, Glenn and Curtis Linton. *Courageous Conversations: A Field Guide for Achieving Equity in Schools*. Thousand Oaks, CA: Corwin Press, 2006.

Smith, Lillian. *Killers of the Dream*. New York: Norton, 1994.

Steele, Claude M. *Whistling Vivaldi and Other Clues to How Stereotypes Affect Us*. New York: W.W. Norton & Company, 2010.

Stone, Douglas, Bruce Patton, and Sheila Heen. *Difficult Conversations: How to Discuss What Matters Most*. New York: Penguin Books, 1999.

Takaki, Ronald T. *Strangers from a Different Shore: A History of Asian Americans*, rev. ed. Boston: Little, Brown, 1998.

Tatum, Beverly Daniel. *"Why Are All the Black Kids Sitting Together in the Cafeteria?" And Other Conversations about Race*, rev. ed. New York: Basic Books, 2003.

Terry, Robert W. *Authentic Leadership: Courage in Action*, San Francisco: Jossey-Bass, 1993.

Terry, Robert W. *For Whites Only*, rev. ed. Grand Rapids, MI: Eerdmans, 1975; reprint 1994.

Terry, Robert W. "The Negative Impact on White Values." In *Impacts of Racism on White Americans*, edited by Benjamin P. Bowser and Raymond G. Hunt. Beverly Hills, CA: Sage Publications, 1981.

Thandeka. *Learning to Be White*. New York: Continuum, 2002.

Thomas, David A. "The Truth about Mentoring Minorities: Race Matters." *Harvard Business Review* 79, no. 4 (2001): 98–107.

Thomas, David A., and John J. Gabarro. *Breaking Through: The Making of Minority Executives in Corporate America*. Boston: Harvard Business School Press, 1999.

Thompson, Becky. *A Promise and a Way of Life: White Antiracist Activism*. Minneapolis: University of Minnesota Press, 2001.

Thompson, Becky, and Sangreeta Tyagi, eds. *Names We Call Home: Autobiography on Racial Identity*. New York: Routledge, 1996.

Timmel, Sally [writing as Sarah Kimmel]. *White on White: A Handbook for Groups Working Against Racism* [unpublished handbook]. New York: YWCA, 1970.

Tuan, Mia. *Forever Foreigners or Honorary Whites?—The Asian Experience Today*. New Brunswick, NJ: Rutgers University Press, 1998.

Tucker, Cynthia. "Media Frenzy isn't Color-blind," *Lansing State Journal*, May 10, 2005.

Turner, Caroline Sotello Viernes, and Samuel L. Myers, Jr. *Faculty of Color in Academe: Bittersweet Success*. Boston: Allyn & Bacon, 2000.

Van Ausdale, Debra, and Joe R. Feagin. *The First R: How Children Learn Race and Racism*. Lanham, MD: Rowman & Littlefield, 2001.

Wall, Vernon A., and Nancy J. Evans, eds. *Toward Acceptance: Sexual Orientation Issues on Campus*. Lanham, MD: University Press of America, 2000.

Ware, Vron. *Beyond the Pale: White Women, Racism and History*. London: Verso, 1992.

Warren, Mark. *Fire in the Heart: How White Activists Embrace Racial Justice*. New York: Oxford University Press, 2010.

Weaver, Toni E. *White to White on Black/White*. Vandalia, OH: Voices Publishing, 1993.

West, Cornel. *Race Matters*. Boston: Beacon Press, 1993.

Wheatley, Margaret J. *Finding Our Way: Leadership for an Uncertain Time*. San Francisco: Berrett-Koehler Publishers, 2005.

Wheatley, Margaret J. *Turning to One Another: Simple Conversations to Restore Hope to the Future*. San Francisco: Berrett-Koehler Publishers, 2002.

Wheatley, Margaret J. and Deborah Frieze. *Walk Out Walk On*. San Francisco: Berrett-Koehler, 2011.

Wijeyesinghe, Charmaine L., and Bailey W. Jackson, III, eds. *New Perspectives on Racial Identity Development: A Theoretical and Practical Anthology*. New York: New York University Press, 2001.

Wildman, Stephanie. *Privilege Revealed: How Invisible Preference Undermines America*. New York: New York University Press, 1996.

Williams, Patricia. *The Alchemy of Race and Rights*. Cambridge, MA: Harvard University Press, 1991.

Williams, Patricia. *The Rooster's Egg: On the Persistence of Prejudice*. Cambridge, MA: Harvard University Press, 1995.

Williams, Patricia. *Seeing a Color-Blind Future: The Paradox of Race*. New York: Noonday Press, 1997.

Williams, Patricia. "Spirit-Murdering the Messenger: The Discourse of Fingerpointing as the Law's Response to Racism." *University of Miami Law Review* 42 (1987): 127–57.

Wilson, Midge, and Kathy Russell. *Divided Sisters: Bridging the Gap between Black Women and White Women*. New York: Doubleday, 1996.

Wise, Tim. *White Like Me: Reflections on Race from a Privileged Son*. Berkeley, CA: Soft Skull Press; revised ed., 2011.

Wolf, Naomi. "The Racism of Well-Meaning White People." *Glamour*, August, 1995, 230–31, 249–50.

Woodward, C. Vann. *The Strange Career of Jim Crow*. New York: Oxford University Press, 1955/2002.

Wu, Frank H. *Yellow: Race in America Beyond Black and White*. New York: Basic Books, 2002.

Wu, Jean Yu-wen, and Min Song, eds. *Asian American Studies: A Reader*. New Brunswick, NJ: Rutgers University Press, 2000.

Yamamoto, Eric K. *Interracial Justice: Conflict and Reconciliation in Post-Civil Rights America*. New York: New York University Press, 1999.

Zia, Helen. *Asian American Dreams: The Emergence of an American People*. New York: Farrar, Straus, & Giroux, 2000.

Zinn, Howard. *A People's History of the United States: 1492–Present*. New York: HarperCollins, 2003.

INDEX